IMAGES
of America

ARLINGTON

ON THE COVER: The Goethals family poses in the middle of Magnolia Avenue around 1907, when it was just a dirt road. Today this part of Magnolia Avenue is in front of the Tyler Mall. Pictured from left to right are Helen, Alberie, Nathalie, Celina, Marie, Cecilia, and their parents, Peter and Amelia Goethals.

IMAGES
of America

ARLINGTON

Georgia Gordon Sercl

ARCADIA
PUBLISHING

ISBN 978-0-7385-5580-5

Published by Arcadia Publishing
Charleston SC, Chicago IL, Portsmouth NH, San Francisco CA

Printed in the United States of America

Library of Congress Catalog Card Number: 2007931267

For all general information contact Arcadia Publishing at:
Telephone 843-853-2070
Fax 843-853-0044
E-mail sales@arcadiapublishing.com
For customer service and orders:
Toll-Free 1-888-313-2665

Visit us on the Internet at www.arcadiapublishing.com

This book is dedicated to my mother, Theresa Leibert Gordon, the real historian of Arlington. A self-published author, she constantly researched the town and kept two cameras with her at all times. My grandmother Marie Leibert was also a historian of Arlington, a writer for the Arlington Times, *and the author of several books.*

CONTENTS

ACKNOWLEDGMENTS

A special acknowledgment goes to my husband, Mike, for his patience and support while spending many hours teaching and helping me with the computer. Lots of encouragement was also provided by family and friends. I am grateful to my editor at Arcadia Publishing, Debbie Seracini, for her ongoing assistance and guidance.

I would like to acknowledge the generosity of those who shared with me: JoAnne Pease-Simpson, Mike Gordon, Norm and Velda Kelley, Frank and Mary Seinturier, John Mata, Steve Lech, Barbara Miller Trujillo, Marion Maxwell Pagliuso, Virginia Pagliuso, Vi Estel, California Baptist University, David Beaird, Marion Alessio Arias, Jim and MaryBelle Neufell Spaulding, Daniel Balboa, Bud and Lois Abraham, Kevin Hallaran, Riverside Metropolitan Museum, Mike Schulte, and Lorene Sisquoc. A special thank-you goes to everyone for their support of this book. Photographs not credited in this book belong to the author.

INTRODUCTION

In 1870, a group of settlers led by Judge John W. North of New York settled in a brush-covered valley near the Santa Ana River in Southern California. A one-square-mile area surrounded by rocky hills was laid out for the new town of Riverside; however, by the time it was incorporated in 1883, the boundaries of this successful town extended seven additional miles to the west.

In 1877, some of Riverside's most prominent businessmen, including Samuel Evans and William Sayward, decided to form another town near the southern border, at the corner of present-day Van Buren Boulevard and Magnolia Avenue. The new town was named Arlington by popular vote, and the entire valley was advertised in Eastern papers as "the land of milk and honey."

Large tracts were soon bought up by growers, many from England, who purchased young orange seedlings for about $2 apiece and established citrus as the valley's main crop. The combination of fertile soil and sunny weather produced a fine quality and sweetness in the fruit, providing newfound wealth for the area's growers. Although Arlington grew and prospered, it was not without disappointment and heartache as the farmers learned to grapple with the devastating spring frosts and summer grasshoppers that often decimated the tender young leaves and buds.

The first business to appear in Arlington was Sanker's blacksmith shop, complete with a water trough outside for the horses. In 1907, a single-horse fire-hose wagon was brought to Arlington and kept in Sanker's barn at the rear of his shop. W. N. Peebles was hired as the first driver. In 1909, Shelby Tabler became captain of the Arlington Fire Department, remaining the main driver and caretaker for the highly prized fire wagon team for several years. The equipment was later moved to new quarters at the rear of the current Arlington Library building. By 1910, Arlington had its own hardware, lumber, grain, and general stores. Extant historic structures include the 1909 library building and the 1911 Jenkins Building. Dr. Jenkins was one of the earliest settlers to the area.

Arlington's first school was a one-room schoolhouse on Miller Street. In 1891, a four-room structure was built on the grounds of present-day Arlington Park. Jessie Gill, the first schoolteacher, rode in daily on horseback from her home in Riverside. Marie Leibert spent many years in Arlington schools, first as a student and then as a teacher from 1901 to 1941. Mary Cell taught for 38 years at the Arlington School. As the town's population grew, a new school was constructed on Hayes Street in 1919 and dedicated to the area boys who served in World War I. Accordingly, it was named the Liberty School. Administrators traveled from far and wide to view this "modern" school with large windows and sliding doors opening onto a beautiful quadrangle.

Many of the original citrus workers, of Italian descent, eventually saved enough money to buy their own properties and bring their wives and families back to America. The Italians were later replaced as grove workers by a large influx of Hispanics, who settled in the *barrio* area of Arlington on Indiana Avenue. Consequently, the area needed a new school with teachers who could speak Spanish. In 1923, this special academy, called Independiente, was built on Indiana Avenue on the future site of Hawthorne Elementary School.

In 1901, the Bureau of Indian Affairs purchased 100 acres at the corner of Jackson Street and Magnolia Avenue for a Native American school. At peak enrollment, 1,200 students attended the school from reservations across the country, representing 80 different tribes. Many went on to attend college. At Fillmore Street and Indiana Avenue, the school maintained a dairy and farm, which allowed the institute to be self-contained and self-sustaining. Many of the original buildings were quite beautiful architecturally, but all have been replaced—with the exception of the old post office, which is now used as a museum. In October 1909, Pres. William Howard Taft made a personal visit to the Sherman Indian Institute. A copy of a letter found in the school archives asked the Bureau of Indian Affairs about the installation of heating in the buildings. The bureau's response was, "Why would you need heating? You live in Southern California." But it can get pretty cold here, as evidenced by the loss of numerous citrus crops over the years due to freezing temperatures.

Chemawa Park, located on Magnolia Avenue next to the Sherman Indian Institute, was built at the end of the Riverside and Arlington Electric Railway and was well known for its small zoo, roller-skating rink, amusement park, polo field, fairgrounds, and tea socials. It served as a destination for the streetcar riders from Riverside who paid special rates to enjoy the park's many attractions. In 1927, the board of education purchased the park and built the Chemawa Junior High School, which opened in 1928.

The General Hospital of Riverside County was constructed in 1893, with the first patient admitted on July 26. In 1898, a fire destroyed the hospital, which was quickly rebuilt and destroyed again in 1899 by an earthquake. The County of Riverside purchased land at Harrison Street and Magnolia Avenue and built a new hospital, destined to be a training facility for nurses and interns. It also included a large tuberculosis ward. After celebrating 100 years at that corner, a new County General Hospital was built in nearby Moreno Valley, while the old hospital was demolished to make way for a shopping center.

At one time, Arlington had all the makings of a typical midsize California town with a small downtown area fronted by all the shops and businesses anyone could need. Older residents fondly remember Abrahams Market and Abrahams Clothing, Carpenter's, Lewis's Grocery, Safeway, Mission Pharmacy–Shilling's Soda Fountain, Keystone Drug, the Arlington 5 and 10 cent store, Arlington Feed, Davenport's Grocery, Cal Stereo, Klas Dressmaking Shop, Schulte's Bakery, the *Arlington Times*, the Chatterbox, the Arlington Theater, and an ice house at the corner of Taft and Magnolia Avenue—all places of the past. Van Buren Boulevard at Magnolia Avenue is now the busiest place in town, as Van Buren is being widened from California State Highway 91 north to Garfield Street. Many of the old businesses have been relocated, completely changing the look of the old downtown section.

Today the historic Arlington Heights Greenbelt area is zoned for large lots to encourage the retention of its citrus groves, but sadly citrus production has diminished even there. One bright note for the area was the creation in 1993 of the California Citrus State Historic Park, at 9400 Dufferin Avenue on the corner of Van Buren Boulevard. This park is a beautiful educational and recreational center celebrating the citrus culture of the area and maintaining a sense of what the town of Arlington once was.

This book will take you back to when businesses were family-run and friendly, when schools were small and everyone knew each other, and when friends and neighbors passing along the road always had time to chat. Those times have changed but will not be forgotten.

One

Businesses of Arlington

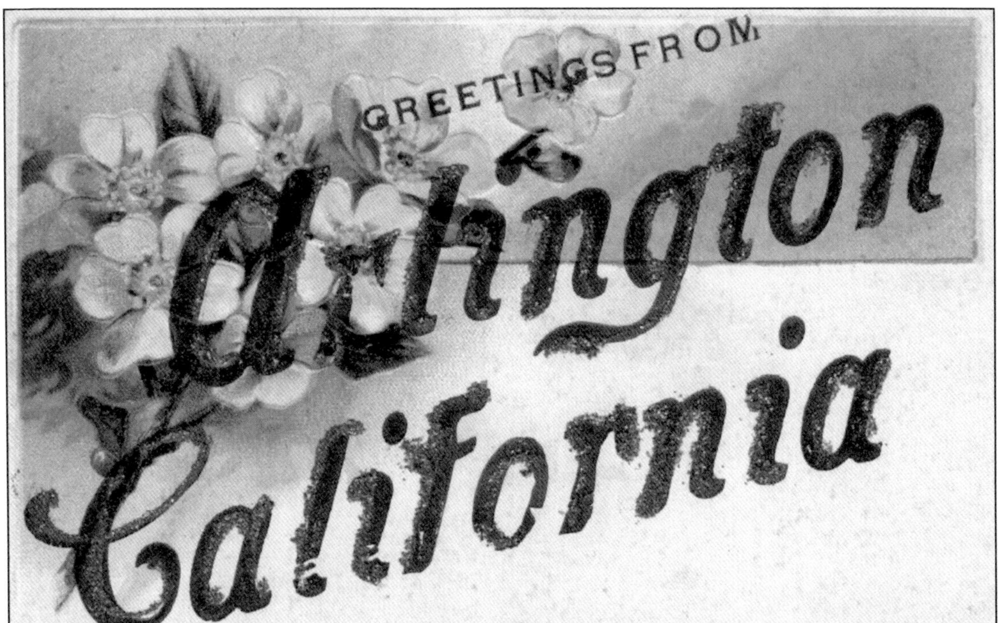

This decorative, rare card reads, "Greetings from Arlington, California." (Courtesy Steve Lech.)

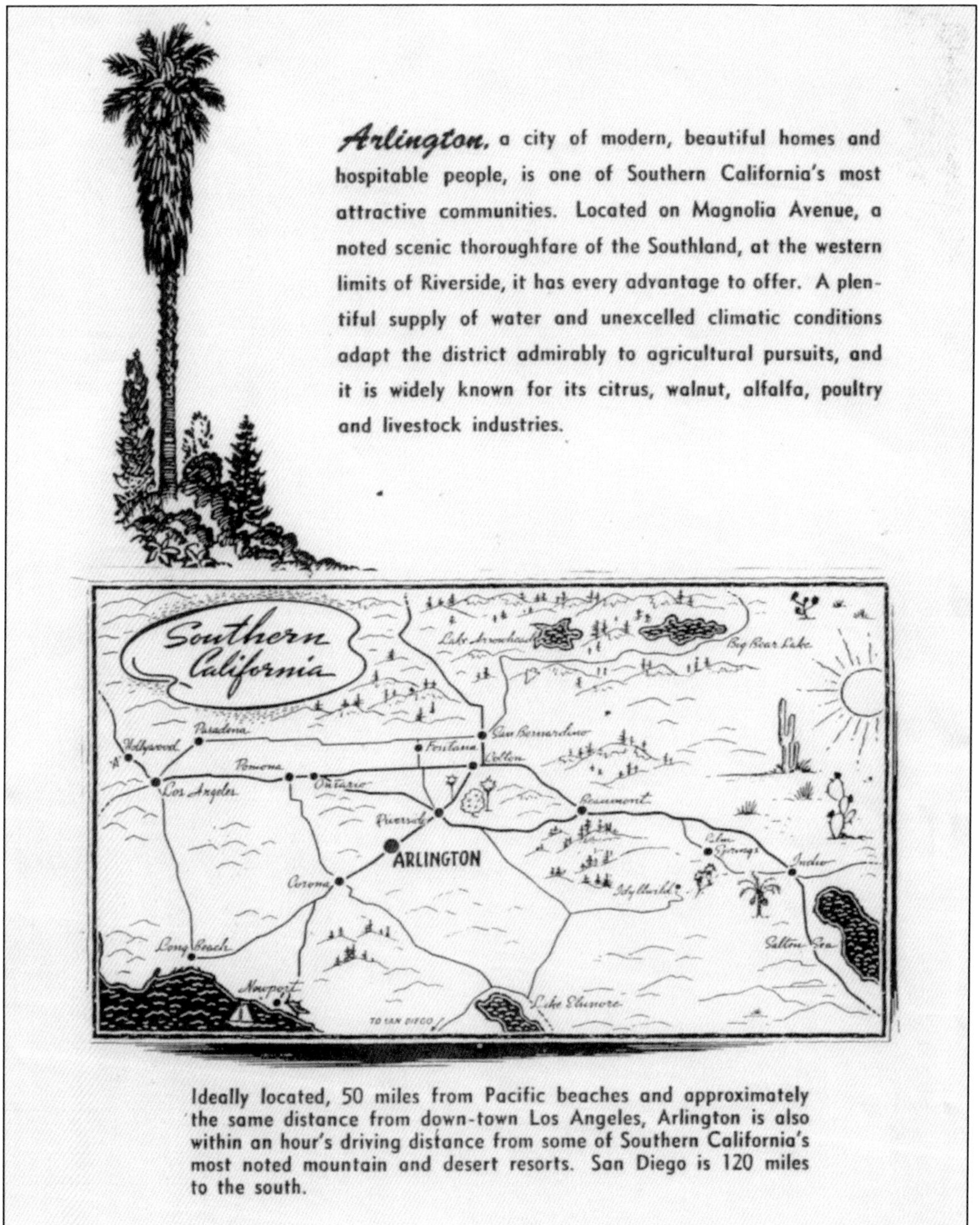

Arlington, a city of modern, beautiful homes and hospitable people, is one of Southern California's most attractive communities. Located on Magnolia Avenue, a noted scenic thoroughfare of the Southland, at the western limits of Riverside, it has every advantage to offer. A plentiful supply of water and unexcelled climatic conditions adapt the district admirably to agricultural pursuits, and it is widely known for its citrus, walnut, alfalfa, poultry and livestock industries.

Ideally located, 50 miles from Pacific beaches and approximately the same distance from down-town Los Angeles, Arlington is also within an hour's driving distance from some of Southern California's most noted mountain and desert resorts. San Diego is 120 miles to the south.

Arlington, a city of modern, beautiful homes and hospitable people, is one of Southern California's most attractive communities. Located on Magnolia Avenue, a noted scenic thoroughfare of the Southland at the western limit of Riverside, it has every advantage to offer. A plentiful supply of water and unexcelled climatic conditions adapt the district admirably to agricultural pursuits such as the citrus, walnut, alfalfa, poultry, and livestock industries. Ideally located 50 miles from Pacific beaches and approximately the same distance from downtown Los Angeles, Arlington is also within an hour's drive from some of Southern California's most noted mountain and desert resorts. San Diego lies 120 miles to the south.

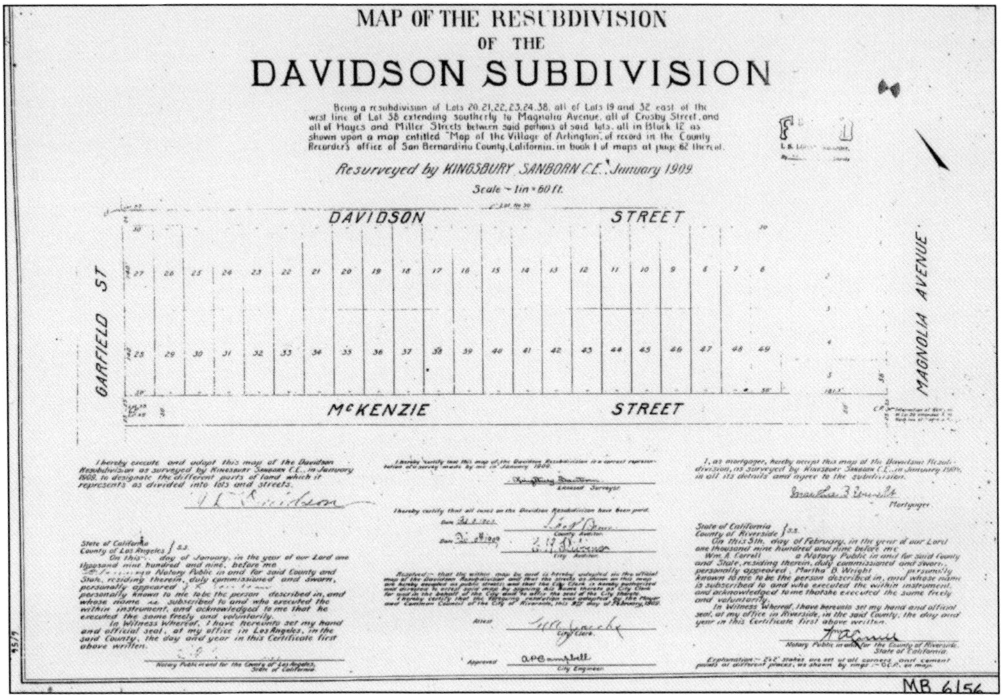

This January 1909 map depicts the Davidson subdivision, located between Magnolia Avenue and Garfield Street in Arlington. Davidson Street is now Everest Avenue, with McKenzie the next street to the west. (Courtesy Mike Gordon.)

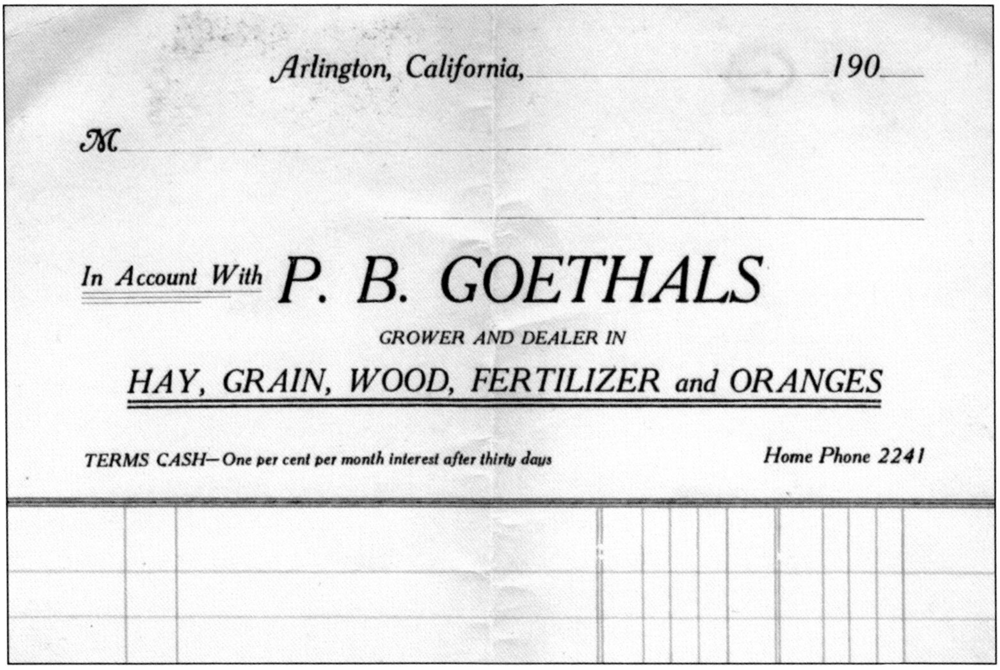

Peter Goethals, one of Arlington's most successful men, made arrangements to create a new lumberyard and wholesale grain business. It operated in conjunction with the Arlington Supply Company about 1905.

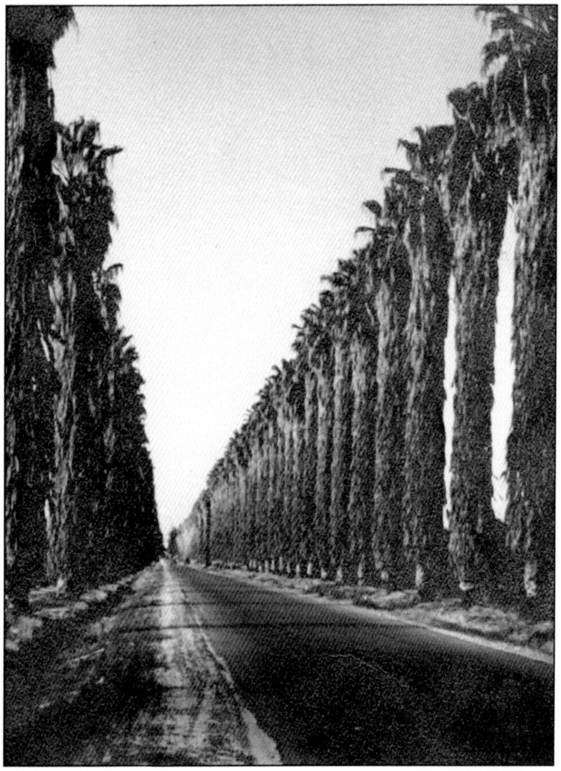

In the 1870s, these trees were planted on the side of the road to be used as landmarks, as one could easily get lost in the back country. Eventually people came to know which trees stood at particular road intersections, making directions a lot easier to follow.

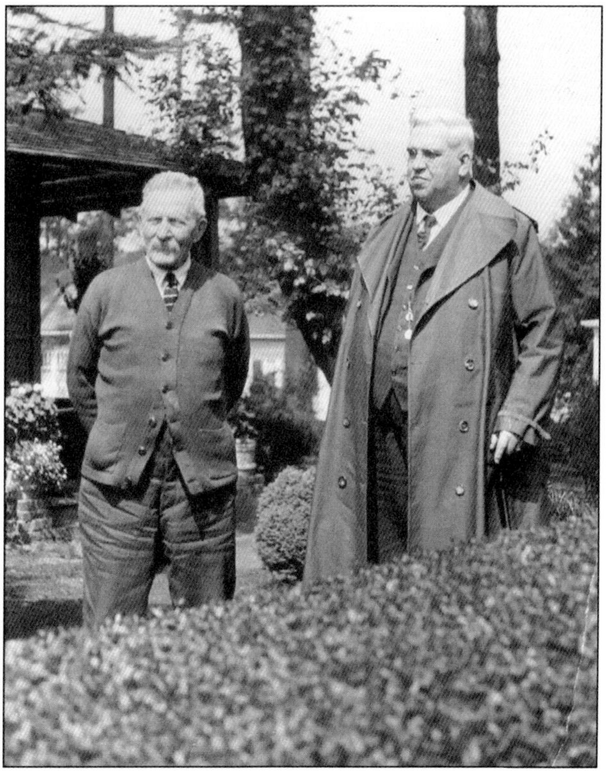

Born in England, William E. and Francis X. Pedley came to Arlington around 1890. Soon becoming local realtors and developers, they had an office on Magnolia Avenue in the heart of Arlington. At the time, the area was growing rapidly as many English people settled in town.

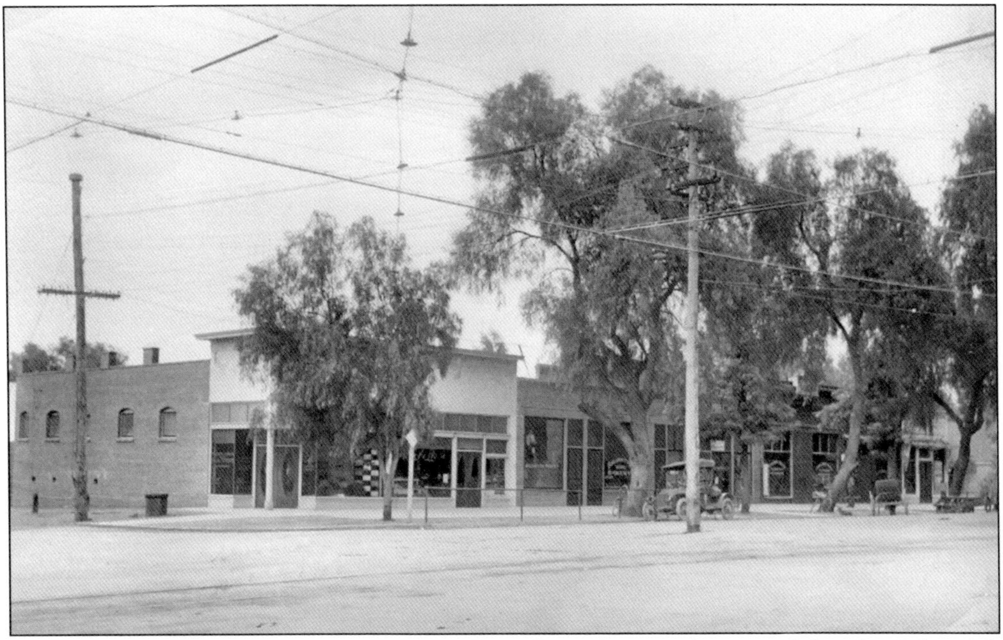

Magnolia Avenue and Van Buren Boulevard are shown here in the second decade of the 20th century. This area was called the McKenzie Block, with McKenzie and Pedley Real Estate–Loan–Insurance listed in the 1907 directory as situated on the corner. Lovely large shade trees provided a place for horses to rest while their owners were buying supplies or conducting business. Notice all the wires above for the trolley car. (Courtesy Steve Lech.)

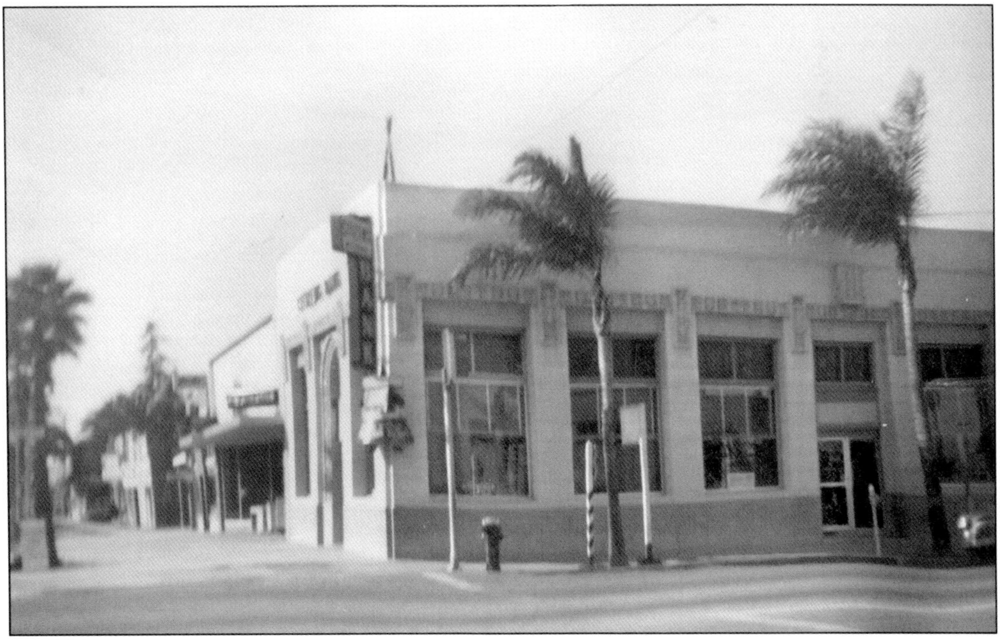

Citizens Bank, known as Citizens National Trust and Savings Bank, served the town of Arlington from 1903 to 1953. It was located at the corner of Van Buren Boulevard and Magnolia Avenue; this photograph shows a view looking west down the block of Magnolia and other businesses around 1950. The building was replaced with a gas station in 1958.

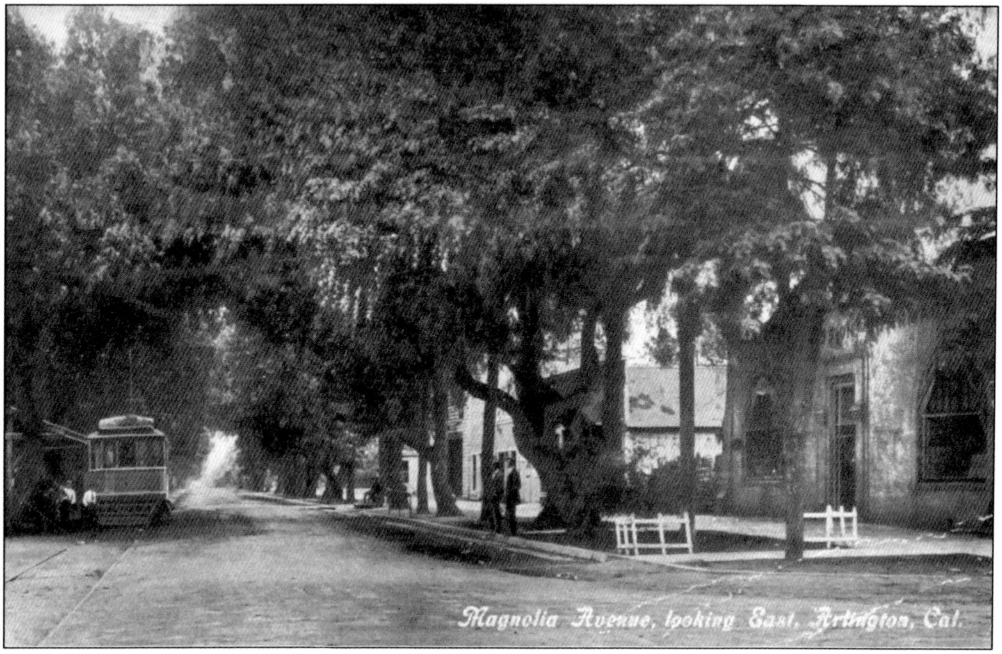

In this 1910 image, both sides of Magnolia Avenue are lined with shade trees, and people are taking advantage of the leaf cover on a hot summer day. As Arlington's main thoroughfare, Magnolia was a busy downtown area with streetcars and businesses. Three people relax by the streetcar, one with his bicycle. On the right is Mission Pharmacy. (Courtesy JoAnne Pease-Simpson.)

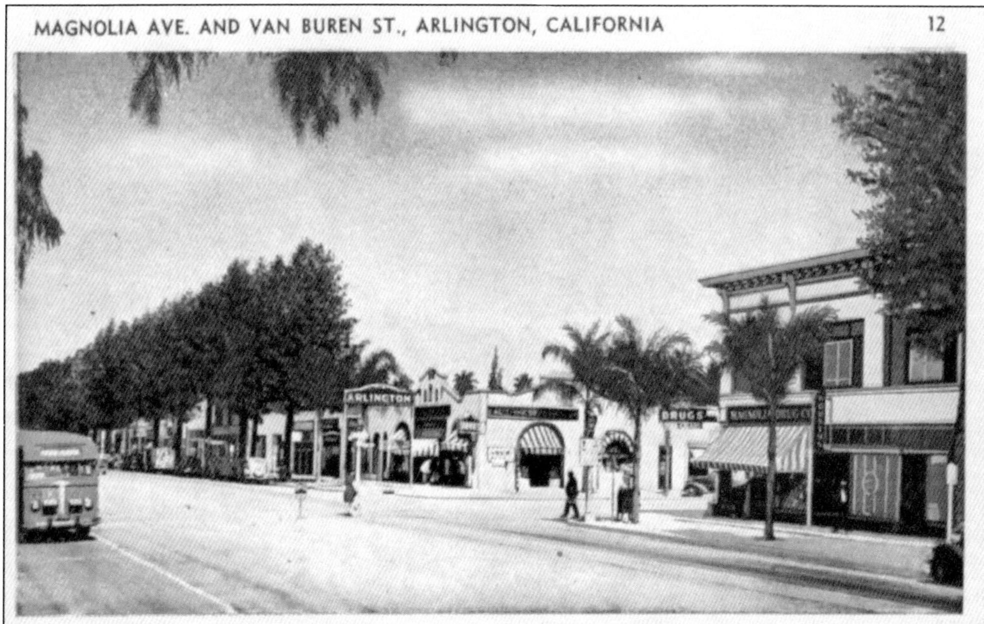

At the intersection of Magnolia Avenue and Van Buren Boulevard, a bus heads west on Magnolia in the 1940s. On the southwest side, Magnolia Drug is located in the Jenkins Building. Large, beautiful trees still line the street. Notice the large Arlington sign. (Courtesy JoAnne Pease-Simpson.)

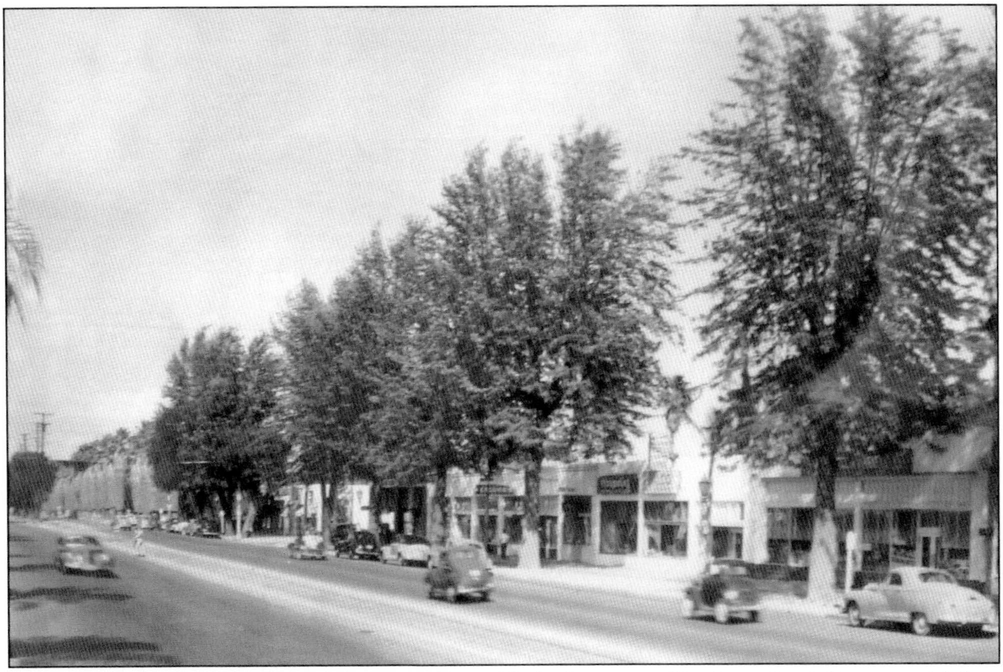

By the 1940s, Magnolia Avenue was a well-established center of business in Arlington with lots of cars coming and going. The street's trees shaded the shopping day.

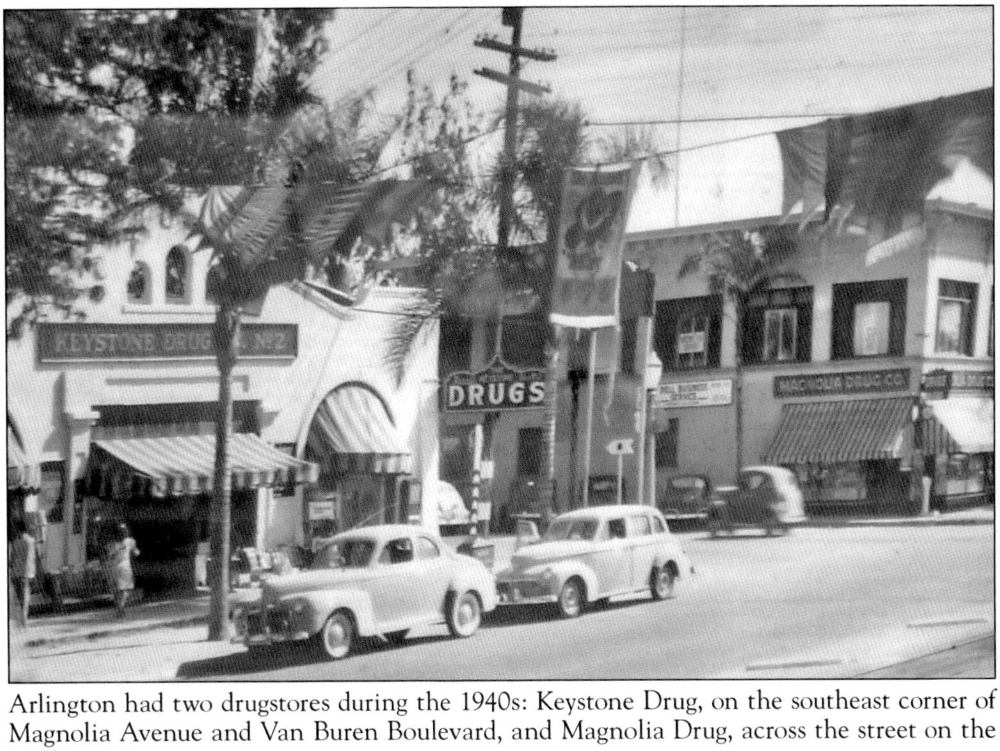

Arlington had two drugstores during the 1940s: Keystone Drug, on the southeast corner of Magnolia Avenue and Van Buren Boulevard, and Magnolia Drug, across the street on the southwest corner.

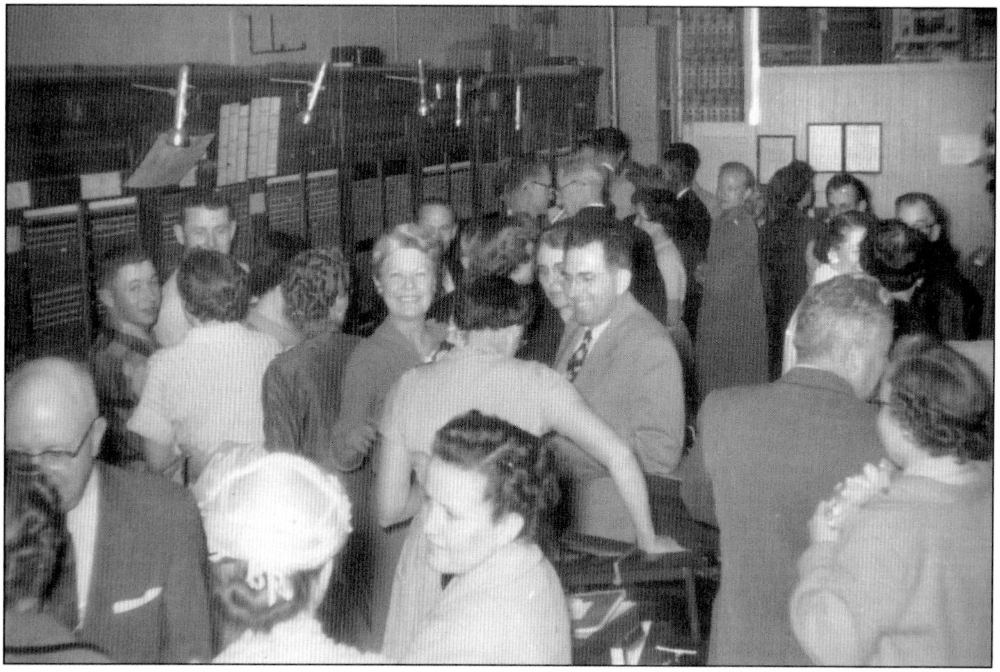

The Arlington-area telephone switchboard (seen below) opened in February 1926 with five employees—mostly women, much more suited by their temperament to work as operators. Jewel Johnson, a former employee of the phone company in Riverside, was appointed chief operator of the Arlington office and worked there until her retirement. Jasie Macquarrie also started in 1926. These two women and many others celebrated (above) "75 years of Women Operators." The firm was backlogged with requests for new telephones. The main switchboard was continuously lit up and jammed due to a lack of available numbers, so a new dial center was established on March 18, 1956, and replaced many operators. Fortunately, none of the operators lost their jobs; they were placed elsewhere within the company. (Courtesy Jim and Mary Belle Neufell Spaulding.)

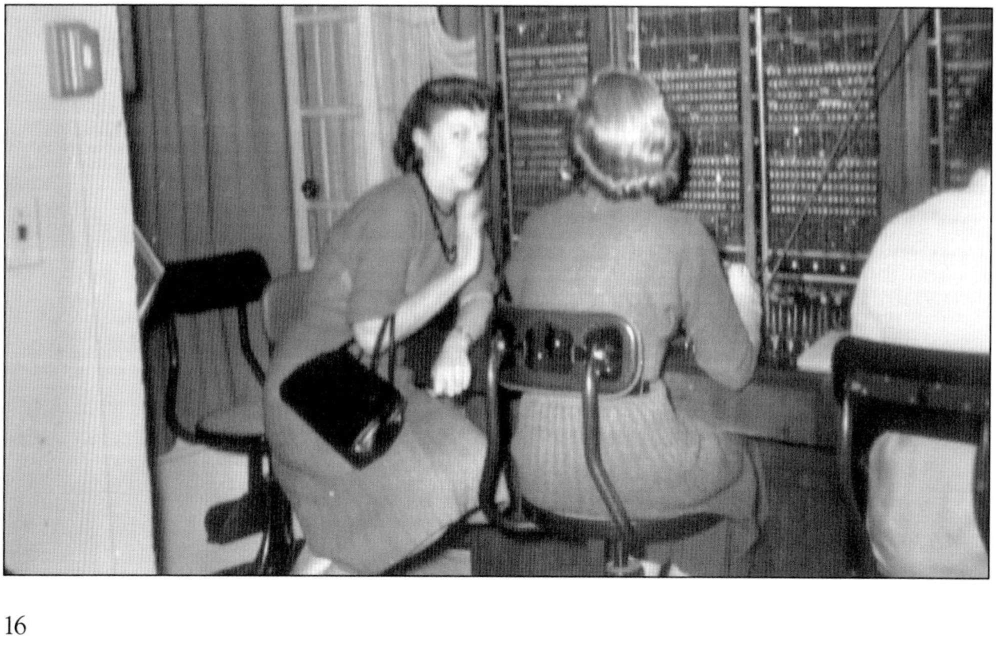

Employees entered this door to access the Pacific Telephone Company of Arlington, located on Van Buren Street (now Boulevard) just south of Magnolia Avenue. The manual switchboard was housed here. When Pacific Telephone went to dial-up, the employees were moved to 9129 Magnolia Avenue because construction took more than a year. (Courtesy Jim and Mary Belle Neufell Spaulding.)

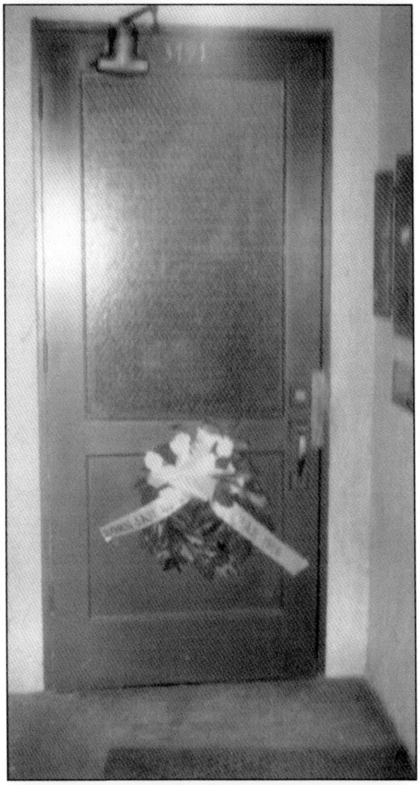

At the Pacific Telephone Company of Arlington, operators were busy with lights always flashing on the switchboard. Every board position was manned all day and night so as to provide good customer service. It was a battle to keep up with the overload of calls. (Courtesy Jim and Mary Belle Neufell Spaulding.)

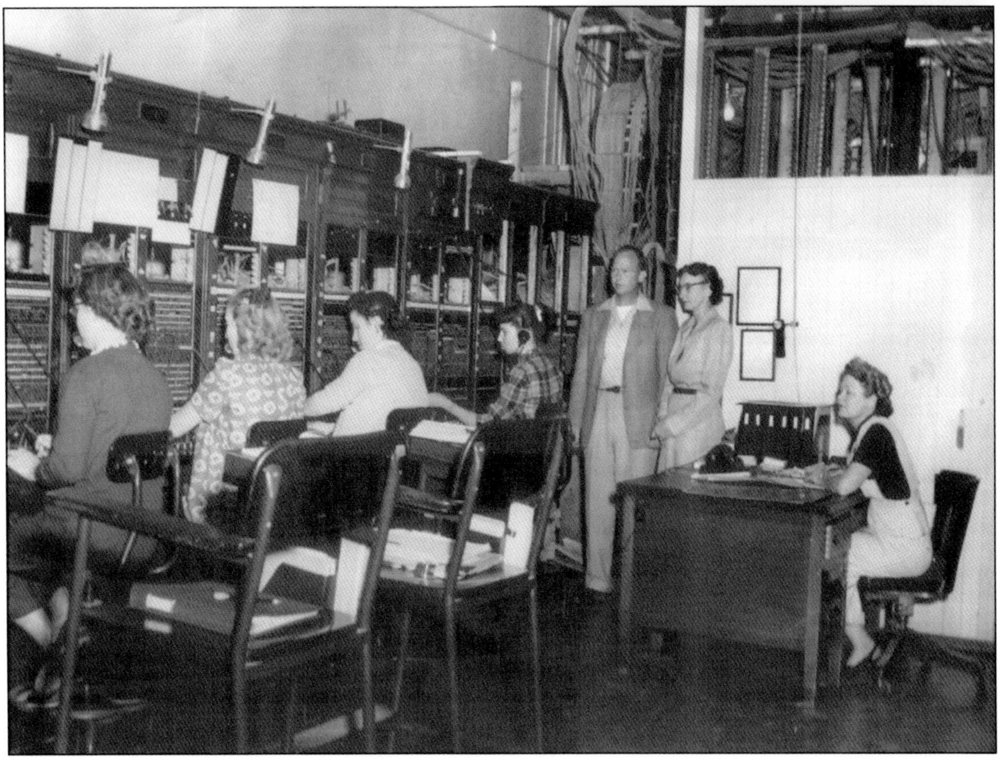

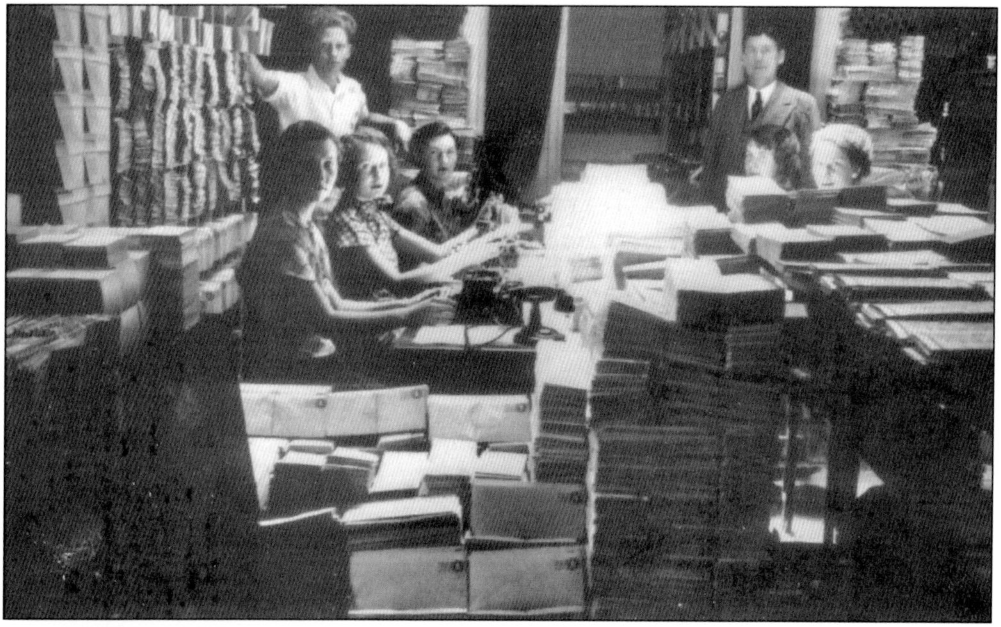

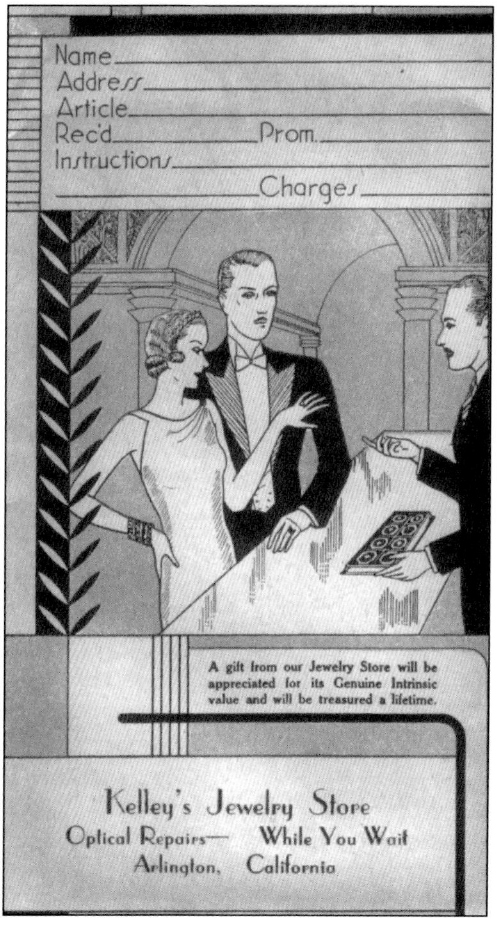

Workers at the Arlington Phototorium received, sorted, and sent out mail daily. The mail was taken to Corona to receive a different postmark because this was a new venture for Guy Kelley, and he was afraid of failure, but the business turned out to be a big success. (Courtesy Norman and Velda Kelley.)

Kelley's Jewelry and the Arlington Phototorium, located adjacent to each other, were both owned by the Kelley family. This would have been the envelope in which to place your jewelry for repairs or to purchase that special gift that would be treasured for a lifetime. (Courtesy Norm and Velda Kelley.)

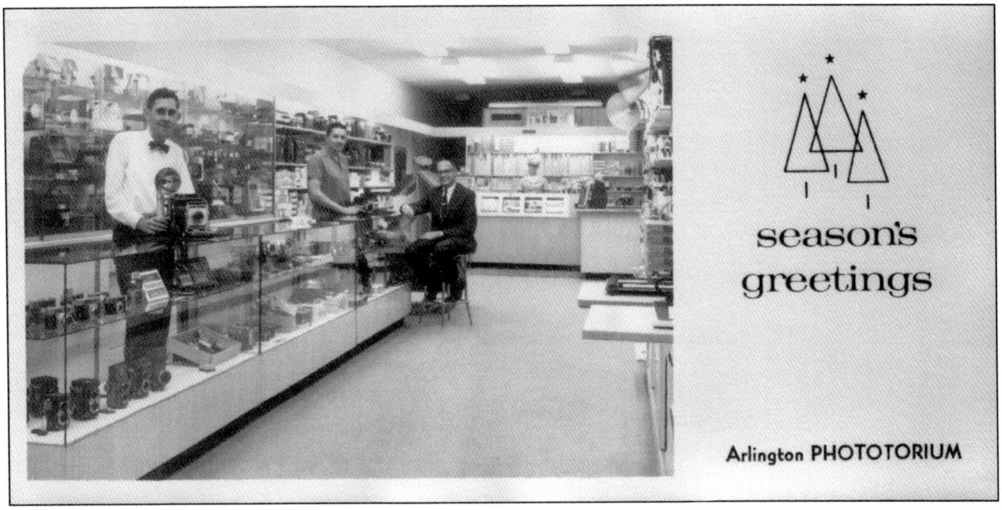

The Arlington Phototorium had special season's greetings cards made like postcards. The friendly, smiling faces of the employees greeted recipients of this photograph just as if they were customers at the Phototorium. (Courtesy Norman and Velda Kelley.)

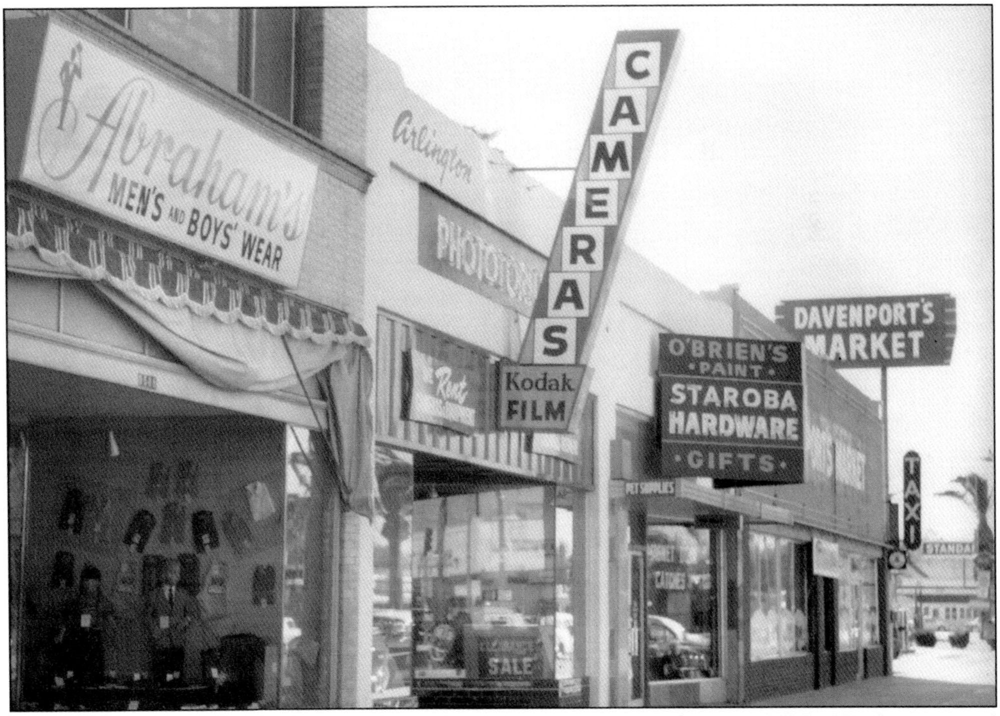

Magnolia Avenue was the main business street in downtown Arlington. Walt Abraham owned Abraham's, a popular men's and boys' clothing shop. Norman Kelley owned the Arlington Phototorium, where everyone bought film and cameras; the other half of the Phototorium was Kelley's Jewelry. Next door were O'Brien's Paint and Staroba Hardware. Davenport's Market offered fresh produce. Residents would walk to Magnolia Avenue to do their shopping and then catch a taxi home with all their goods. (Courtesy Norman and Velda Kelley.)

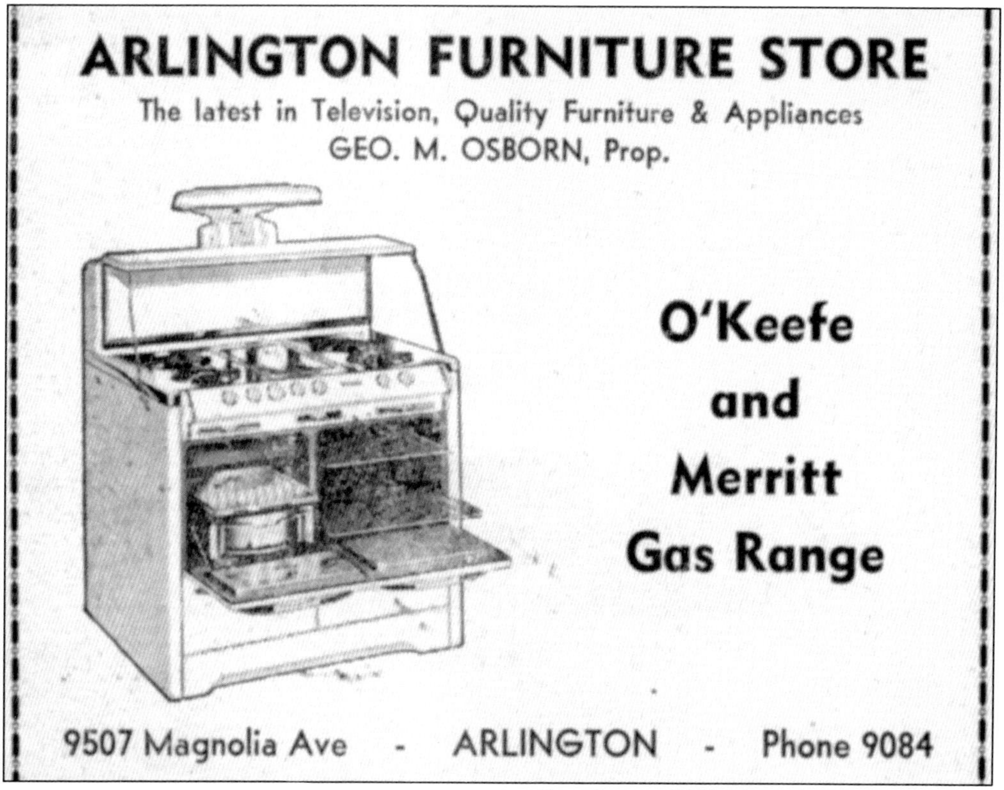

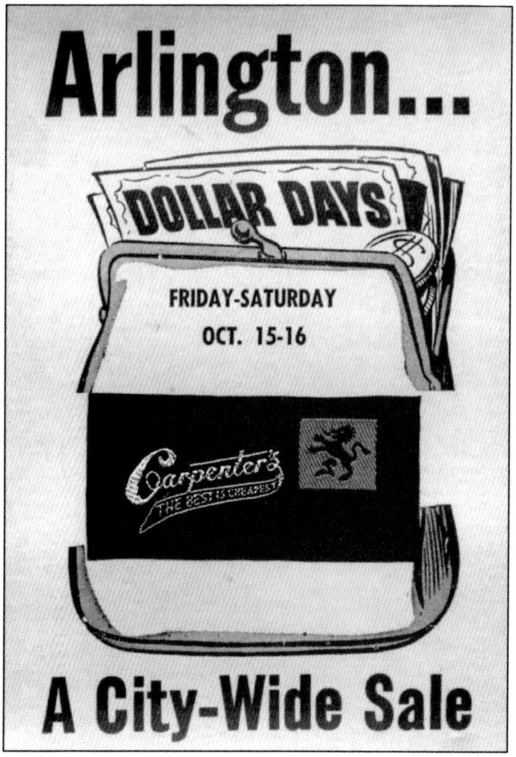

Standing at 9507 Magnolia Avenue, Arlington Furniture boasted a large selection of televisions, furniture, and appliances in the 1940s. In 1935, records were broken with the sales of electric ranges. Now the shop just carries televisions and a line of appliances. Styles sure have changed through the years.

Carpenter's department store was located at 9377 Magnolia Avenue in Arlington. The shop carried the best clothing in town, from dressy to casual, with departments for men, women, and children. Dollar Days highlighted their specials on Friday and Saturdays.

H. W. HAILS BRACE SHOP

Artificial Limbs — Surgical Corsets — Arch Supports
Braces — Repairs
Wheel Chairs E. & J. AND INVALID Walkers
Sales and Rentals
3815 Holden at Magnolia ARLINGTON Phone 9459-W

Arlington seemed to have a shop for everything. H. W. Hails Brace Shop, at 3815 Holden at Magnolia Avenue, coordinated sales, rentals, and repairs for carrier medical supplies, artificial limbs, surgical corsets, arch supports, braces, wheelchairs, and walkers.

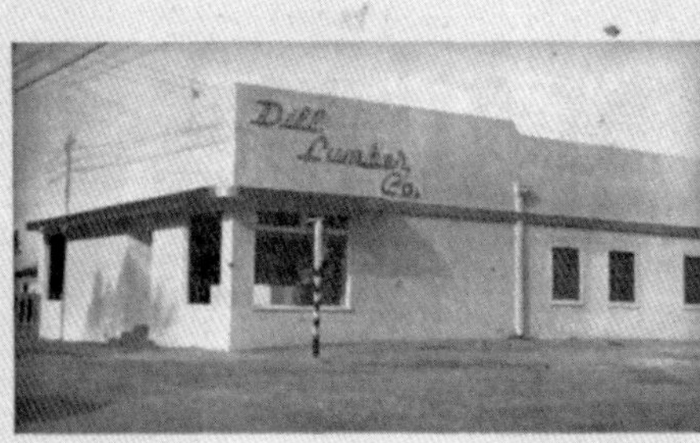

LUMBER

BUILDING MATERIALS
Paint -- Hardware
Sash -- Doors
ALSO STEEL SASH
Wallboard and Insulation

Dill Lumber Company

3839 Van Buren ☆ Arlington, Calif. ☆ Phone 9000

Dill Lumber Company, seen here in the 1940s, stood at 3839 Van Buren Boulevard, north of Magnolia Avenue. With the growth of the town, building supplies were always needed. Dill Lumber carried construction materials, paint, hardware, sash, doors, steel sash, wallboard, and insulation.

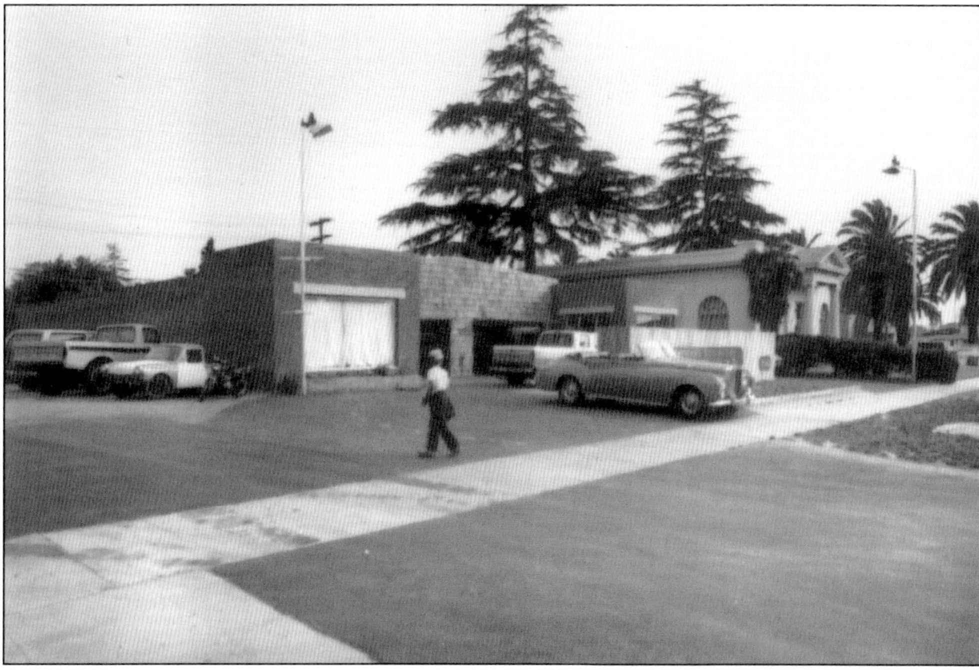

Many local residents took their cars to the Arlington Garage on Magnolia Avenue for routine maintenance and repairs. Eventually the garage was removed to allow for the new addition to the public library, which is expected to reopen at the end of 2007 or beginning of 2008. The historic part of the main library will remain the same. (Courtesy Norman and Velda Kelley.)

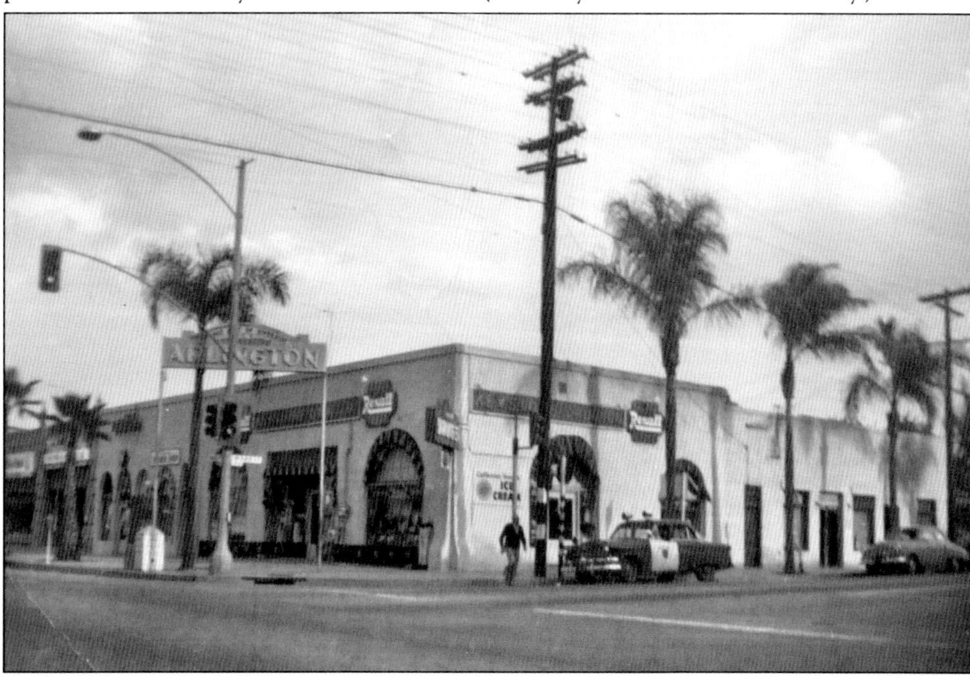

The popular Keystone Drug was located at the southeast corner of Magnolia Avenue and Van Buren Boulevard. In the 1950s, just about everybody frequented this favorite hangout—even the local police! Note the Arlington sign next to the store.

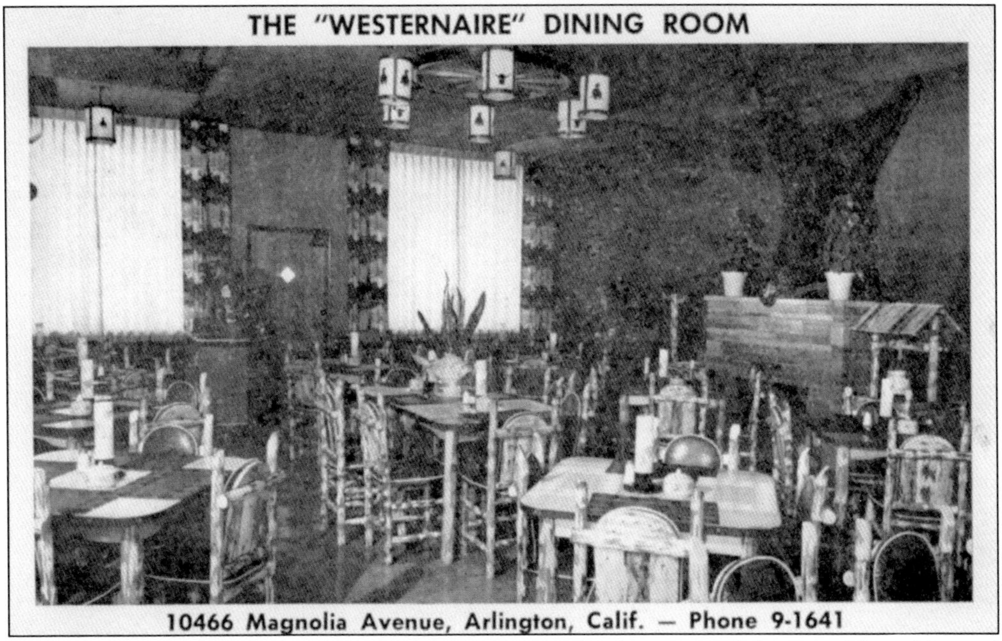

The Westernaire Dining Room stood at 10466 Magnolia Avenue in Arlington. The tables and chairs were fashioned from round pieces of tree limbs, contributing to a very rustic feeling in the restaurant. If someone wanted to make reservations, all he had to do was dial phone number 9-1641. (Courtesy Steve Lech.)

John H. Jacobs Shoe Repair

Up-to-date shoe repairing, using the finest materials.
Our work guaranteed and prices right.

KIWI SHOE SHINE & DYEING PARLOR

9511 MAGNOLIA ARLINGTON, CALIFORNIA

John H. Jacobs Shoe Repair was situated at 9511 Magnolia Avenue. Using the finest and most up-to-date materials, Jacobs guaranteed his work at reasonable prices. The Kiwi Shoe Shine and Dyeing Parlor was housed in the same building.

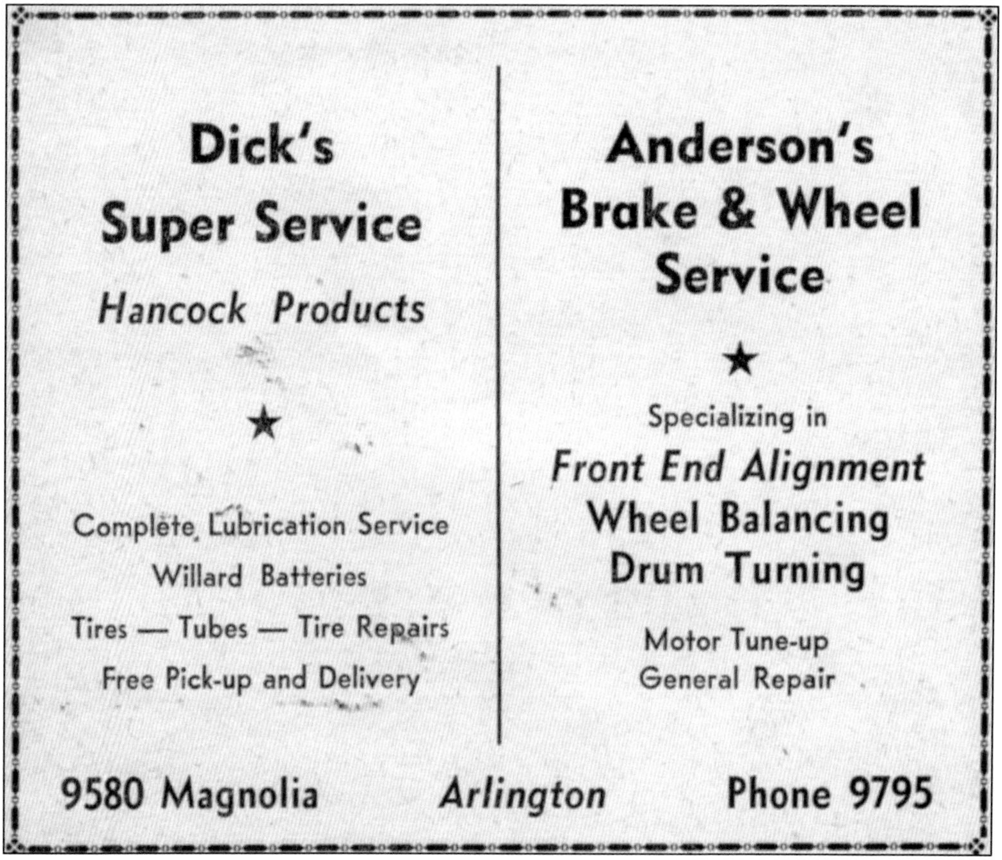

Dick's Super Service and Anderson's Brake and Wheel Service were located at 9580 Magnolia Avenue in Arlington. Dick's provided a complete lubrication service, tubes and tire repair, and free pickup and delivery. Anderson's specialized in front-end alignment, wheel balancing, drum turning, motor tune-up, and general repair.

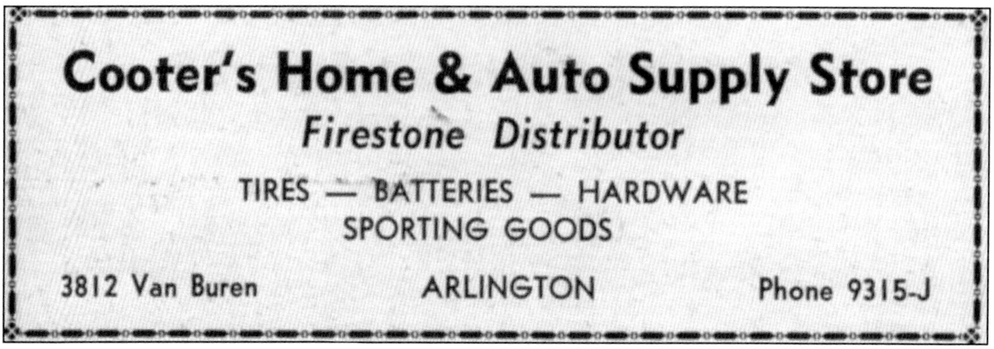

Cooter's was a home and auto supply store at 3812 Van Buren Boulevard in the 1940s. The business's advertisement reads, "TIRES–BATTERIES–HARDWARE–SPORTING GOODS."

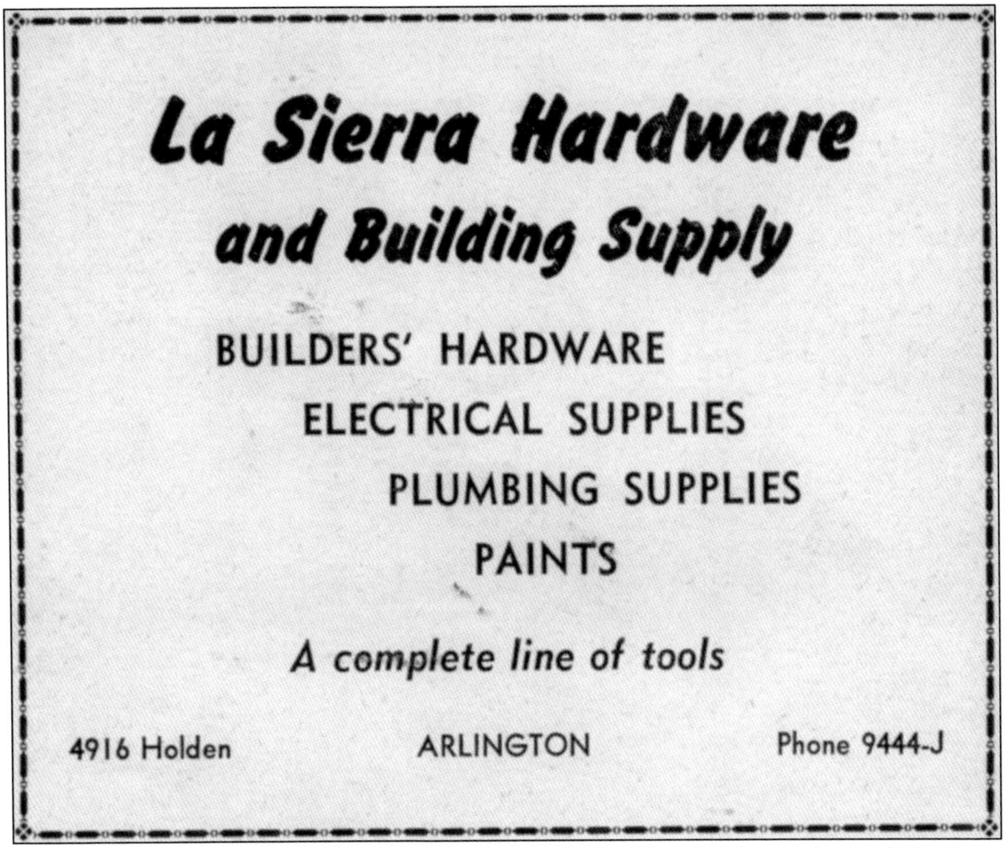

La Sierra Hardware, at 4916 Holden in Arlington, provided building, hardware, electrical, plumbing, and paint supplies plus a complete line of tools.

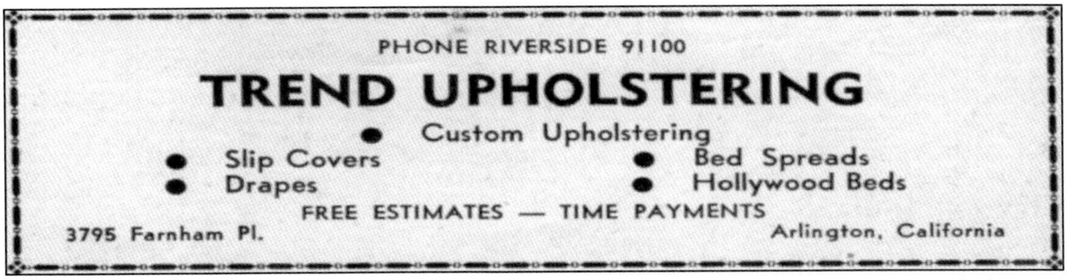

Trend Upholstering stood at 3795 Farnham Place. The business not only reupholstered furniture, but also created slipcovers, drapes, bedspreads, and covers for Hollywood beds. Trend Upholstering would come to customers' homes to give free estimates and allow them to make planned payments if needed.

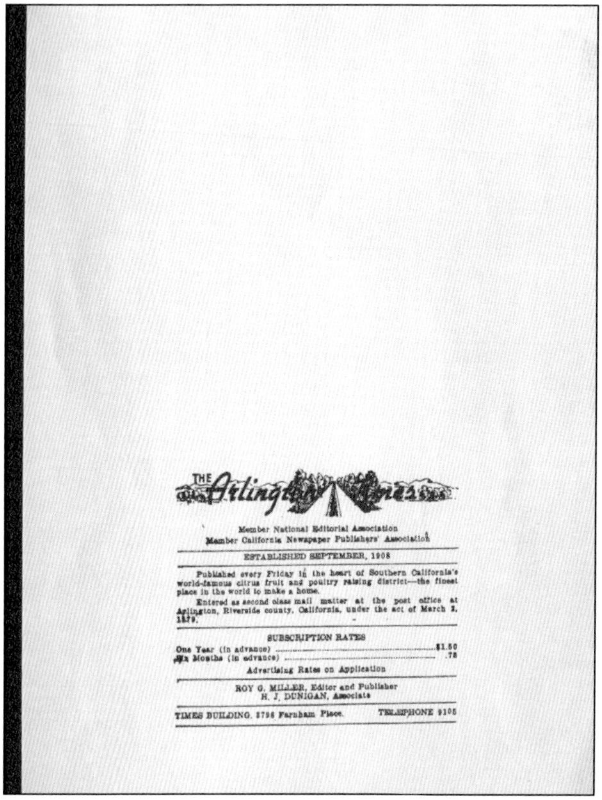
THE Arlington Times

Member National Editorial Association
Member California Newspaper Publishers' Association

ESTABLISHED SEPTEMBER, 1908

Published every Friday in the heart of Southern California's world-famous citrus fruit and poultry raising district—the finest place in the world to make a home.

Entered as second class mail matter at the post office at Arlington, Riverside county, California, under the act of March 3, 1879.

SUBSCRIPTION RATES

One Year (in advance)	$1.50
Six Months (in advance)	.75

Advertising Rates on Application

ROY G. MILLER, Editor and Publisher
H. J. DUNIGAN, Associate

TIMES BUILDING, 3796 Farnham Place. TELEPHONE 9105

The *Arlington Times*, established in September 1908, served as the weekly newspaper for the town and included local and national news. The subscription rates were one year (in advance) $1.50 or six months (in advance) 75¢. The newspaper was located at 3796 Farnham Place, just south of Magnolia Avenue.

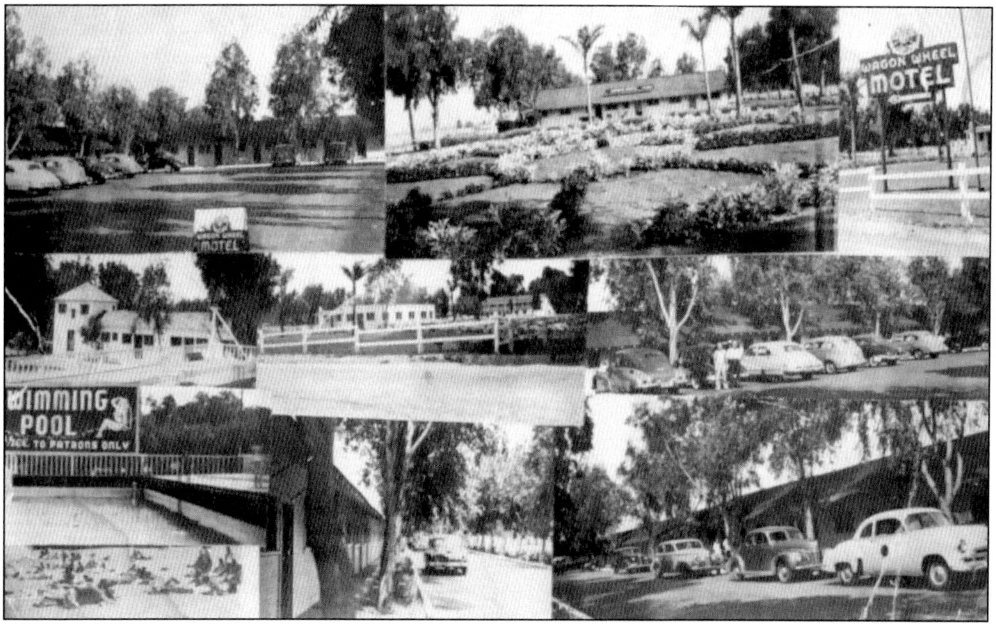

The Wagon Wheel Motel, at 10299 Magnolia Avenue at the northeast corner of Tyler Street, was the only motel in town for a time. Sammy Davis Jr. owned the business in the 1940s. Situated on the main highway, the motel offered many amenities for travelers: a refreshing swimming pool, a little kitchen for meals, and parking right in front of the rooms.

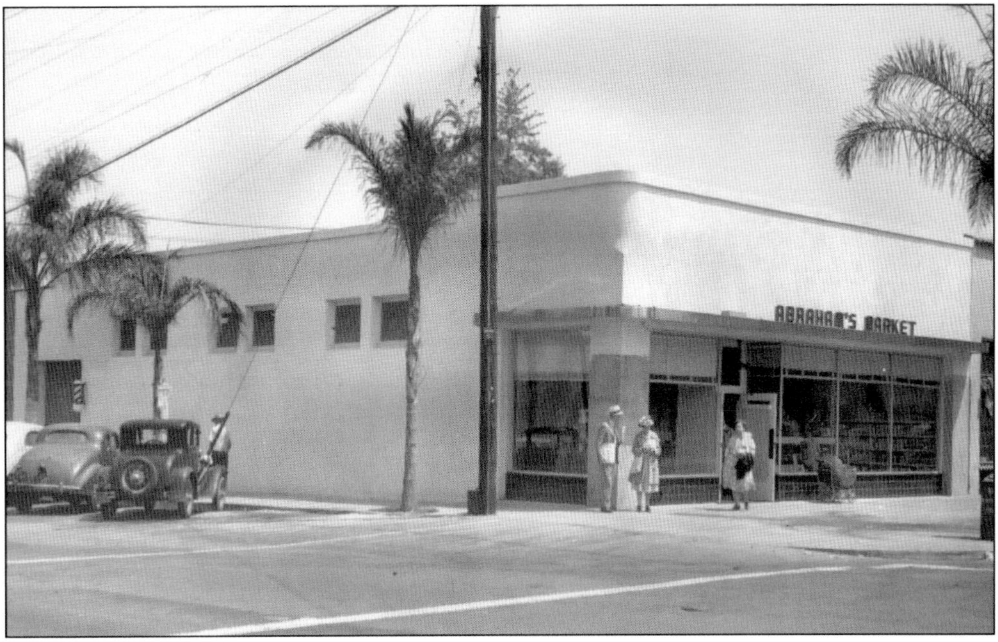

Opening on May 10, 1923, in a corner of Carpenter's department store, Abraham's Market was owned and operated by Ted and Rose Abraham. Ted would bicycle through the area with grocery orders each morning and deliver the food that afternoon in his 1922 Ford. In those days, 90 percent of the business was by delivery. Ted and Rose's three sons—Ted Jr., Bud, and Jed—also worked there. Below, the store later moved to the old Arlington Furniture building and then across the street to the corner of Magnolia Avenue and Van Buren Boulevard (above). (Courtesy Bud and Lois Abraham.)

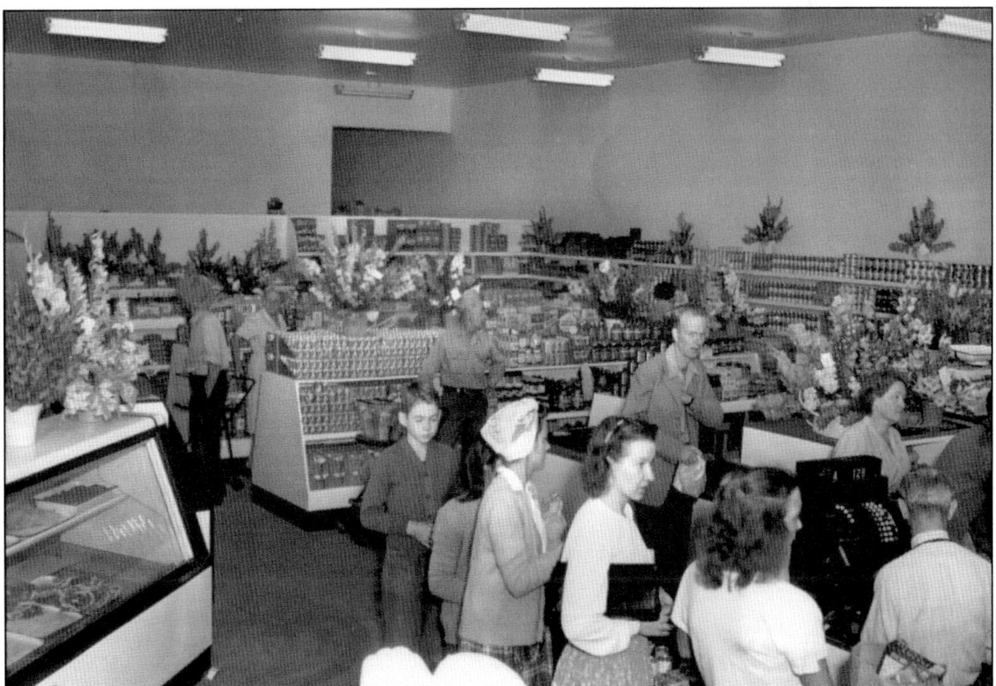

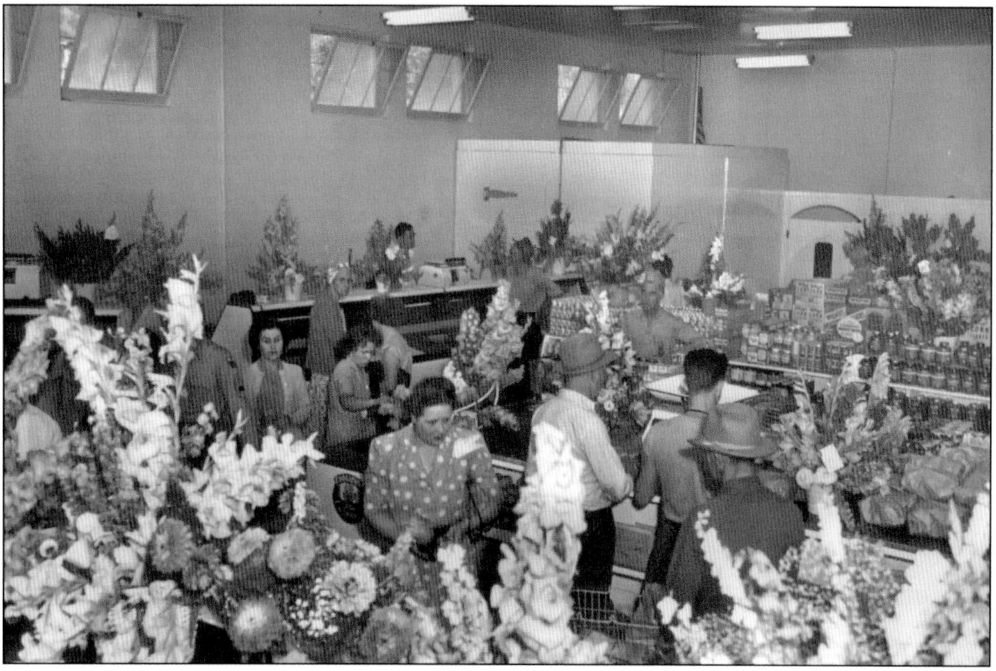

Abraham's Market was doing a good business, its shelves always filled with fresh food and flowers (above). But on June 29, 1945, a gas leak in the basement caused an explosion that blew up the building (below). The gas company rebuilt the structure but took an inordinately long time in doing so. The market was closed for one year and one week before reopening. Ted Sr. then turned the operation over to his three boys. Abraham's Market was in business for 48 years before the family hung up the closed sign for the last time on June 30, 1971, marking the end of an era for neighborhood grocery stores in Arlington. (Courtesy Bud and Lois Abraham.)

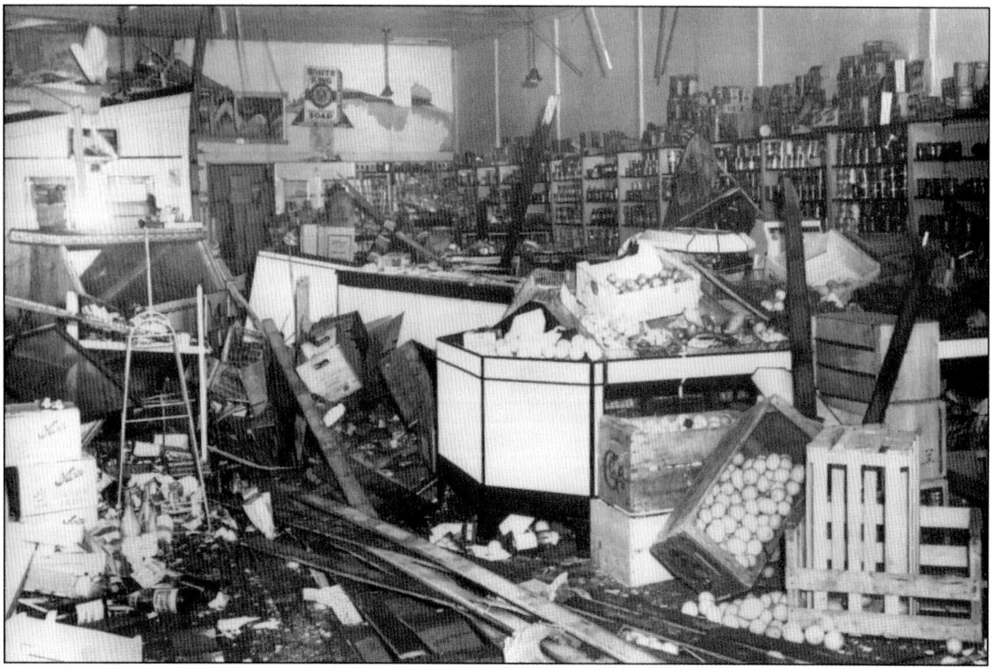

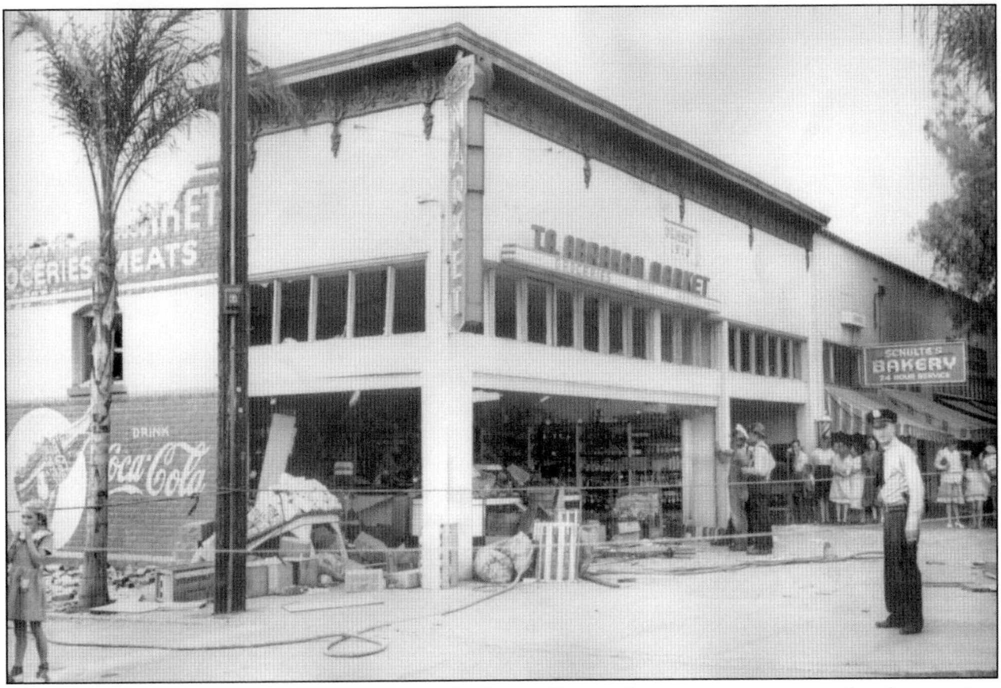

The day after the explosion, so many people from all over the area came to see the destruction that the area had to be contained with rope. A policeman was posted out front to keep a close eye out for any mishaps. (Courtesy Bud and Lois Abraham.)

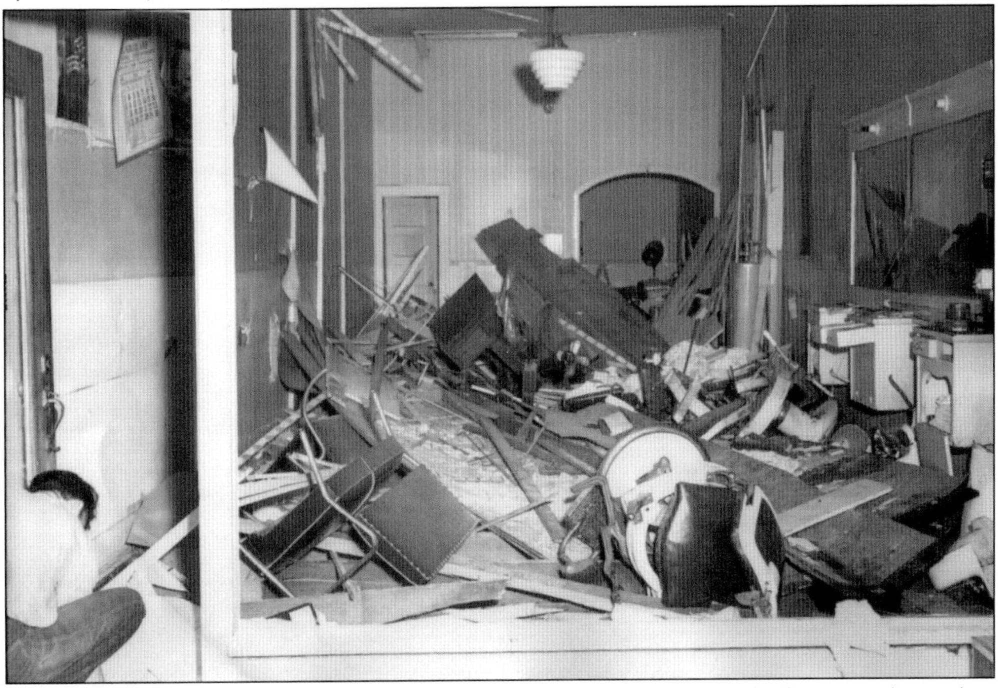
The gas explosion not only rocked the town of Arlington, but destroyed Abraham's Market and an adjacent barbershop as well. The barber chair flew to the ceiling and crashed into the middle of the floor. The front wall and windows were also blown out. (Courtesy Bud and Lois Abraham.)

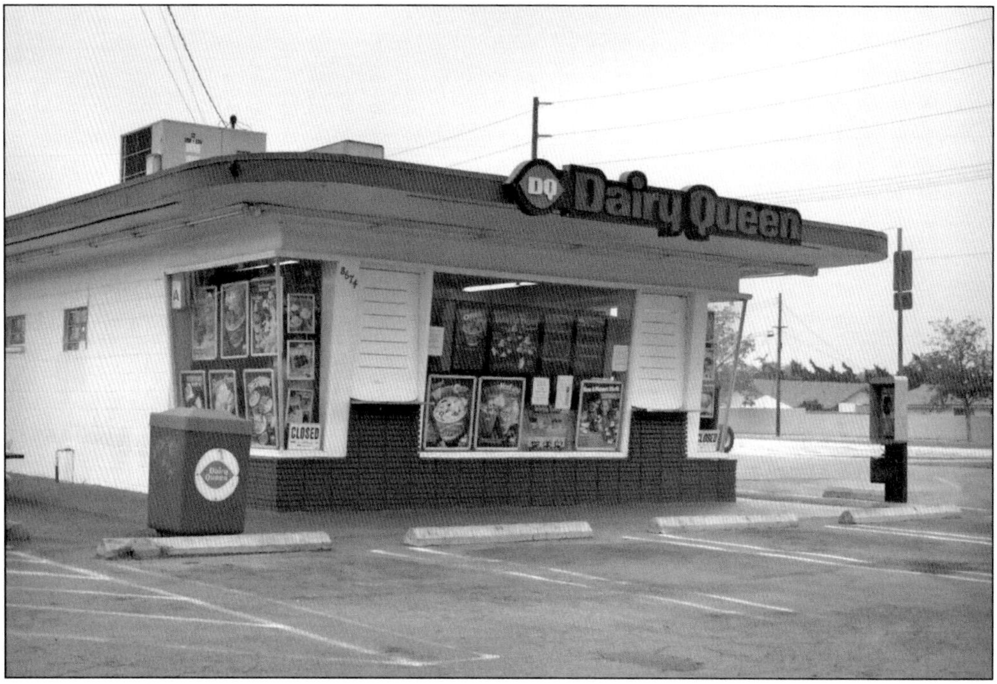

Dairy Queen, located at the corner of California and Monroe Streets, was the locals' favorite place for a special treat on a hot day. The business specialized in hot fudge sundaes, shakes, banana splits, root beer floats, dilly bars, and many other ice cream treats.

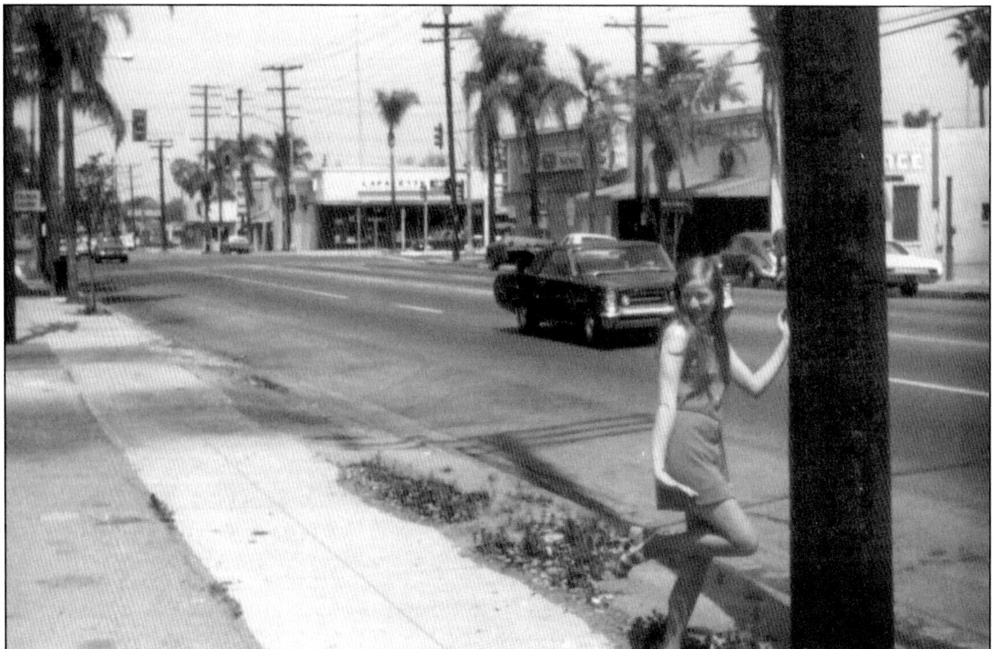

In this northward view of Van Buren Boulevard in the 1960s, a young lady poses by the power pole as cars pass. All the businesses are now gone; they had to be demolished in order to widen the street. (Courtesy Norm and Velda Kelley.)

Two

Many Schools

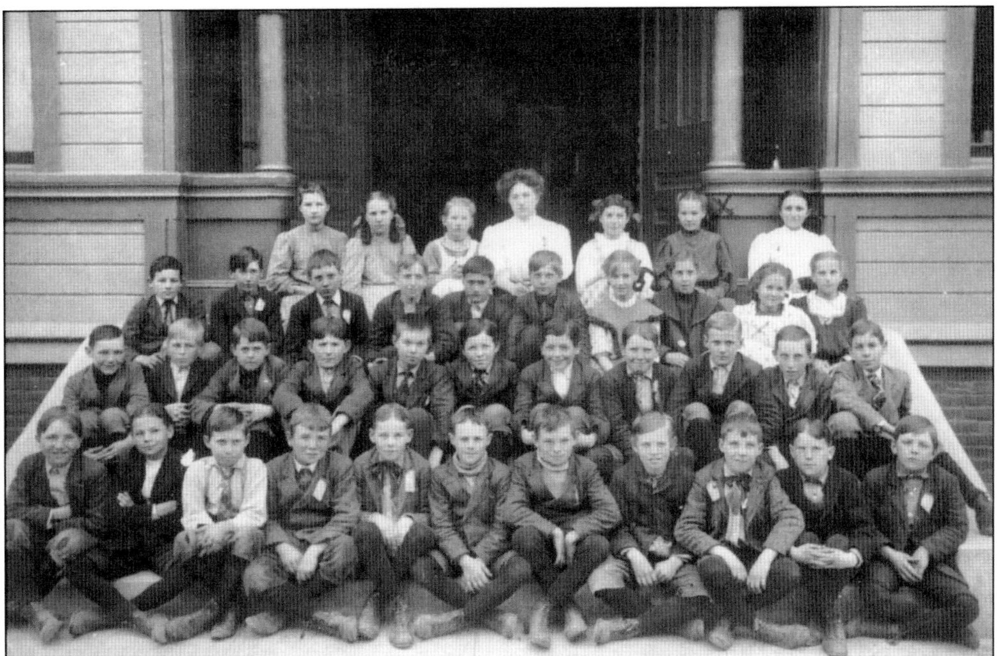

Shown here around 1906 is the fourth-grade class at Magnolia School, later renamed Arlington School. Teacher Helen Bass had a very large class consisting mostly of boys. In the fourth row, sixth from the left, is the author's great-aunt Helen Goethals. The school stood one block north of Magnolia Avenue on the site now occupied by Arlington Park.

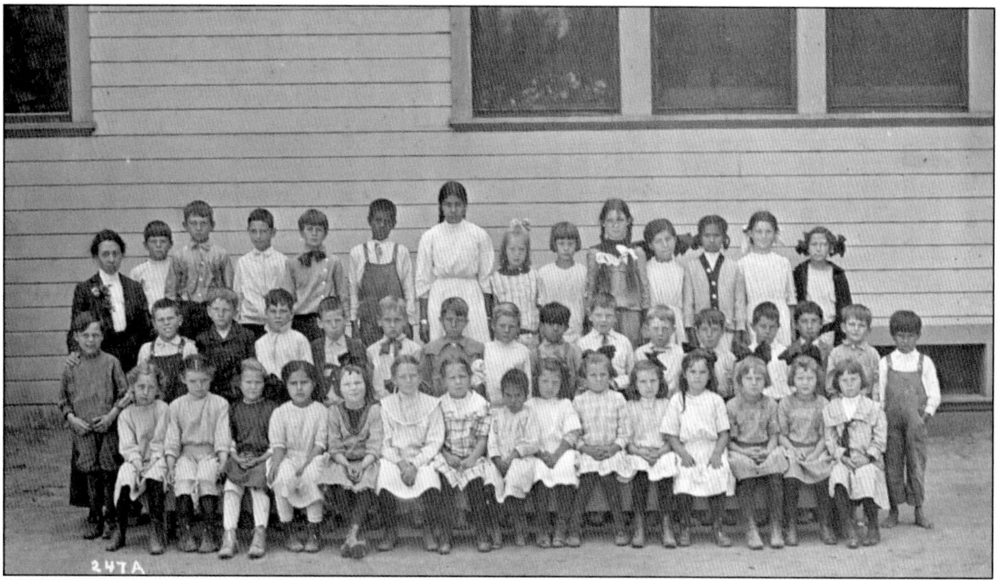

Mrs. Copeland taught the first grade at Arlington School. Children of all ages were often in the same class, as there were not enough students of one age group to put together a single class. In 1911, Mrs. Copeland had 44 pupils under her care.

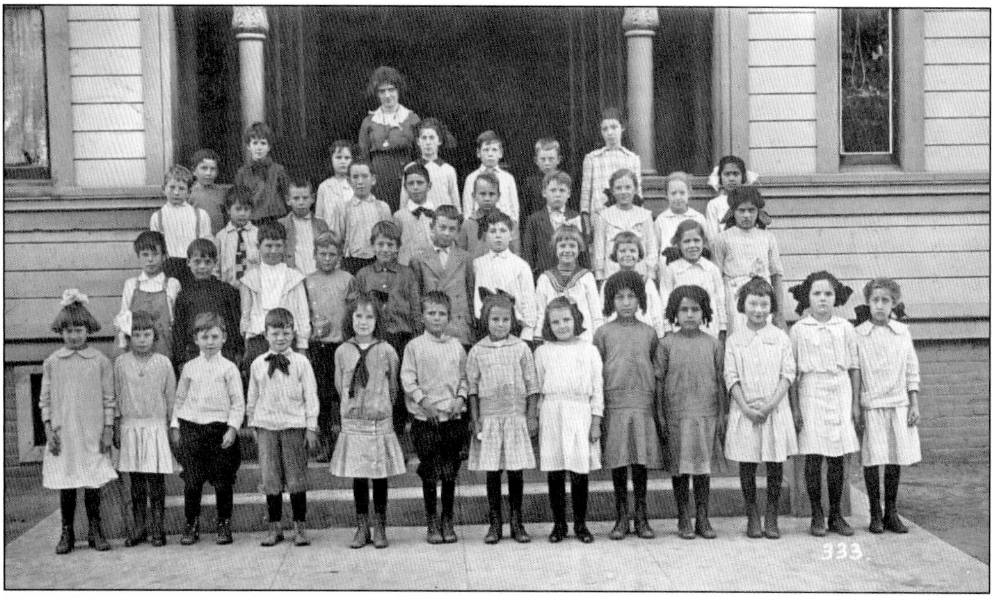

Miss Wilson's third-grade class at Arlington School poses for a photograph in 1913. Almost all of the young girls wear large bows in their hair and long-waisted dresses; some of the boys wear bow ties.

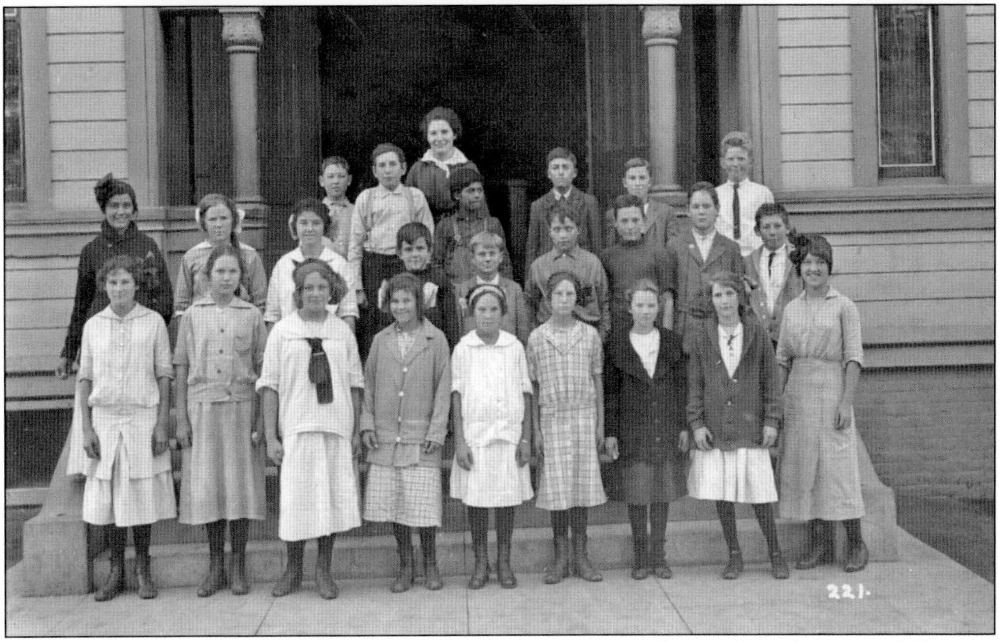

Marie Goethals (in the fourth row) spent her first year teaching this sixth-grade class at Arlington School during 1914–1915.

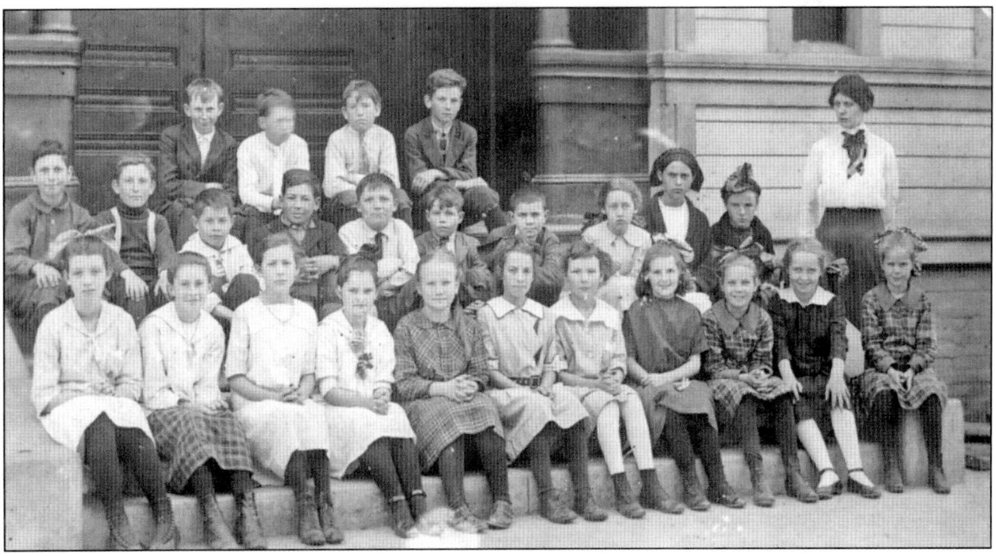

The Arlington School fifth-grade class was taught by Miss R. Robb (right) in 1916. Here the 25 students are all seated on the front steps of the school, ready and waiting for their portrait to be taken.

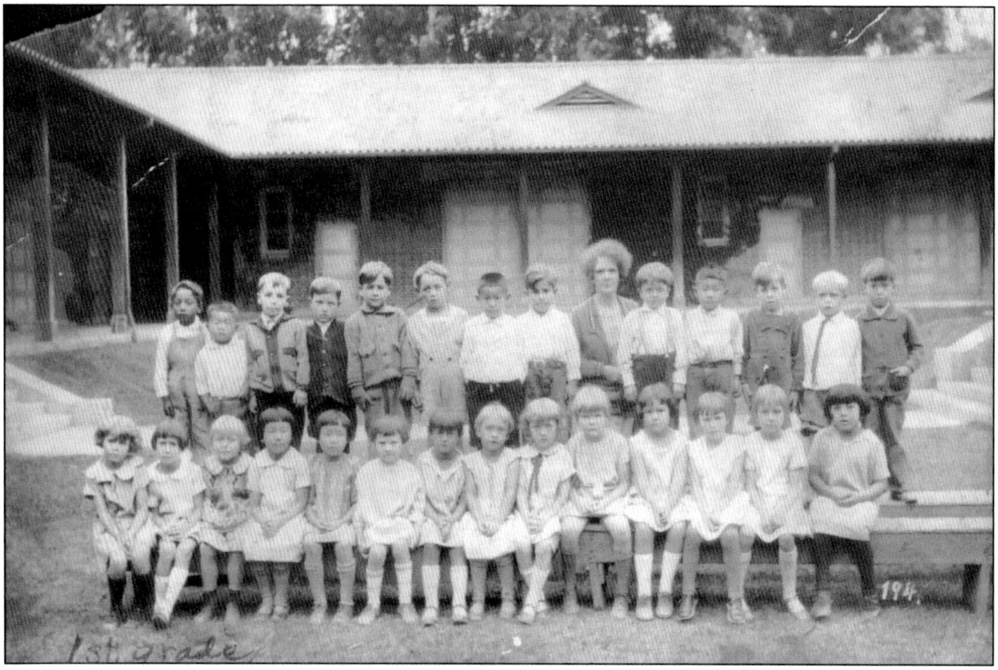

This c. 1926 photograph shows 27 first-grade students sitting and standing on benches in Liberty Elementary School's back courtyard. Their teacher is seen in the second row, ninth from the left.

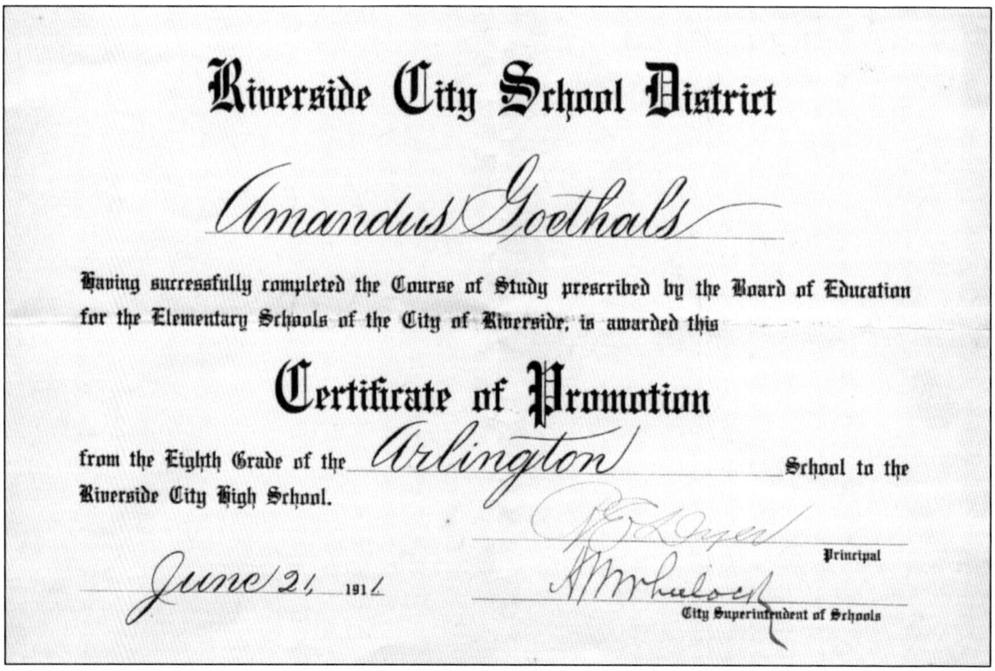

Riverside City School District

Amandus Goethals

Having successfully completed the Course of Study prescribed by the Board of Education for the Elementary Schools of the City of Riverside, is awarded this

Certificate of Promotion

from the Eighth Grade of the Arlington School to the Riverside City High School.

Principal

June 21, 1911

City Superintendent of Schools

A certificate of promotion was issued to Amandus Goethals by the Riverside City School District on June 21, 1911. Amandus successfully completed the eighth-grade courses at Arlington Elementary School in Arlington, allowing him to attend the Riverside City High School.

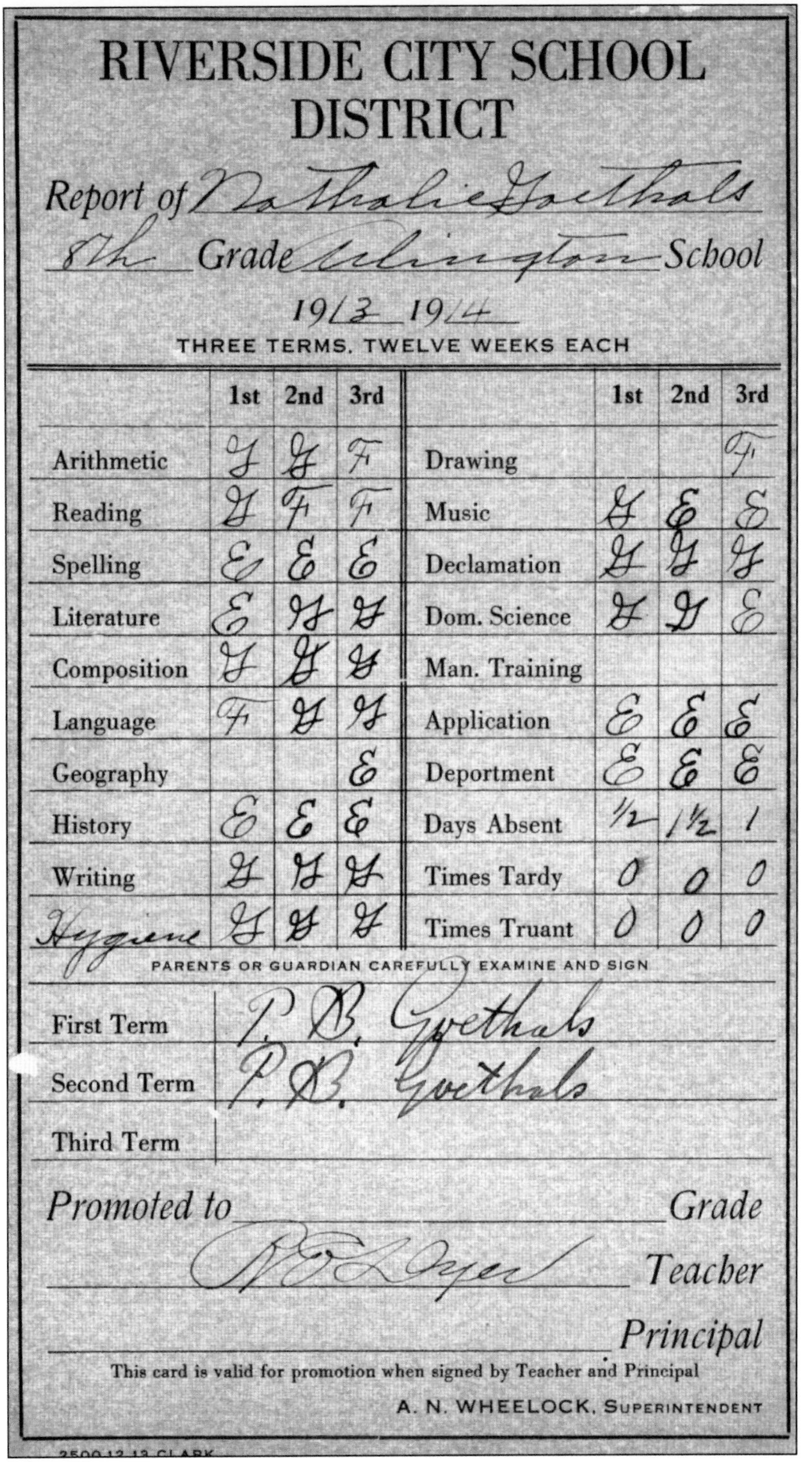

RIVERSIDE CITY SCHOOL DISTRICT

Report of Nathalie Goethals

8th *Grade* Arlington *School*

1913 1914

THREE TERMS, TWELVE WEEKS EACH

	1st	2nd	3rd		1st	2nd	3rd
Arithmetic	G	G	F	Drawing			F
Reading	G	F	F	Music	G	E	E
Spelling	E	E	E	Declamation	G	G	G
Literature	E	G	G	Dom. Science	G	G	E
Composition	G	G	G	Man. Training			
Language	F	G	G	Application	E	E	E
Geography			E	Deportment	E	E	E
History	E	E	E	Days Absent	1/2	1 1/2	1
Writing	G	G	G	Times Tardy	0	0	0
Hygiene	G	G	G	Times Truant	0	0	0

PARENTS OR GUARDIAN CAREFULLY EXAMINE AND SIGN

First Term	P. B. Goethals
Second Term	P. B. Goethals
Third Term	

Promoted to ________ *Grade*

R. O. L. Dyer *Teacher*

________ *Principal*

This card is valid for promotion when signed by Teacher and Principal

A. N. WHEELOCK, SUPERINTENDENT

2500-12-13 CLARK

This Arlington School report card belongs to Nathalie Goethals, an eighth-grade student in 1913–1914. It shows many more classes than the standard reading, writing, and arithmetic. Just like today, parents had to sign the cards along with the teacher.

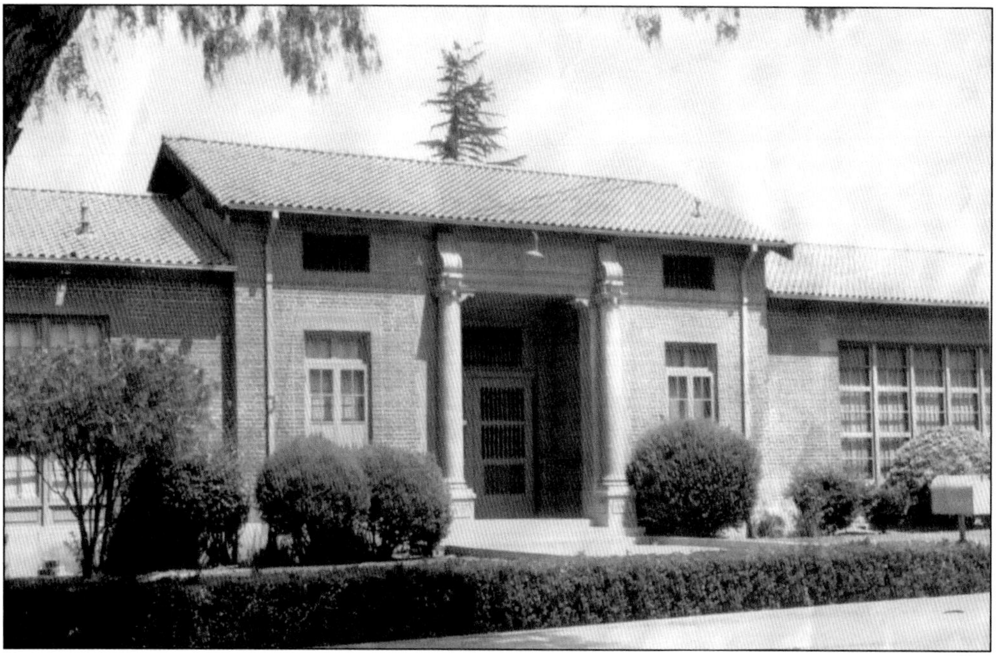

During the second decade of the 20th century, Arlington experienced population growth, requiring larger facilities at the elementary school. A new, modern facility was built on Hayes Street in 1917 and named Liberty Elementary School in remembrance of those who served during World War I. The prior school was a simple, four-room schoolhouse on Van Buren Boulevard (now Arlington Park).

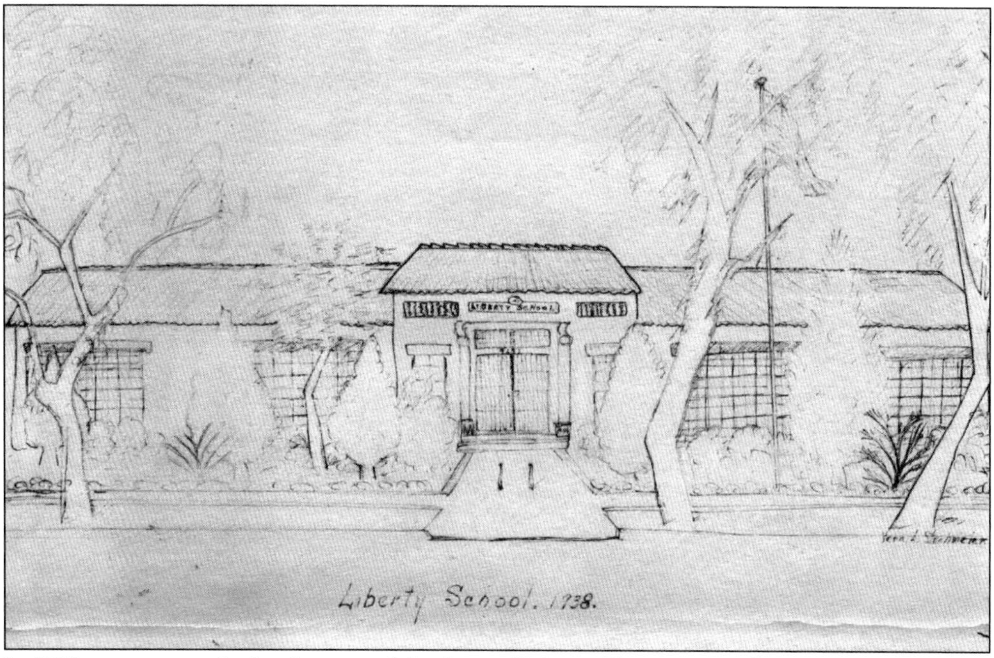

In 1938, an artist made this drawing of the front of Liberty Elementary School with lots of detail, right down to the name on the front of the building and the trees and flagpole. The drawing was found in a scrapbook of newspaper articles concerning the school.

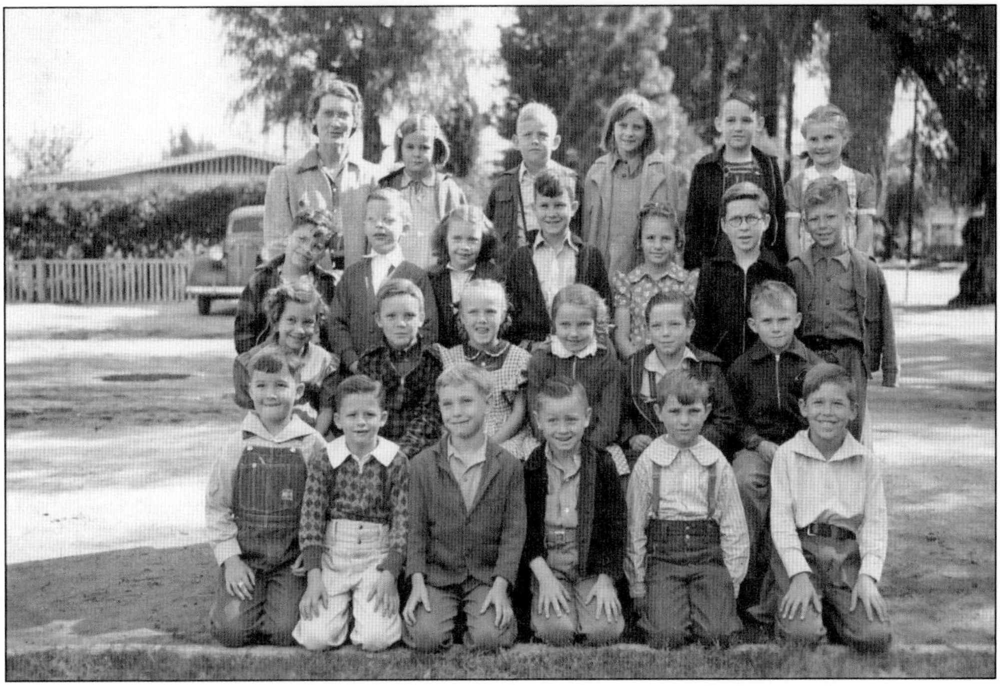

The Liberty Elementary School second-grade class of 1940 poses with their teacher, Miss Reaper (fourth row, left). At 25 students, this class is much smaller than most of the time. Patsy Leibert stands in the fourth row on the right.

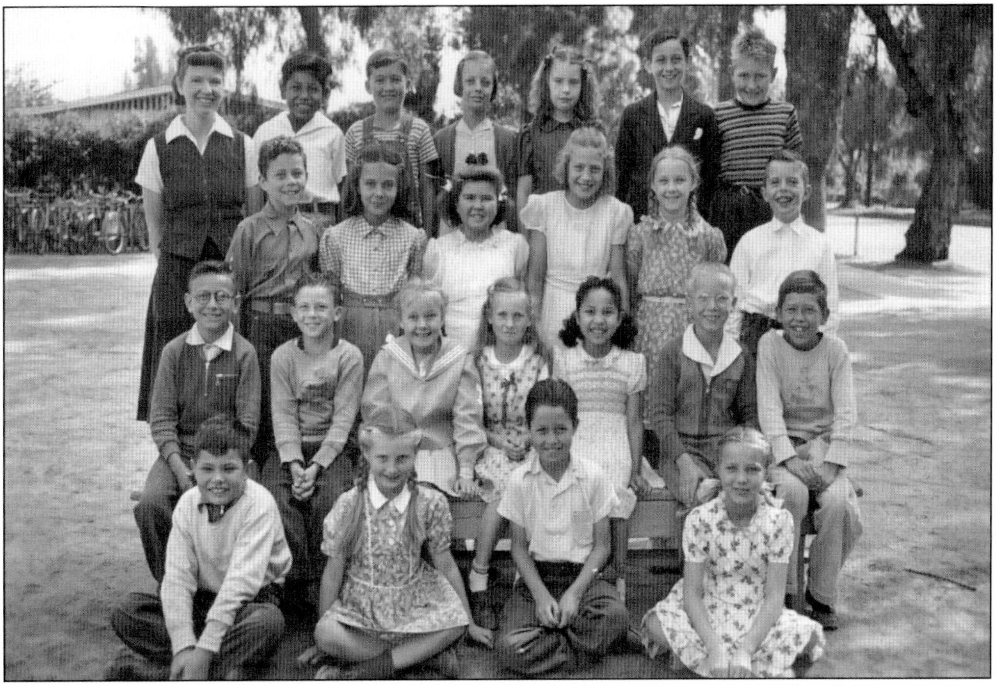

In this c. 1941 photograph taken in the side yard of Liberty Elementary School, Patsy Leibert (first row, second from the left) wears her hair in long blond braids and dons a beautiful, ancestral Dutch smile. The grins on all of the children's faces must reflect the love for their teacher.

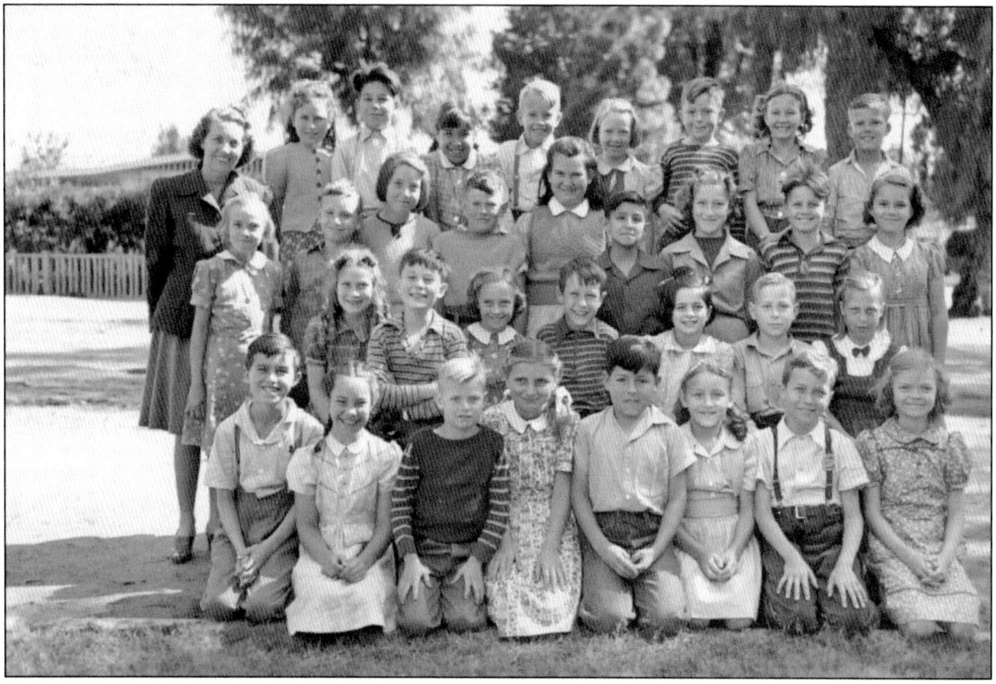

This Liberty Elementary School class portrait was taken in the school yard about 1939. The teacher stands on the left with her very large class of 32 students. The author's aunt, Nathalie Leibert, appears in the first row, fourth from the left.

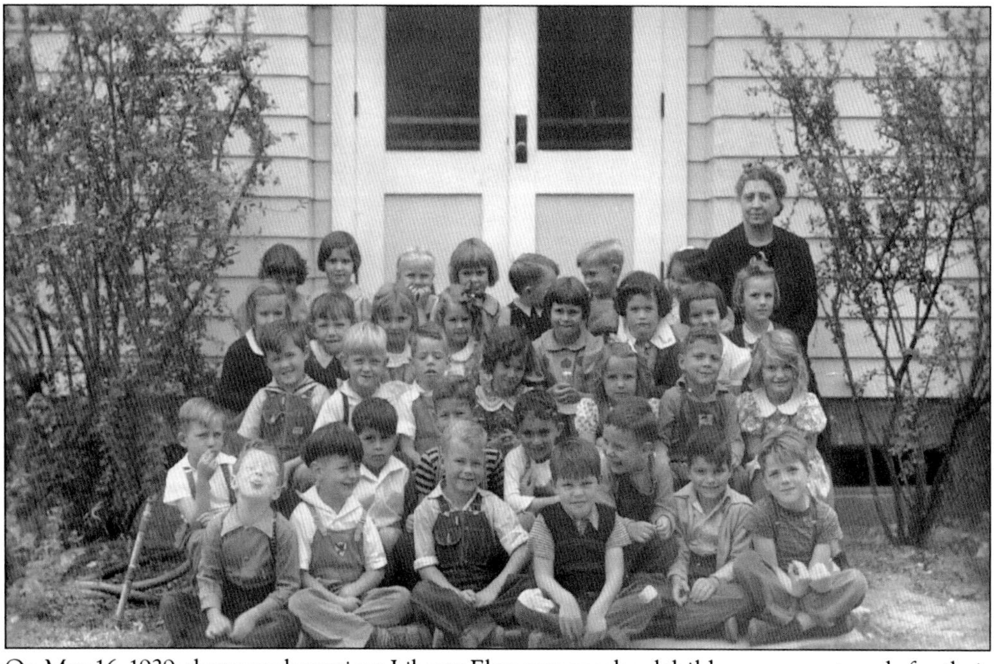

On May 16, 1939, these rambunctious Liberty Elementary schoolchildren were not ready for their photograph to be taken, as evidenced by the laughing, sticking out of tongues, hiding of faces, and closing of eyes. This image is one that will not be forgotten very soon. Their patient teacher stands in the fifth row to the right.

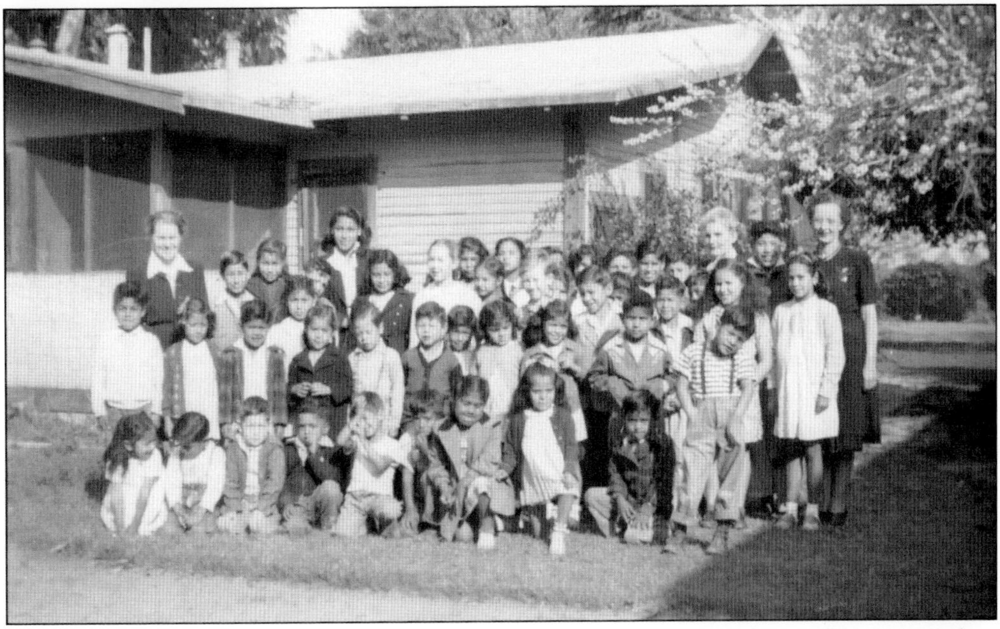

Independiente School, pictured around 1945, was established in 1924 due to the overcrowding conditions that developed at Liberty School in Arlington. *Independiente* means "liberty" in Spanish; thus, the new facility was named after Liberty Elementary School. Most of the children that attended Independiente were Hispanics whose parents worked in the nearby orange groves. The site at 9174 Indiana Avenue is now occupied by Hawthorne School, previously located at 9170.

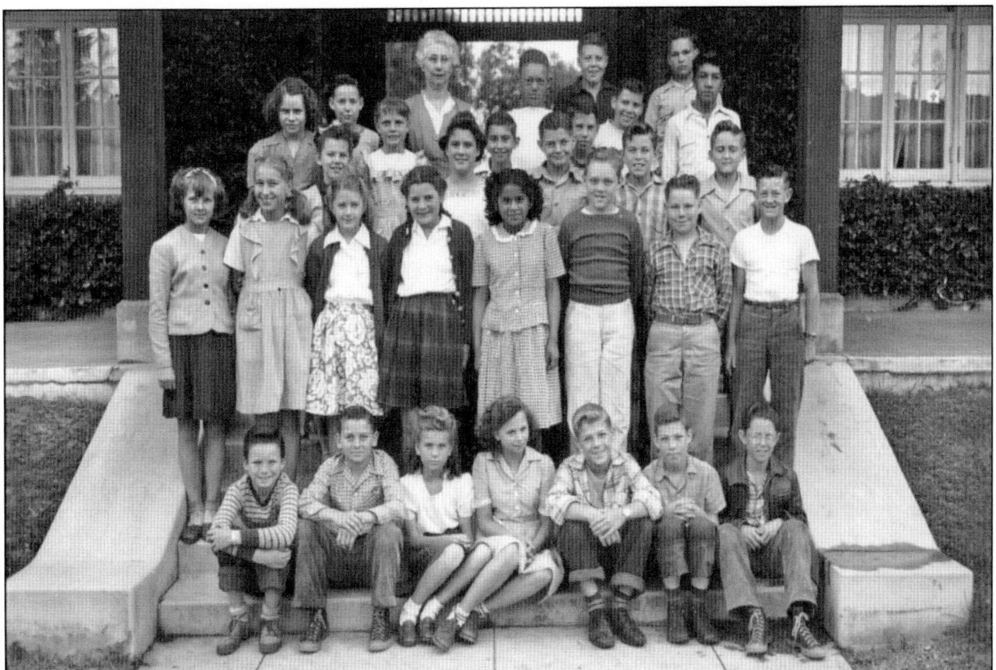

Mrs. McQuin's class poses on the front steps of Liberty Elementary School in the early 1940s. The building had a lovely entrance and large windows. The author's aunt, Agnes Leibert, stands in the second row, fourth from the left.

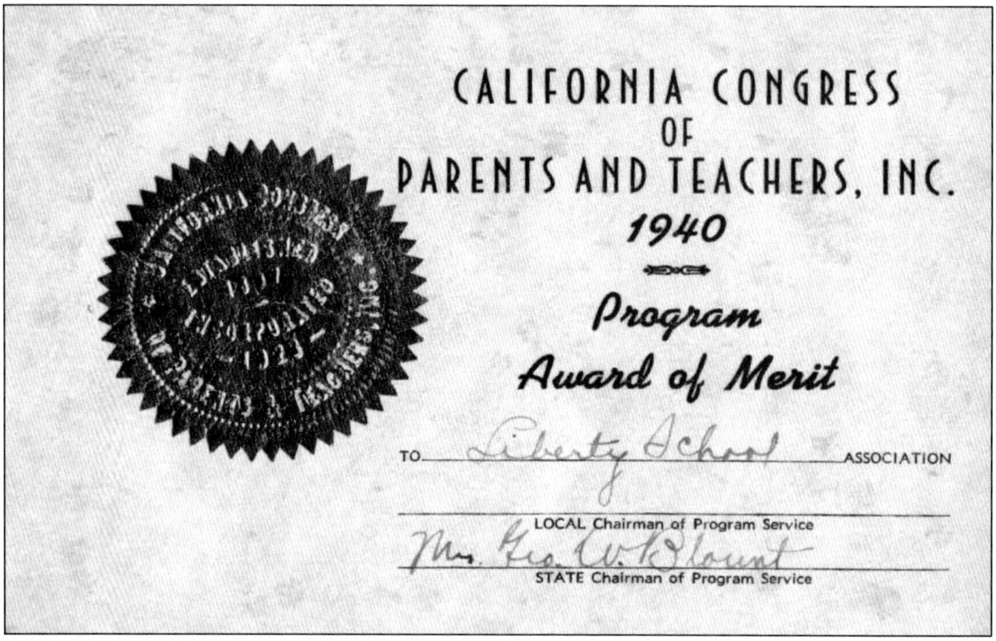
CALIFORNIA CONGRESS
OF
PARENTS AND TEACHERS, INC.
1940

Program
Award of Merit

TO Liberty School ASSOCIATION

LOCAL Chairman of Program Service

Mrs. Geo. W. Blount
STATE Chairman of Program Service

In 1940, Liberty Elementary School was presented an Award of Merit by the California Congress of Parents and Teachers. The award was signed by Mrs. George W. Blount, state chairwoman of program service.

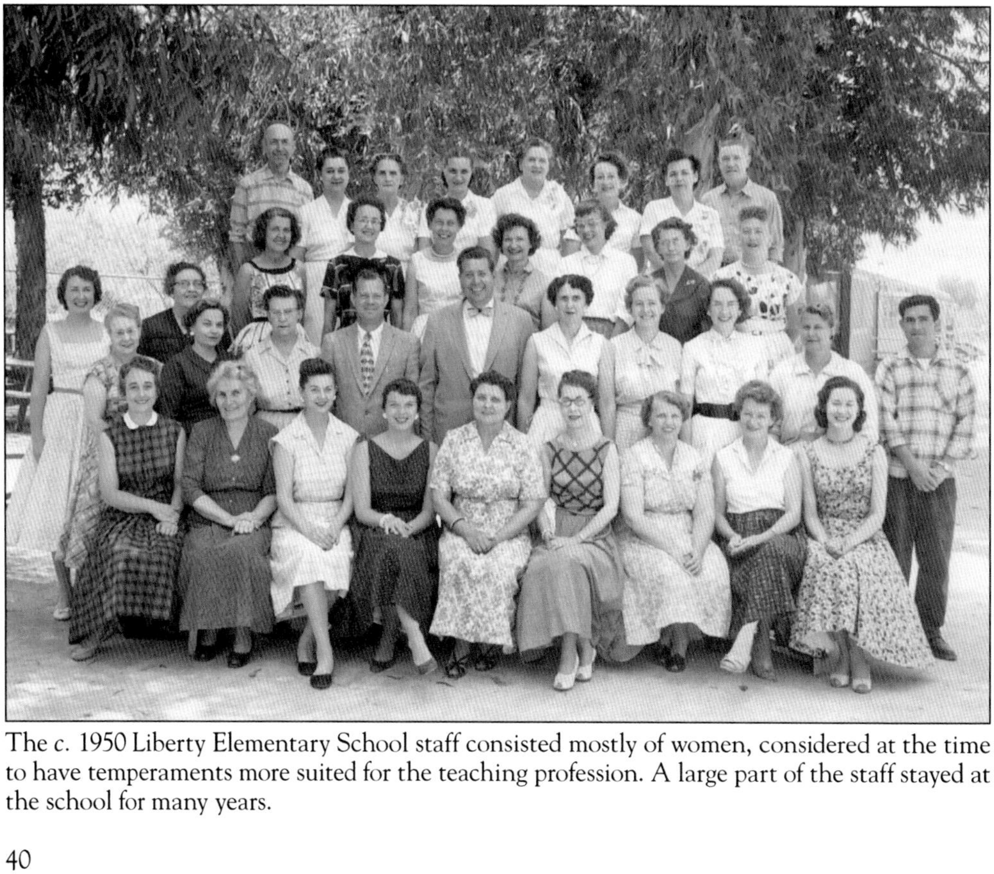

The *c.* 1950 Liberty Elementary School staff consisted mostly of women, considered at the time to have temperaments more suited for the teaching profession. A large part of the staff stayed at the school for many years.

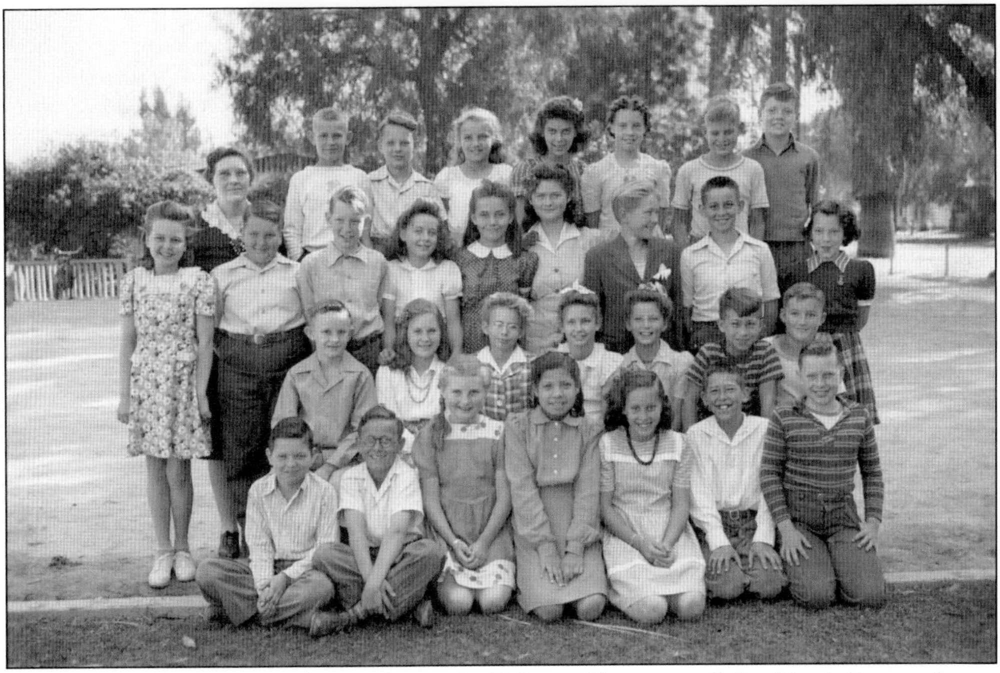

Class portraits were often taken in the yard of Liberty Elementary School in Arlington. It was a beautiful day for this *c.* 1942 photograph, in which the author's aunt, Patsy Leibert, appears in the first row, third from the left, and the teacher in the fourth row, left.

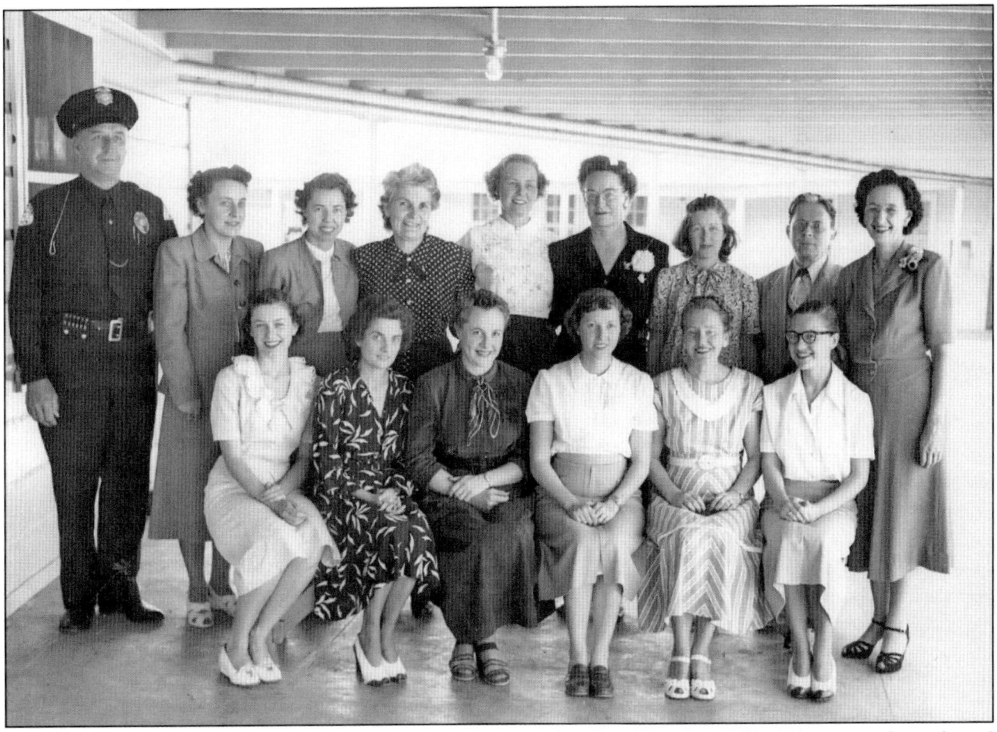

Arlington's local police officer poses with the Liberty School staff in the 1950s. They must have loved their teaching days, because they all look very happy and stayed at the school for many years.

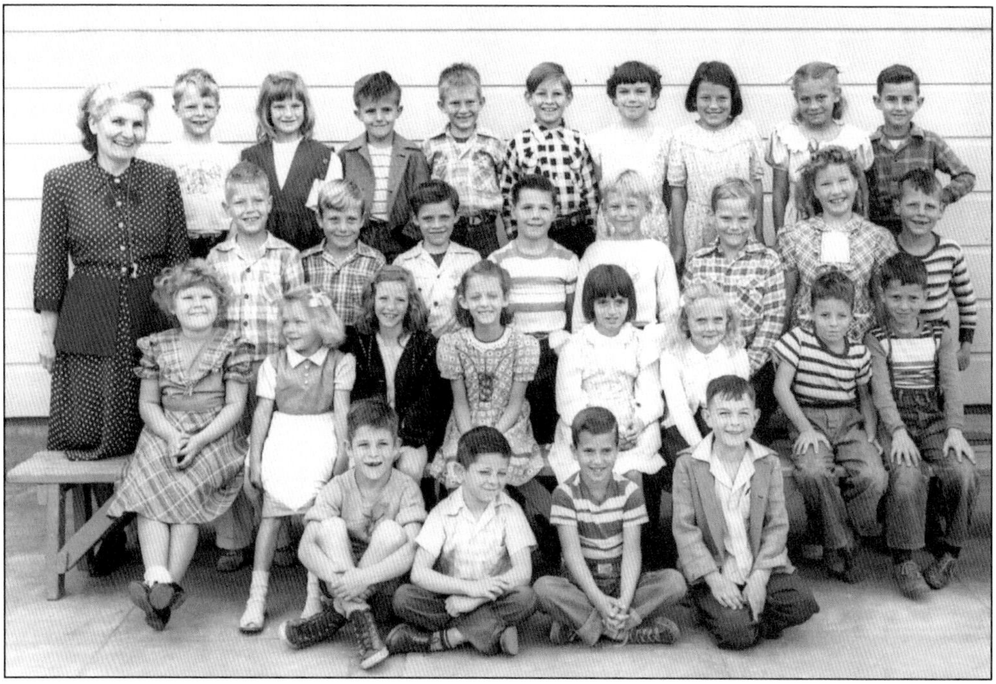

In this 1950s portrait, Marie Leibert stands to the left of her third-grade class of 29 students. She was known for teaching the third grade, as she loved the children's young, fresh minds and willingness to learn. Mrs. Leibert, well liked by her pupils and their parents, would conduct private lessons in her home after school for those who needed special help.

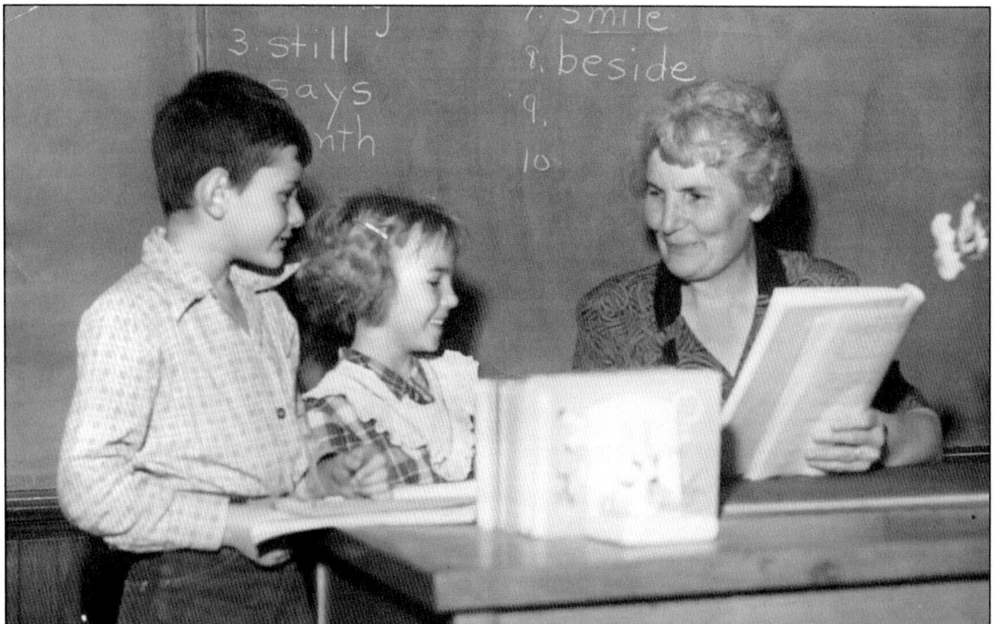

Marie Leibert starts a new day in 1953 with her third-grade class. She enjoyed making the school day a fun learning time—and succeeded, as evidenced by the smiling faces of Roger Noble (left) and Sally Kuntz (right).

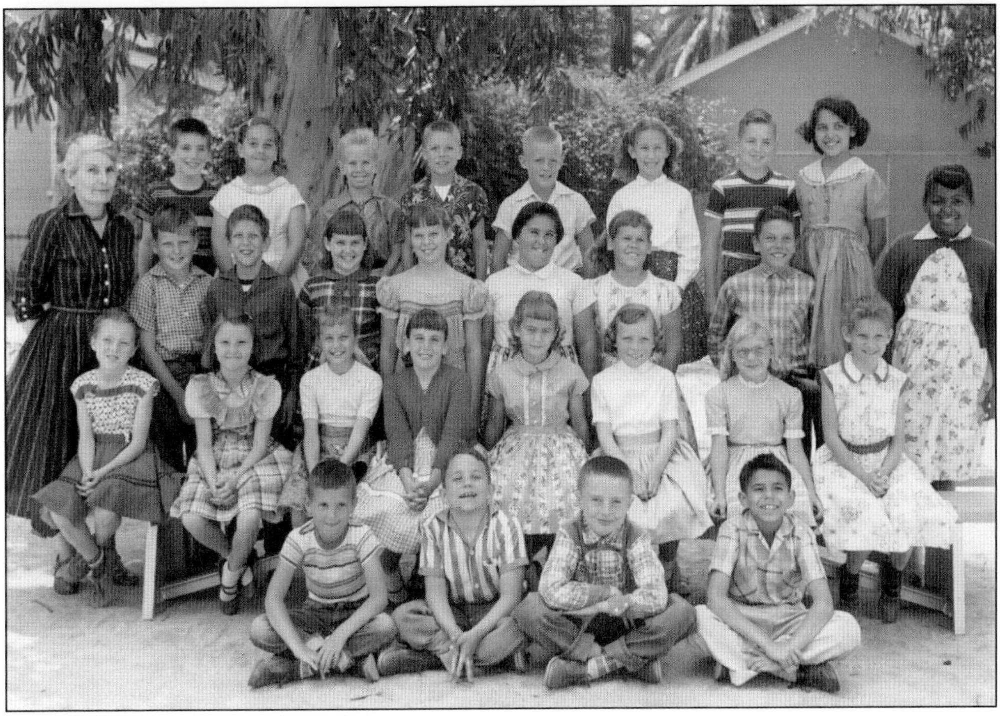

Taken in the side yard of Liberty School, this 1956 photograph depicts Marie Leibert standing to the left of her third-grade class of 28 students. Just look at all the happy smiles on their faces.

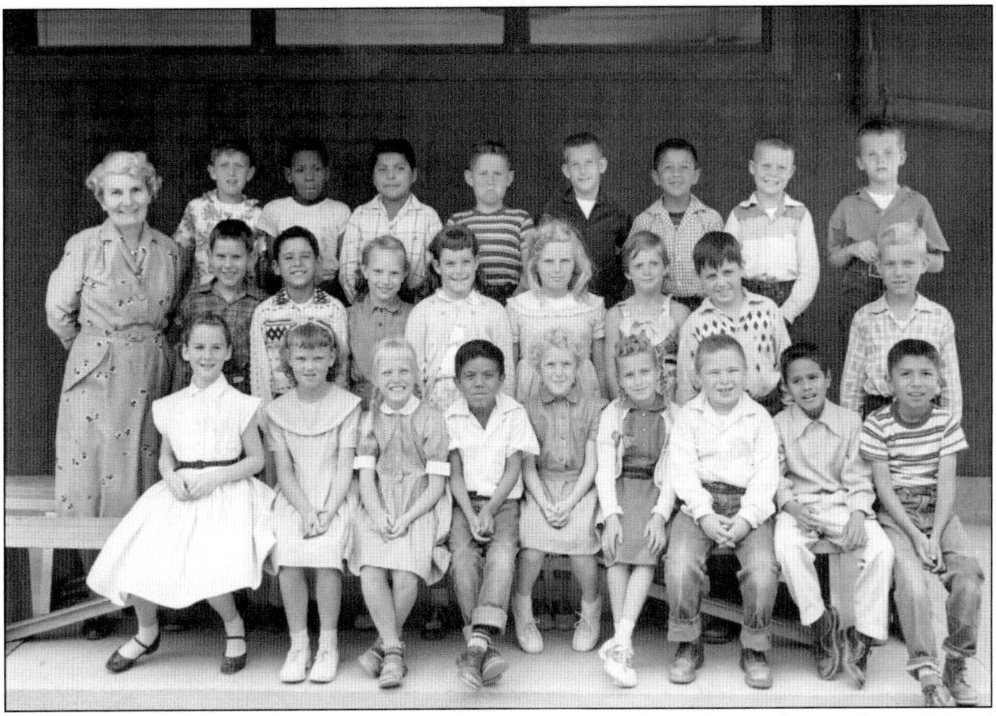

Marie Leibert (left) served as the teacher to this third-grade class of 25 students. Liberty School was located just one block north of Magnolia Avenue on Hayes Street.

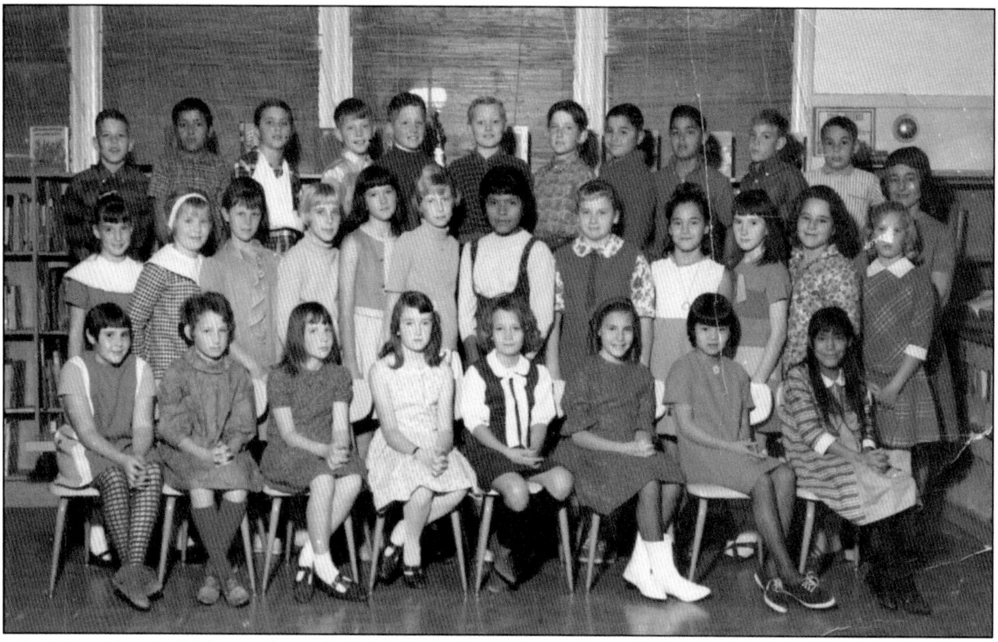

Mrs. Hamilton's fifth-grade students at Liberty Elementary School are pictured here in January 1968. Mrs. Hamilton stands on the right of her class, consisting of 20 girls and 11 boys. Michael Gordon, the author's brother, appears in the middle of the third row.

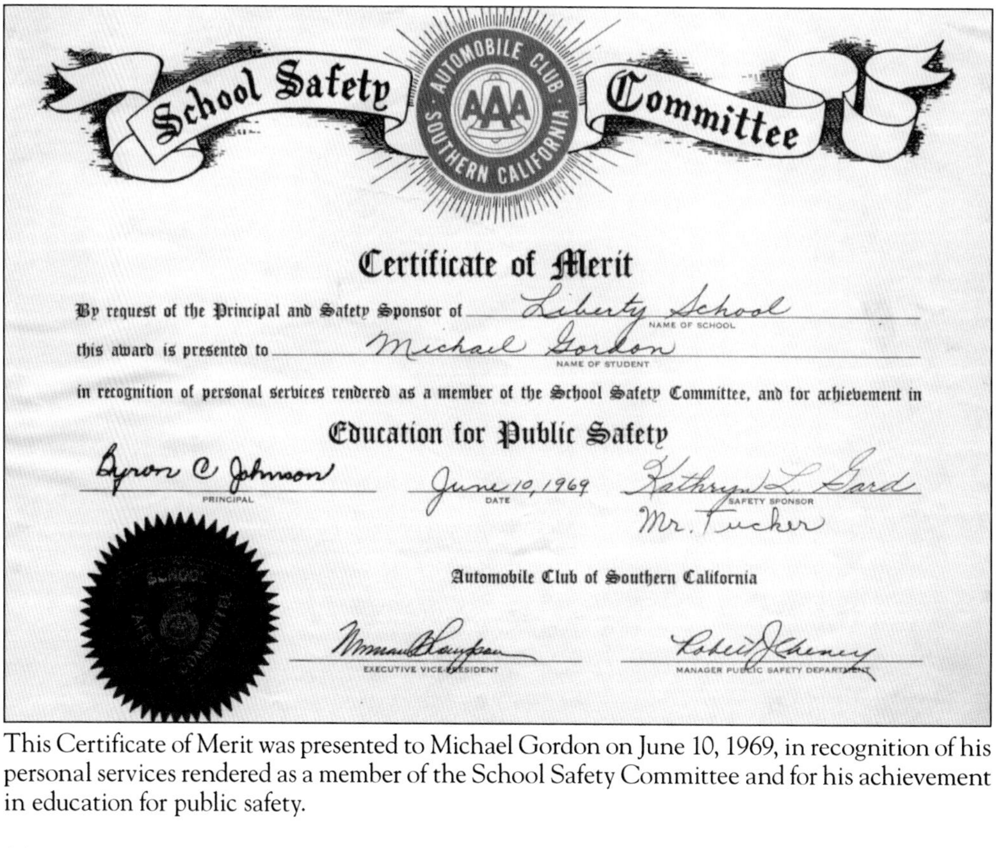

School Safety Committee

AUTOMOBILE CLUB AAA SOUTHERN CALIFORNIA

Certificate of Merit

By request of the Principal and Safety Sponsor of Liberty School
NAME OF SCHOOL

this award is presented to Michael Gordon
NAME OF STUDENT

in recognition of personal services rendered as a member of the School Safety Committee, and for achievement in

Education for Public Safety

Byron C Johnson — PRINCIPAL

June 10, 1969 — DATE

Kathryn L. Gard — SAFETY SPONSOR

Mr. Tucker

Automobile Club of Southern California

EXECUTIVE VICE-PRESIDENT

MANAGER PUBLIC SAFETY DEPARTMENT

This Certificate of Merit was presented to Michael Gordon on June 10, 1969, in recognition of his personal services rendered as a member of the School Safety Committee and for his achievement in education for public safety.

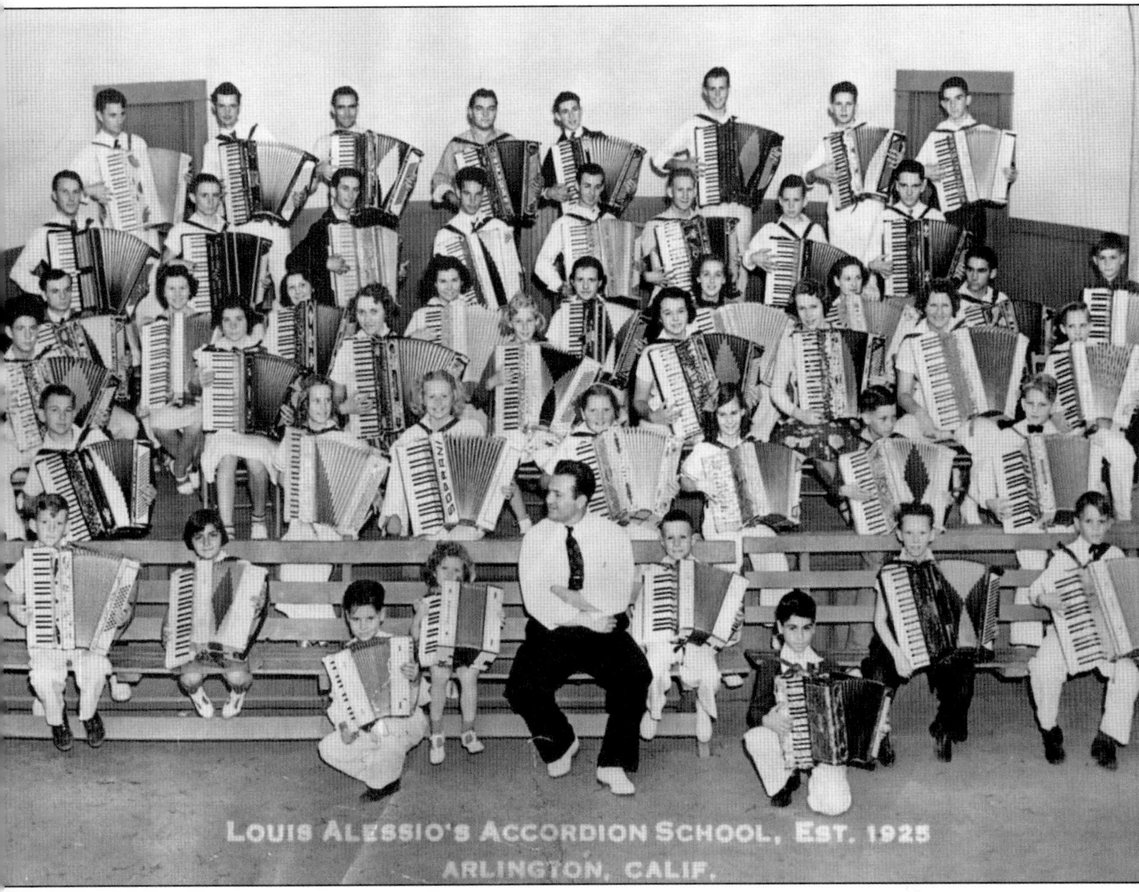

Louis Alessio's Accordion School opened in Arlington in 1925 at the corner of Van Buren Boulevard and Hoag Street, now Primrose Drive. Music teacher Louis Alessio is seated in the middle of the first row at a recital performed by children of all ages. He traveled from home to home to give private accordion lessons. (Courtesy Marion Alessio Arias.)

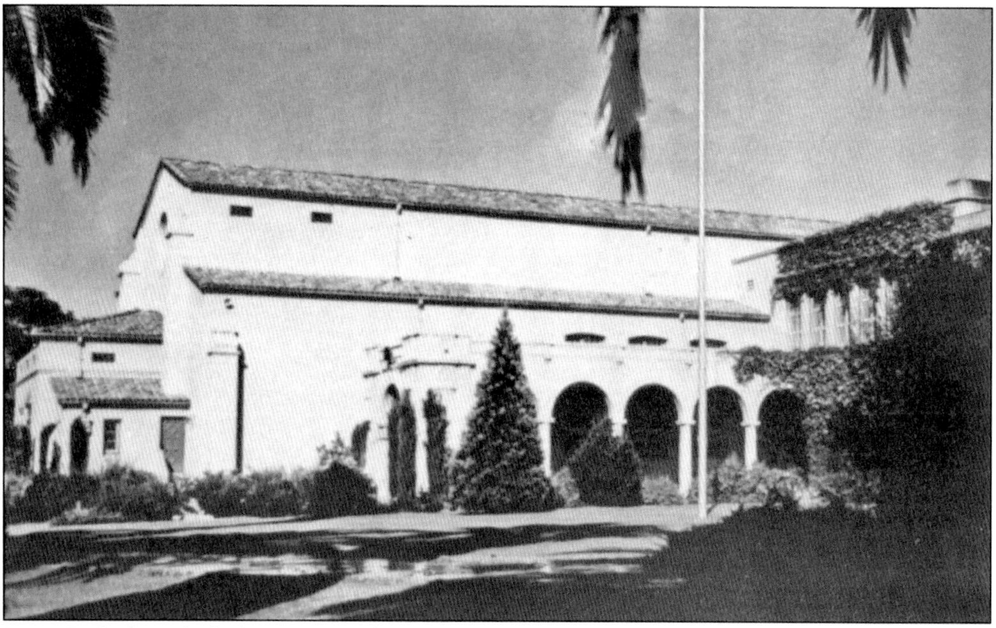

In 1927, the board of education purchased Chemawa Park and opened Chemawa Middle School on the site in the fall of 1928. The grounds were filled with trees and shrubbery. The school had a large auditorium that seated 700 students, a library, a principal's office, seven classrooms on the first floor, and 261 enrolled students. Harold B. Walker served as principal for 40 years. Many generations of Arlingtonians knew him.

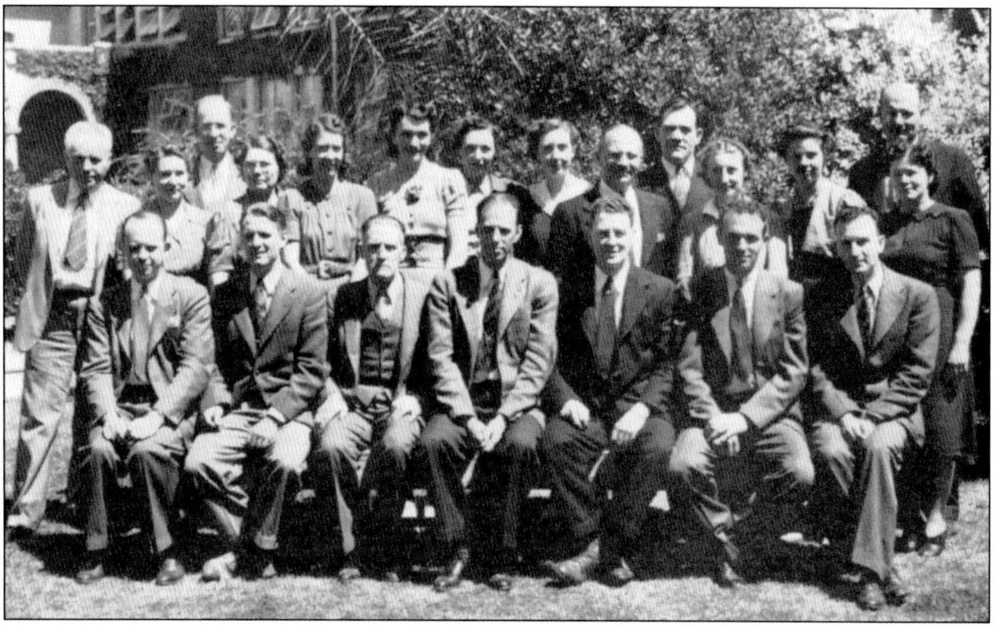

The 1940 Chemawa Junior High School faculty included Harold Walker, Florence Montgomery, Mildred Andrews, George Bromell, Leland DePriest, Kyle Esgate, Anne Horsley, Robert Jackson, Ray Johnson, Sarah Kennedy, Arthur Knopf, Rachel Loveday, Elizabeth Minkel, Myra Crawford, Hazel Phillips, Henry Roselle, Doris Rowlands, Frederick Schmidt, Garland Smith, John Stewart, and Lewis Wickens.

This Chemawa Junior High School guide booklet was printed in the spring of 1939. Such handbooks were given to students to allow them to become more acquainted with the school. Chemawa Junior High was located at 8830 Magnolia Avenue in Arlington.

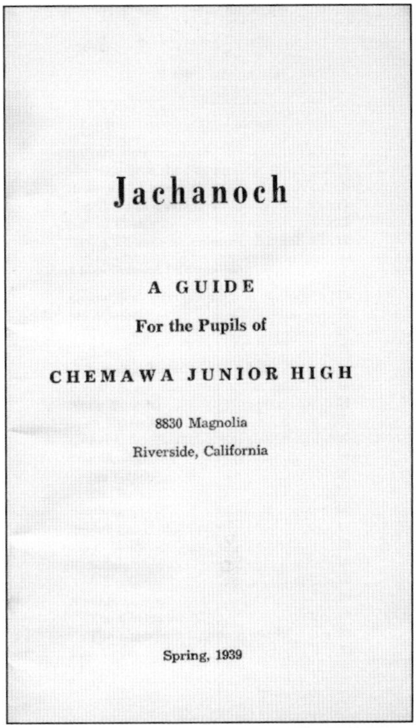
Jachanoch

A GUIDE

For the Pupils of

CHEMAWA JUNIOR HIGH

8830 Magnolia

Riverside, California

Spring, 1939

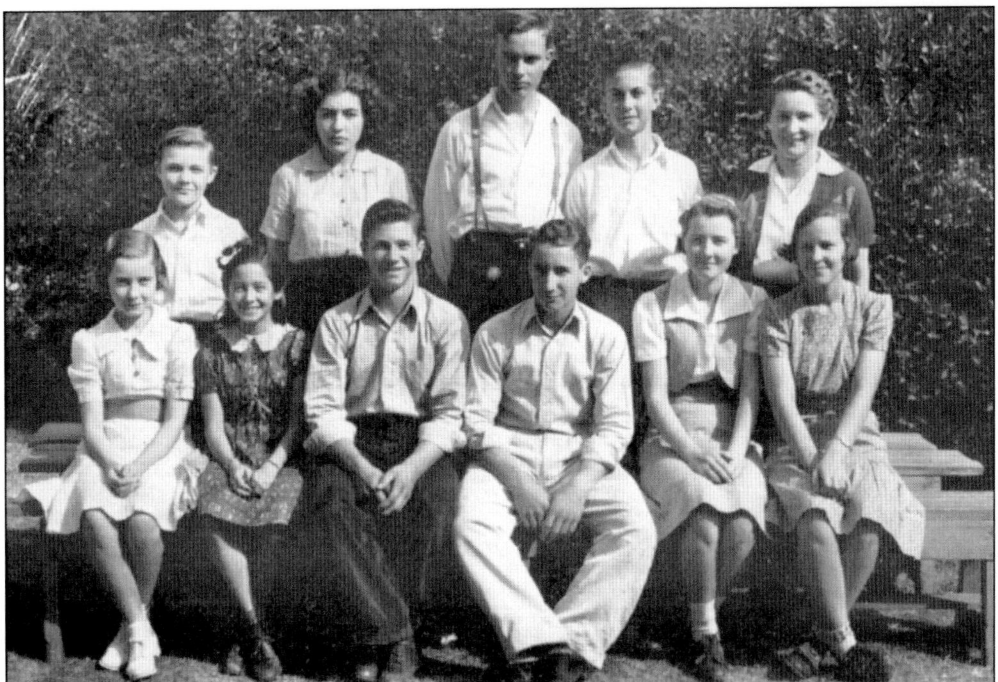

The 1939 Chemawa Junior High School Student Council was comprised of a group of students who met twice a month to discuss problems and approve amendments to the school's constitution. Hollis Bascom (first row, fourth from left) served as president, with Mrs. Montgomery (second row, far right) as student advisor.

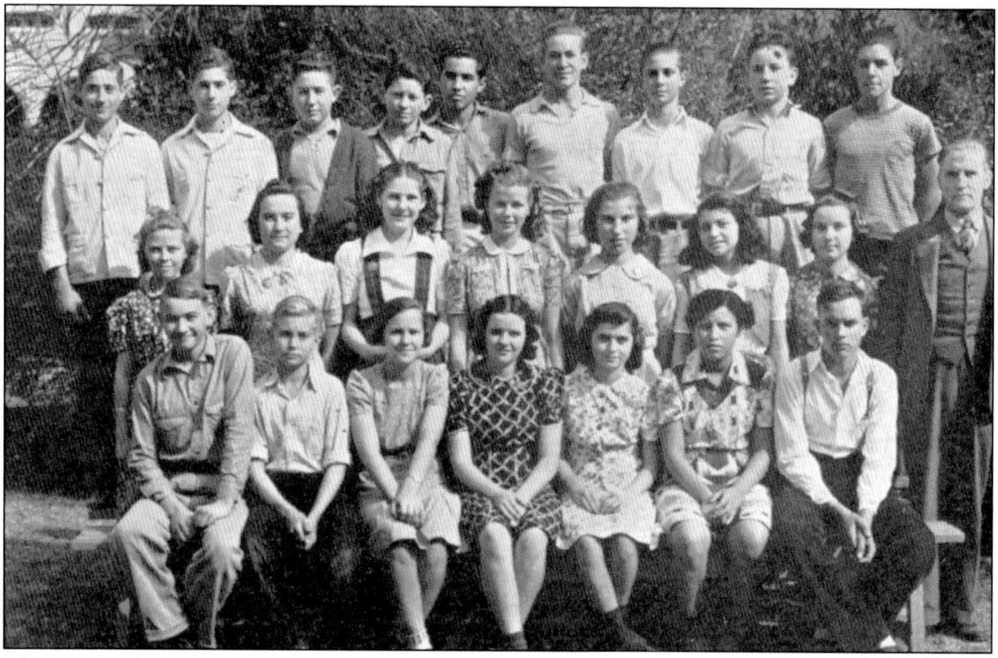

The 1939 Safety Committee included Vivian Barnes, Margaret Bellezza, Iva Mae Bowers, Talona Byrnes, Joyce Davis, Rose Ferraro, Wayne Fraser, John Gaynor, Lily Luce, Utahanna Martin, Matilde Martinez, Rosie Mendoza, Dorothy Parrick, Joe Sanchez, Richard Sandretto, Mary Santo, Frank and Fred Seinturier, Robert Stebbins, Sterling Stott, Leone Thompson, and Billy Williamson.

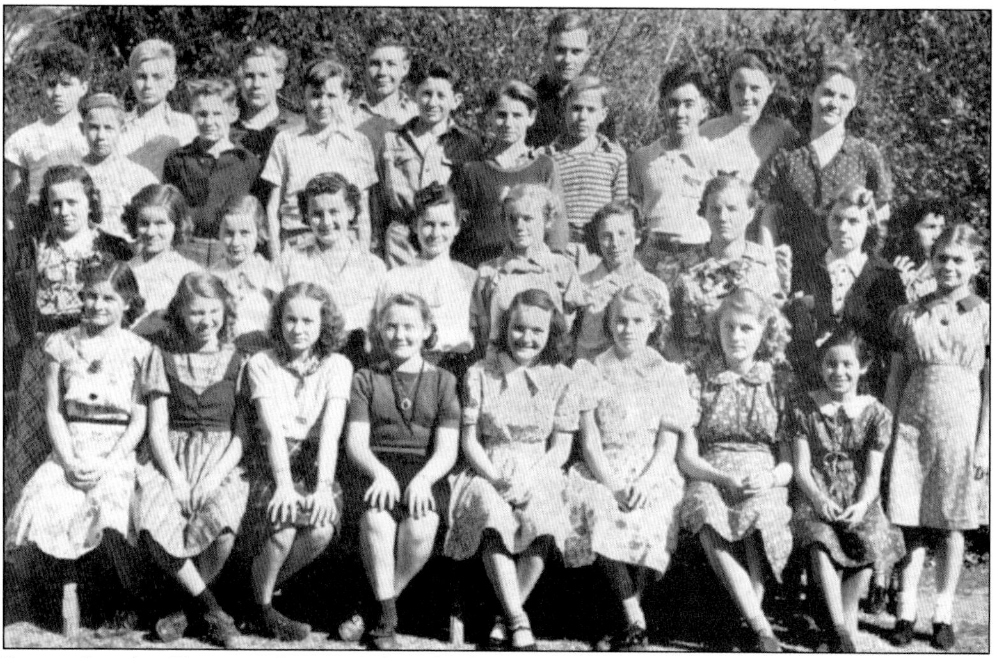

Pictured in the Chemawa Junior High School annual *Iyaneka* is the eighth-grade class of 1939, consisting of 33 students. Class presidents were Ben Hammer (fourth row, second from the left) and Fay Titus (fourth row, fifth from the left); senators were Fay Titus and Billy Metzel (second row, left).

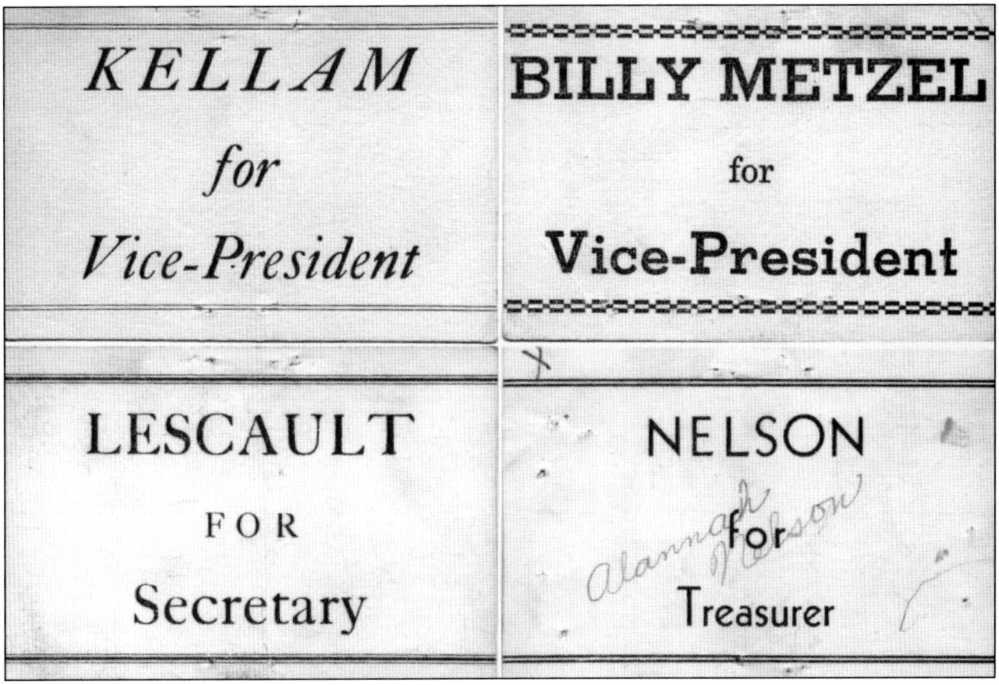

For the 1938 reelections of new officers at Chemawa Junior High School, these nametags were made for the candidates. Some of the students who ran for office were Alannah Nelson for treasurer, Ted Lescault for secretary, Billy Metzel for vice president, and Jimmy Kellam for vice president.

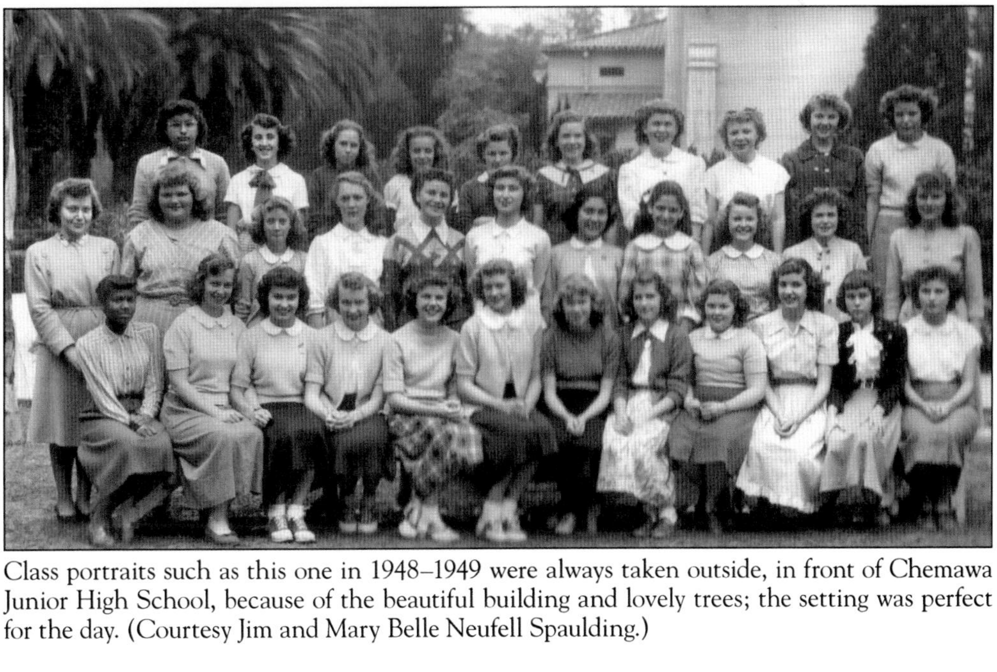
Class portraits such as this one in 1948–1949 were always taken outside, in front of Chemawa Junior High School, because of the beautiful building and lovely trees; the setting was perfect for the day. (Courtesy Jim and Mary Belle Neufell Spaulding.)

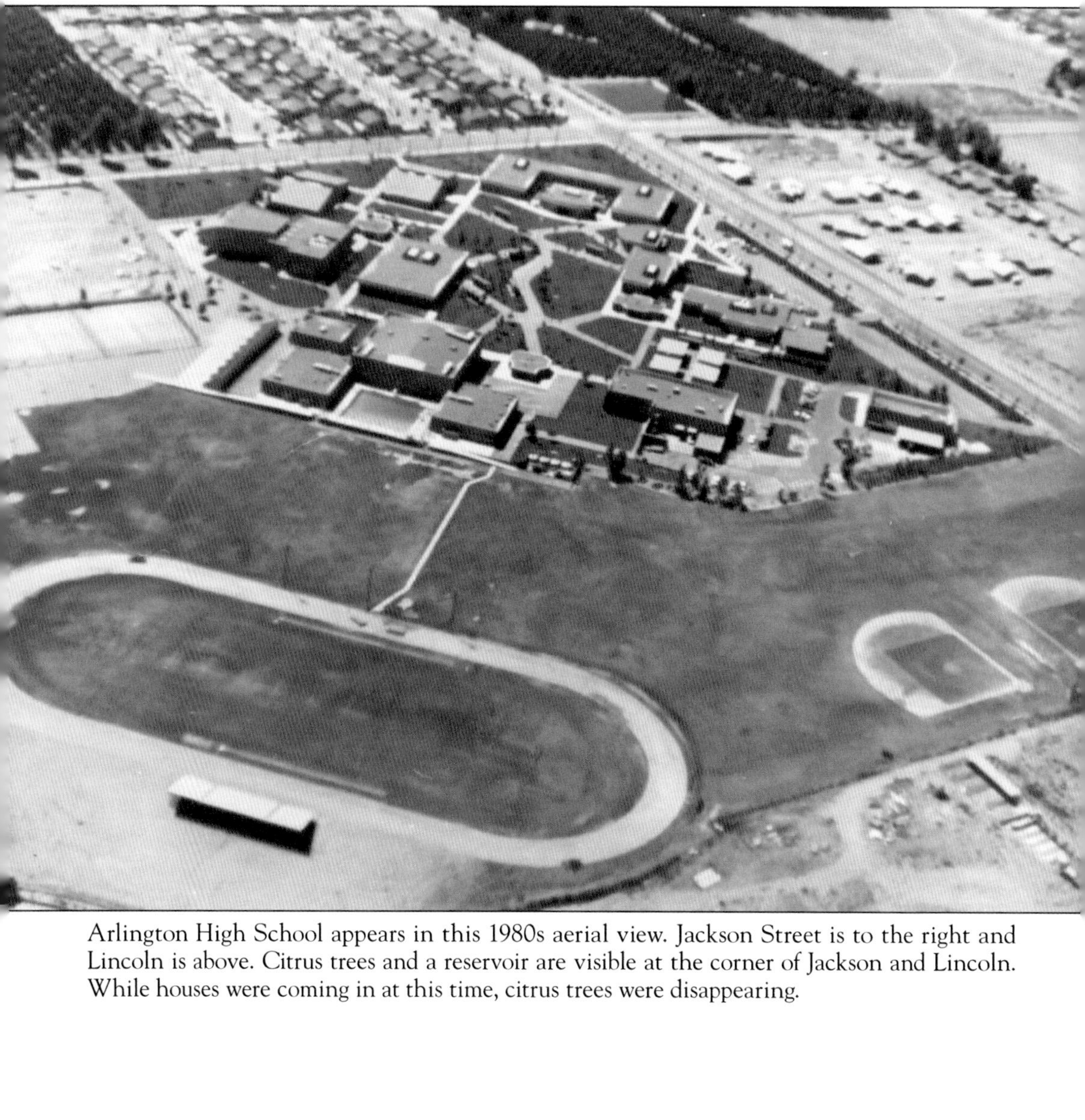

Arlington High School appears in this 1980s aerial view. Jackson Street is to the right and Lincoln is above. Citrus trees and a reservoir are visible at the corner of Jackson and Lincoln. While houses were coming in at this time, citrus trees were disappearing.

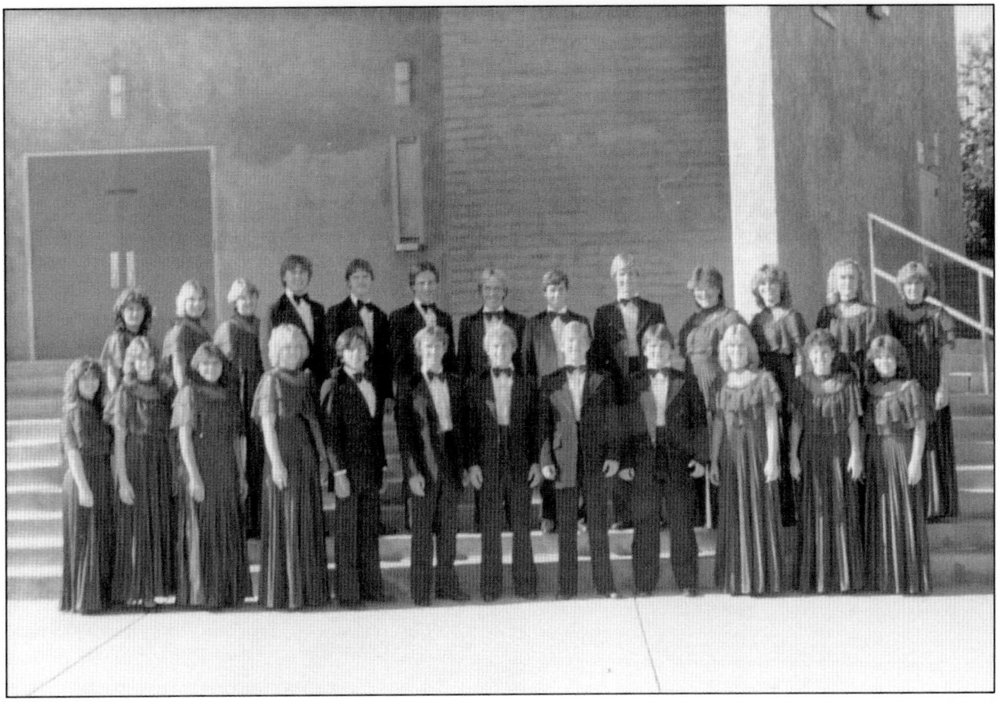

The 1983–1984 Arlington High School Chamber Singers were the best singers at the school and performed at different places in the city. The students wear their formal attire: girls in long dresses and young men in tuxedos.

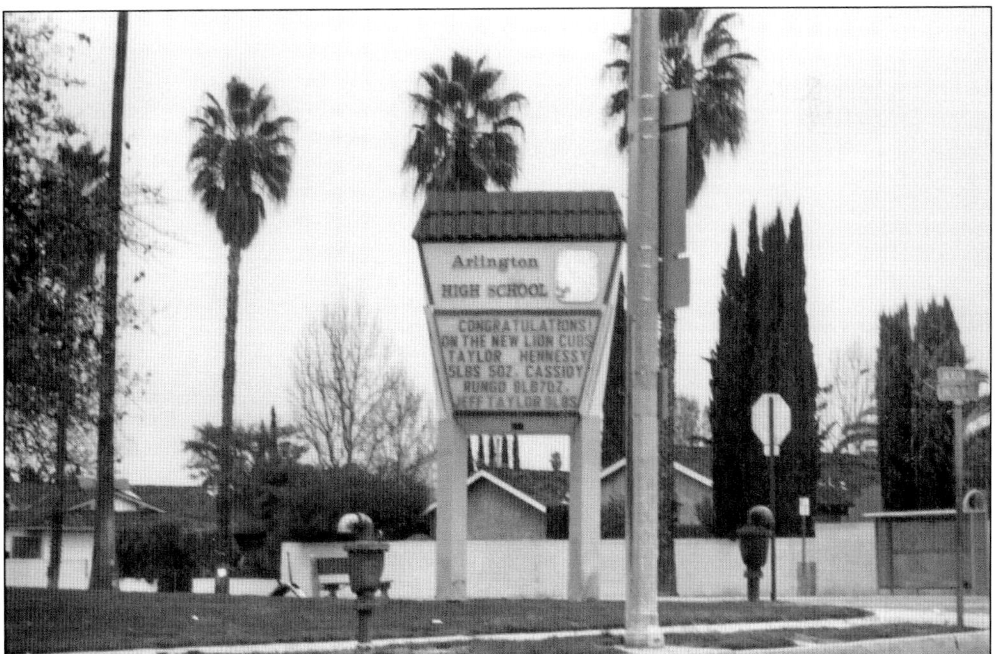

Shown here in the 1970s is Arlington High School, located at the corner of Jackson and Lincoln Streets in Arlington.

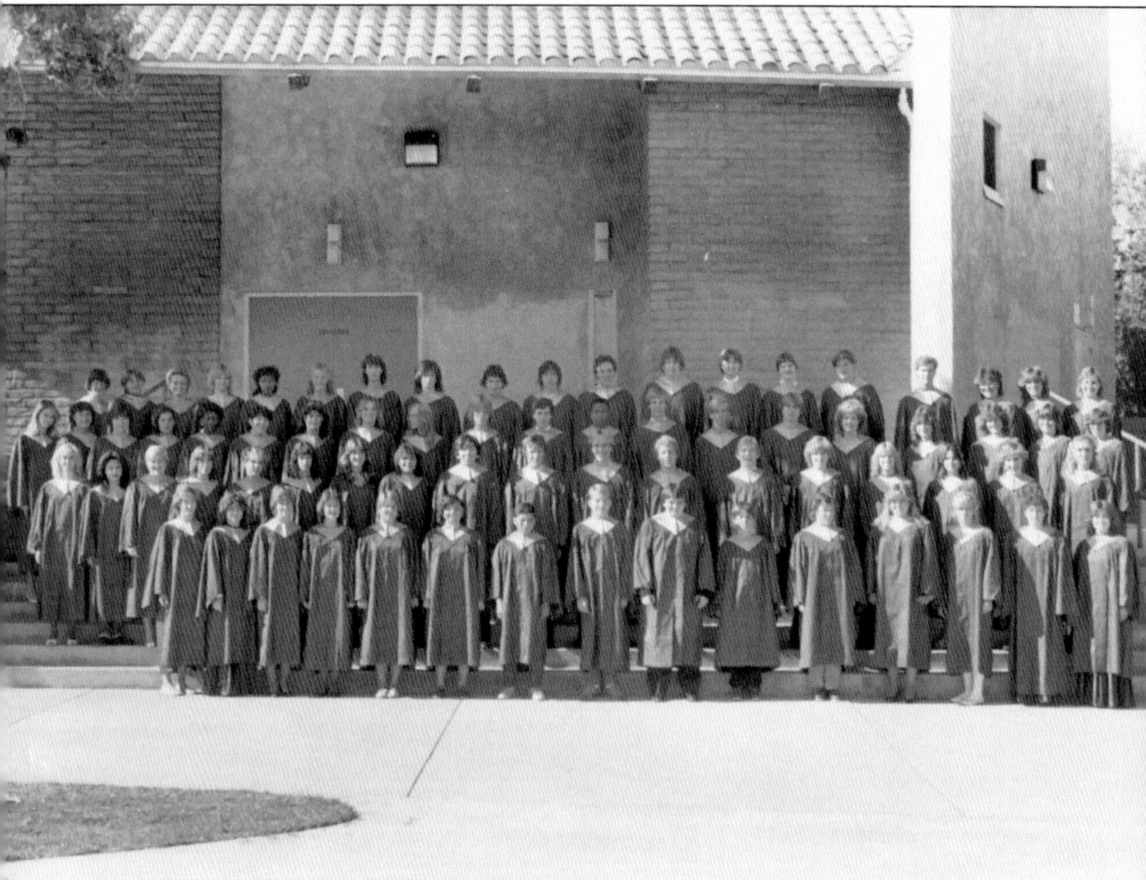

The Arlington High School Concert Choir, pictured in 1983–1984, was made up of all the singers at the school. The students don long, matching robes.

Three

THE SHERMAN INDIAN INSTITUTE

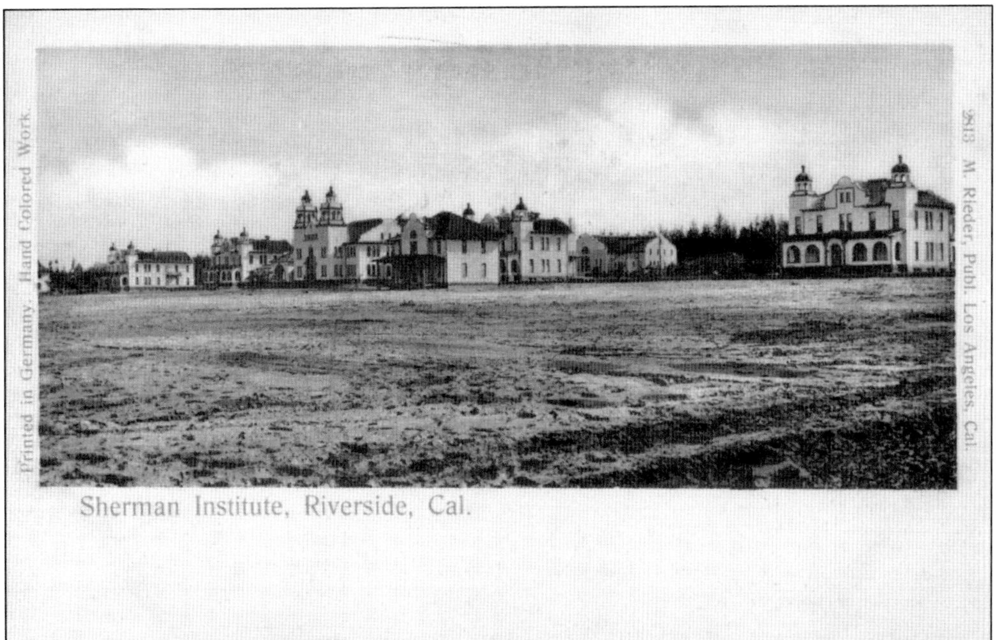

In June 1901, the Sherman Indian Institute's main building was laid out on the southeast corner of Magnolia Avenue and Jackson Street, and the following year, nine buildings were completed. Eighteen Pima Indians from the Pima Reservation came to live there in the fall of 1902, and enrollment was full. (Courtesy Steve Lech.)

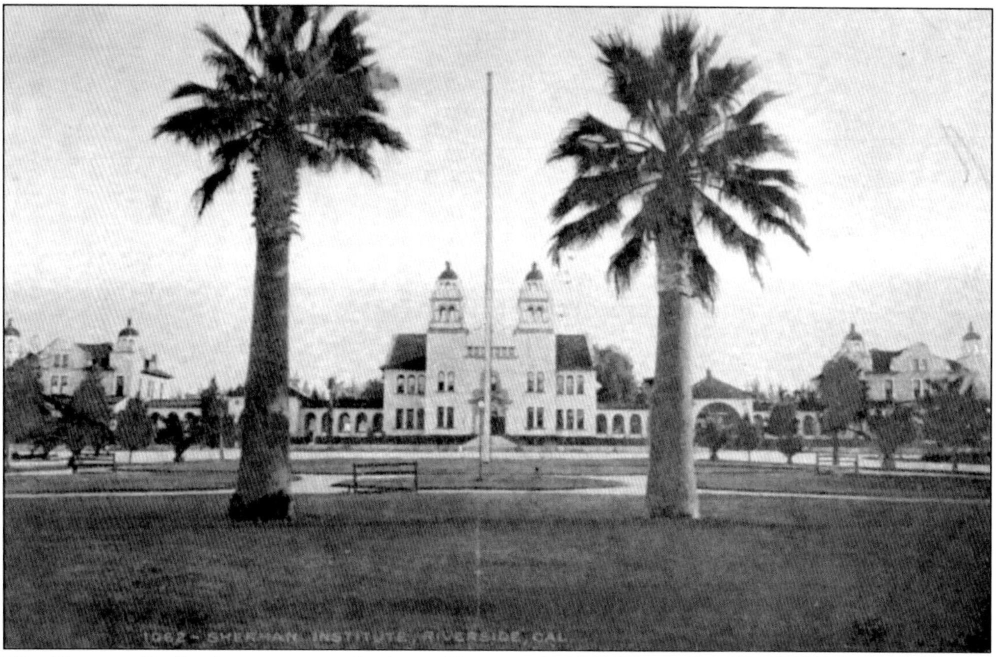

The Sherman Indian Institute was the first off-reservation boarding school in California established for Native Americans and administered by the federal government with the purpose to assimilate tribal students into American society. The original school was built in 1892 in the nearby city of Perris. (Courtesy JoAnne Pease-Simpson.)

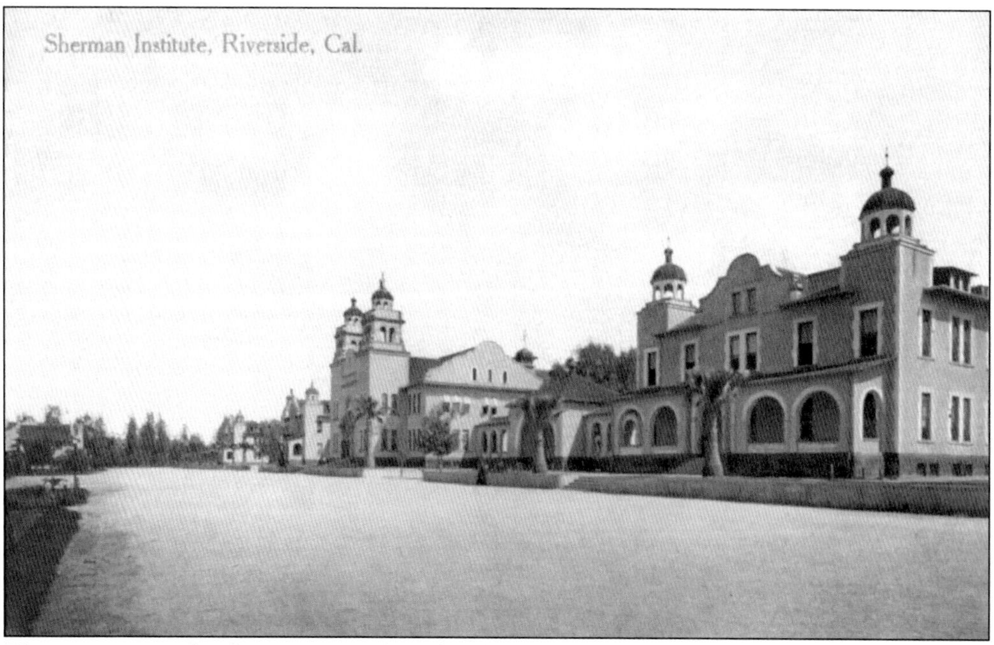

The cornerstone for the new Spanish-style school was laid on July 1, 1901. The school's only remaining original structure today is the administration building, which now houses the Sherman Indian Museum. (Courtesy JoAnne Pease-Simpson.)

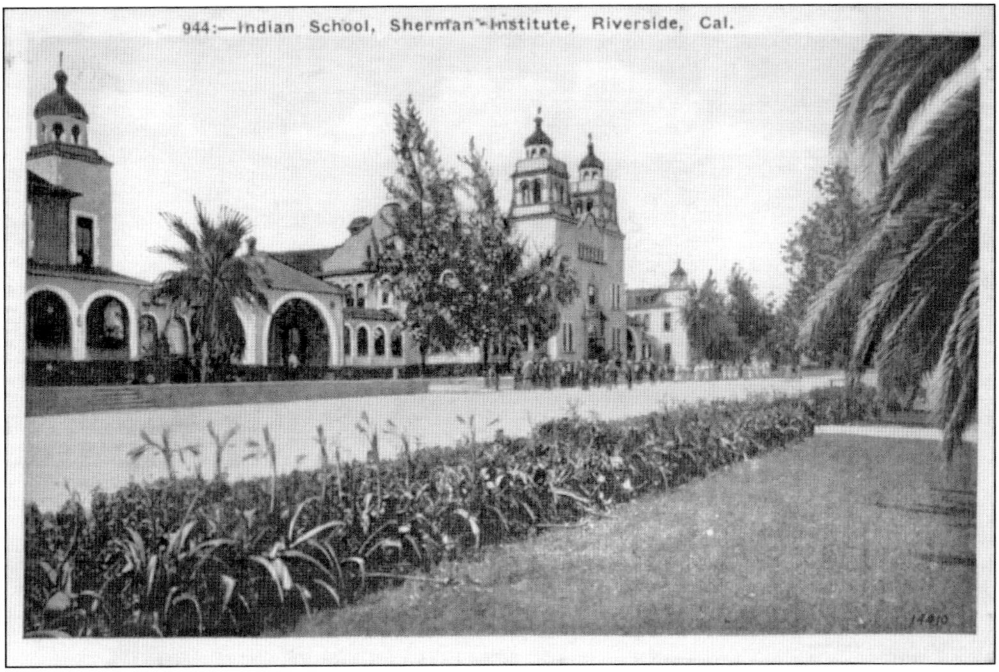

The Sherman Indian Institute was constructed with large, mission-style arches. The Native American students had their own band and would often practice in front of the school and perform for different events around town. (Courtesy JoAnne Pease-Simpson.)

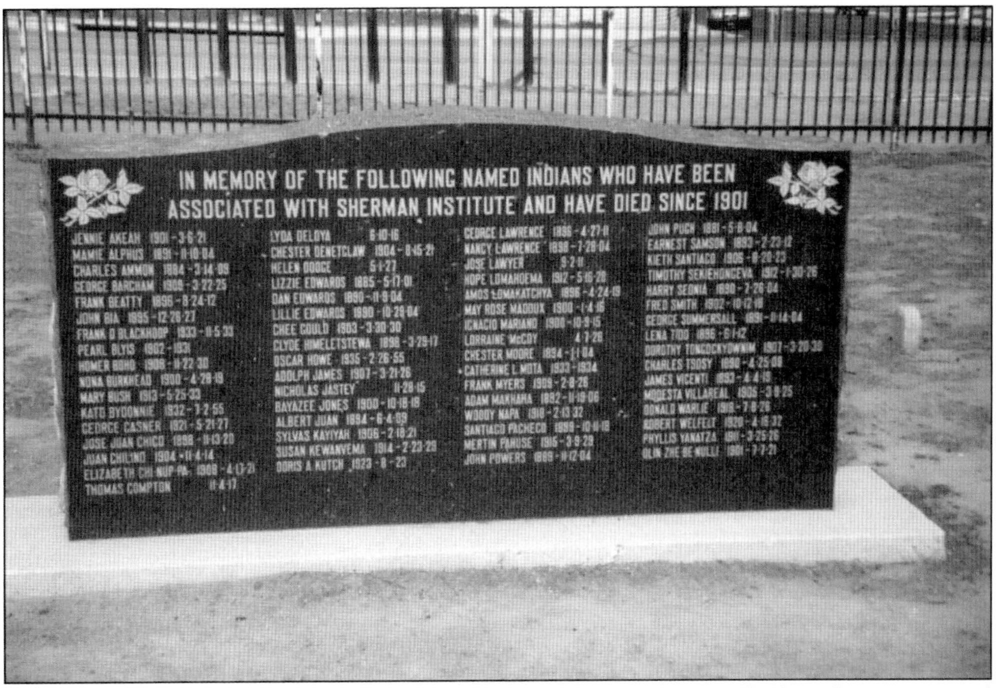

This Sherman Indian School Memorial names the Native Americans who have been associated with the institute and have died since 1901. There are 65 names on this headstone. The school cemetery is located on old farmland on Indiana Avenue.

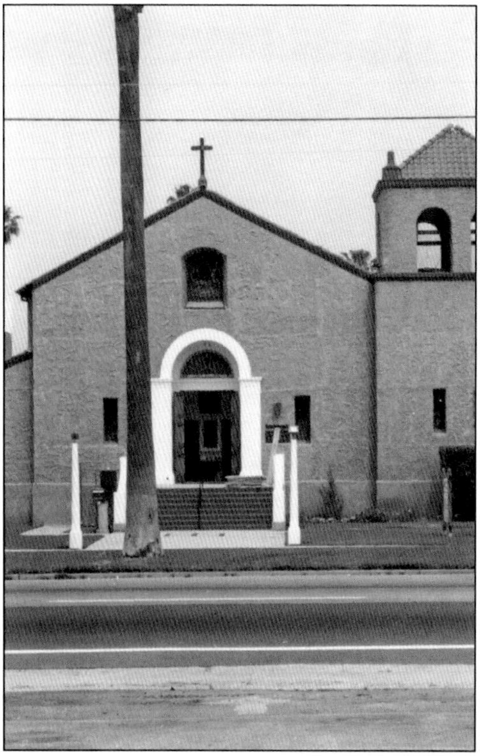

The Sherman Protestant Chapel was built on Magnolia Avenue for the use of Sherman Indian Institute students. The chapel, designed in the mission style with a bell tower, stands across the street from the school.

Pictured here around 1935 are students from Sherman Indian High School. During the week, they attended school; on Friday evening and Saturdays, they would make their way down to the Arlington Theater to see a movie. Sundays saw them dressed for church.

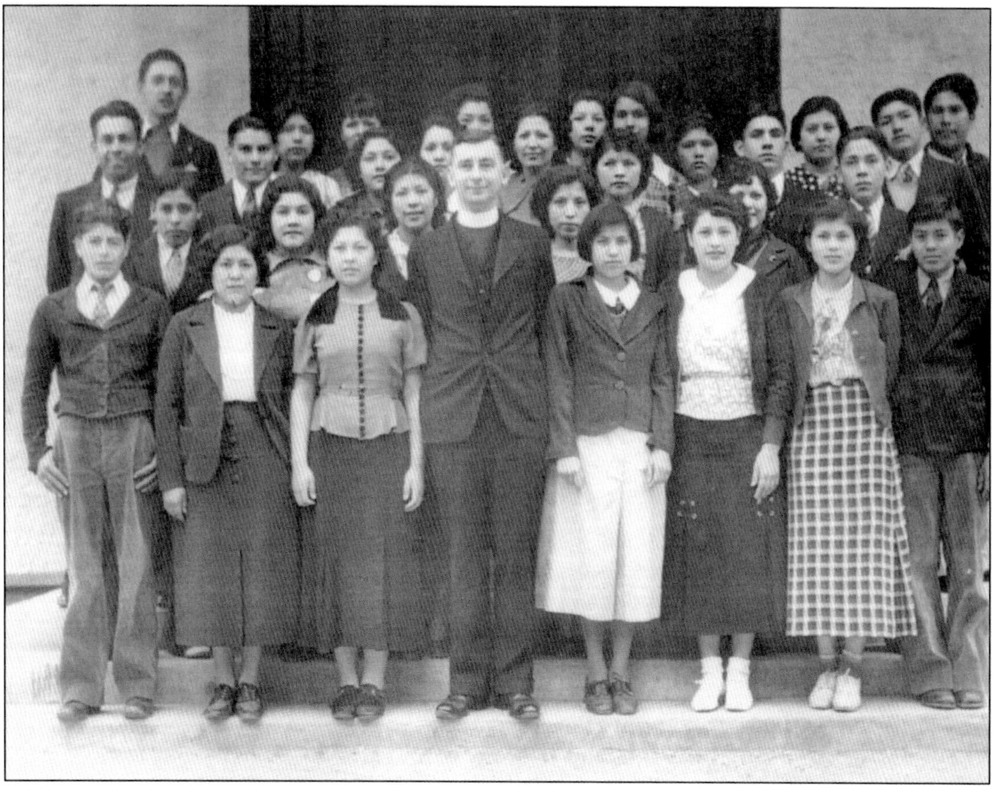

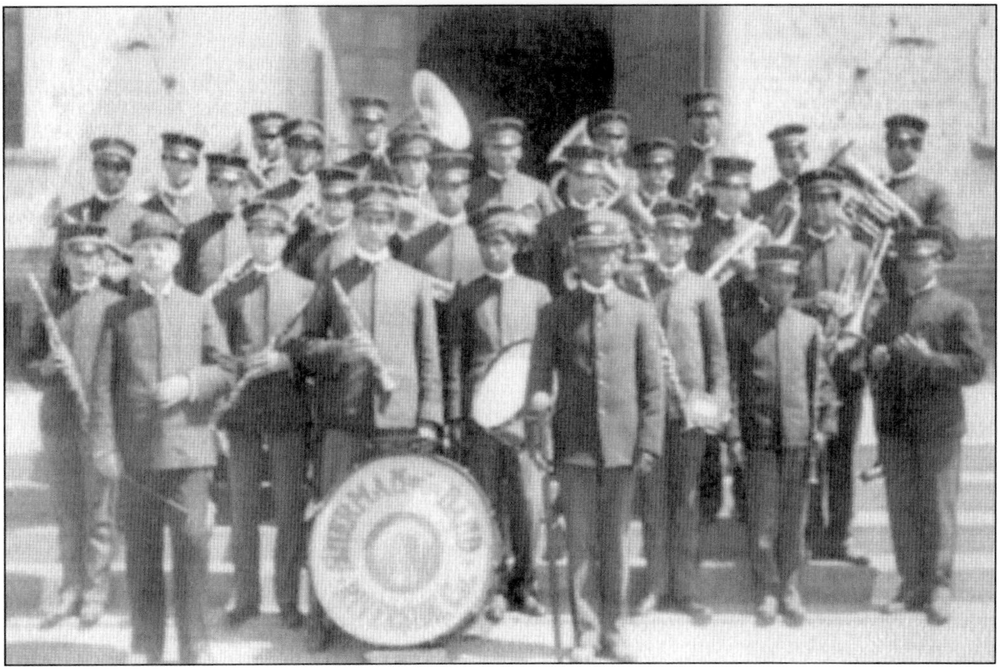

The Sherman Indian Institute's band is pictured here around 1901. The group, full of many different instruments, performed at local events. (Courtesy Sherman Indian Museum.)

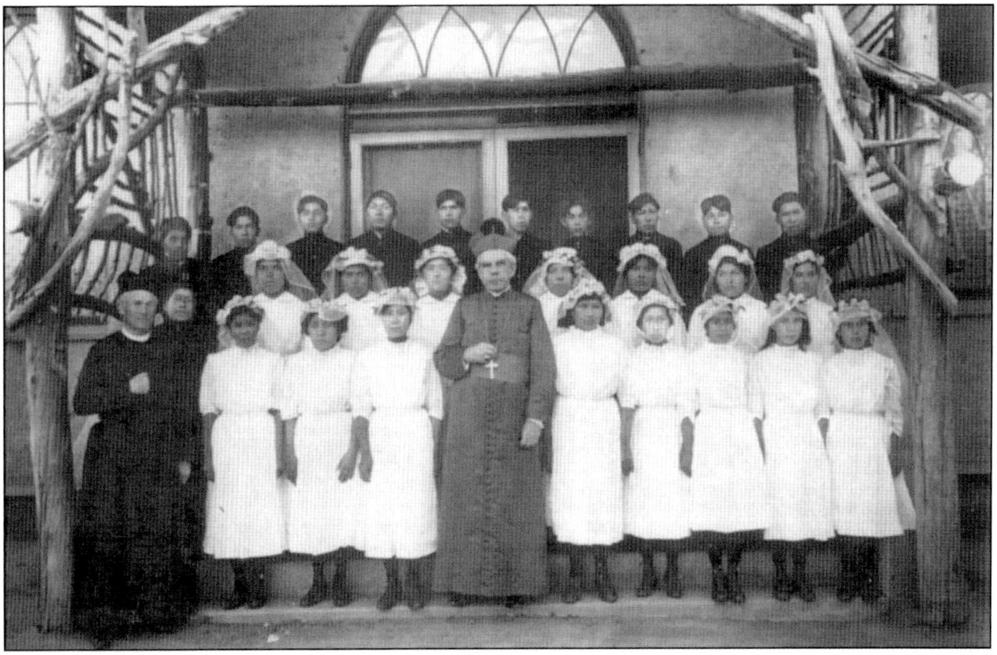

Native Americans from the Sherman Indian Institute stand in an archway with Father Jureck (left) and Bishop Cantwell (center). Attending St. Thomas Catholic Church, they received the sacrament of confirmation on May 1918 in an important Roman Catholic ceremony. The boys are dressed in black and the girls in white with veils on their heads.

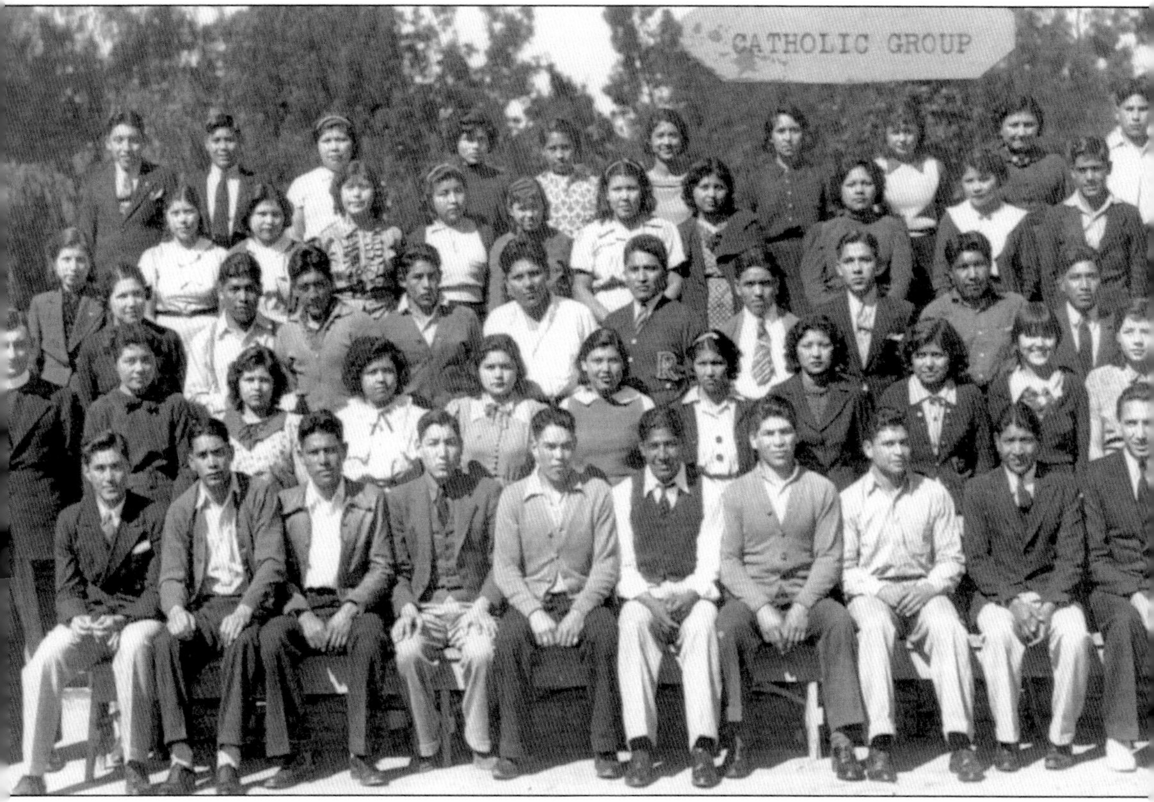

A large group of Native American men and women from the Sherman Indian Institute poses about 1937 with Fr. Michael Bryne, who taught them about the Roman Catholic faith.

Four

PEOPLE OF THE TIMES

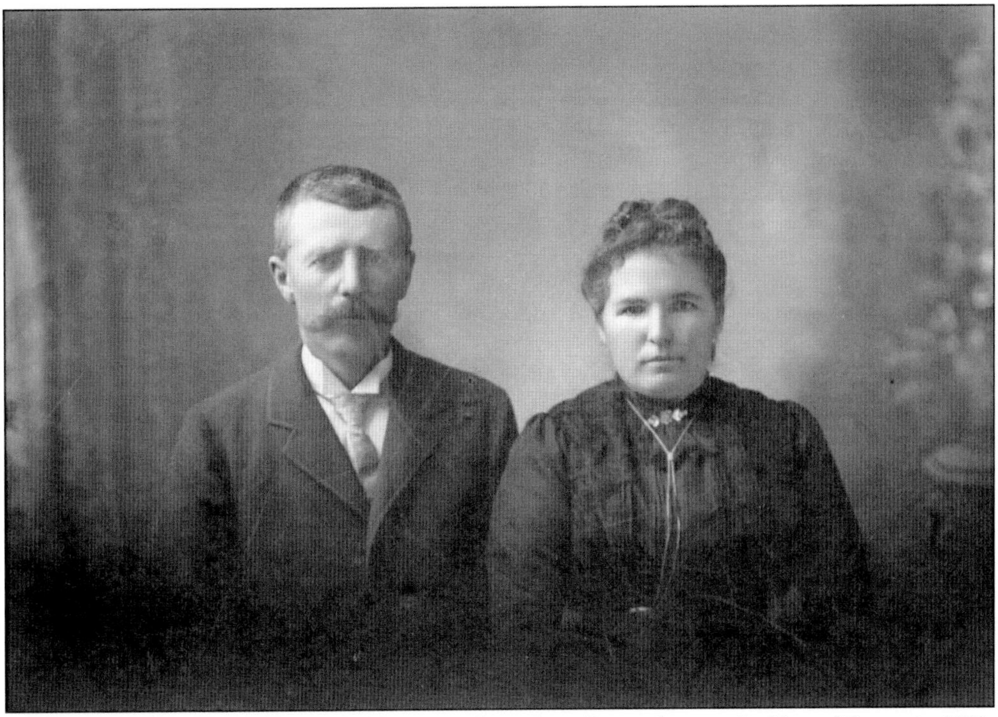

Peter and Amelia Goethals traveled by ocean liner from Rotterdam to the United States in 1890. They came to Riverside and stayed at the Kincell Rooming House at Orange and Ninth, where the Riverside Post Office now stands. Real estate men were on hand to show land. Peter and Amelia bought 10 acres in Arlington, with a house under construction and groves around.

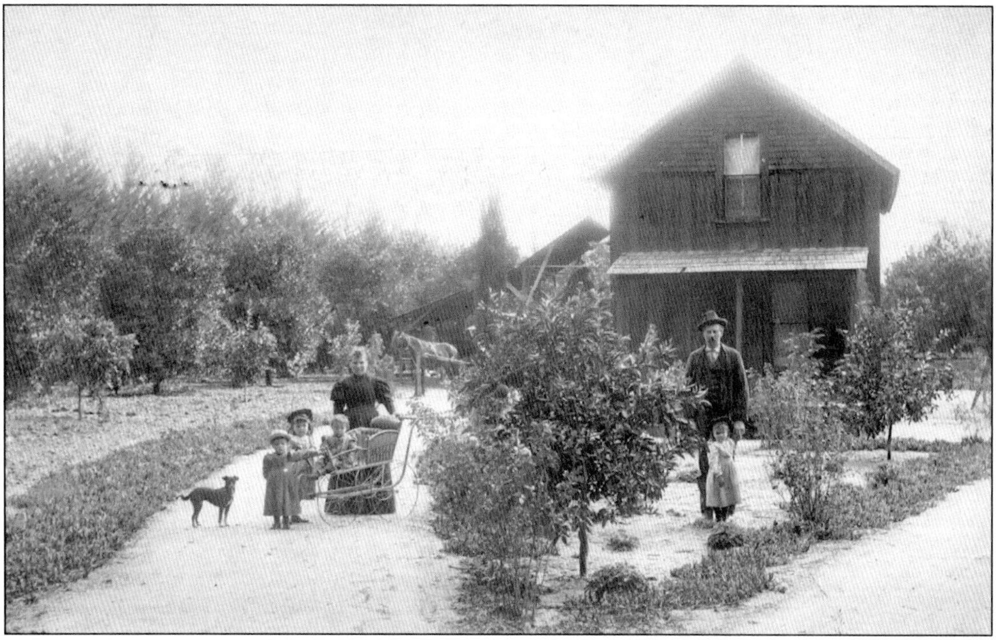

Shown in 1897 is the Goethals family homestead at 970 Magnolia Avenue. In 1890, Peter Goethals purchased two 10-acre orange groves from Samuel C. Evans, an early developer of the area. A two-story unfinished house, built with square nails, was located in one of the orange groves. This is where Peter and Amelia lived for 51 years and raised their family of eight children.

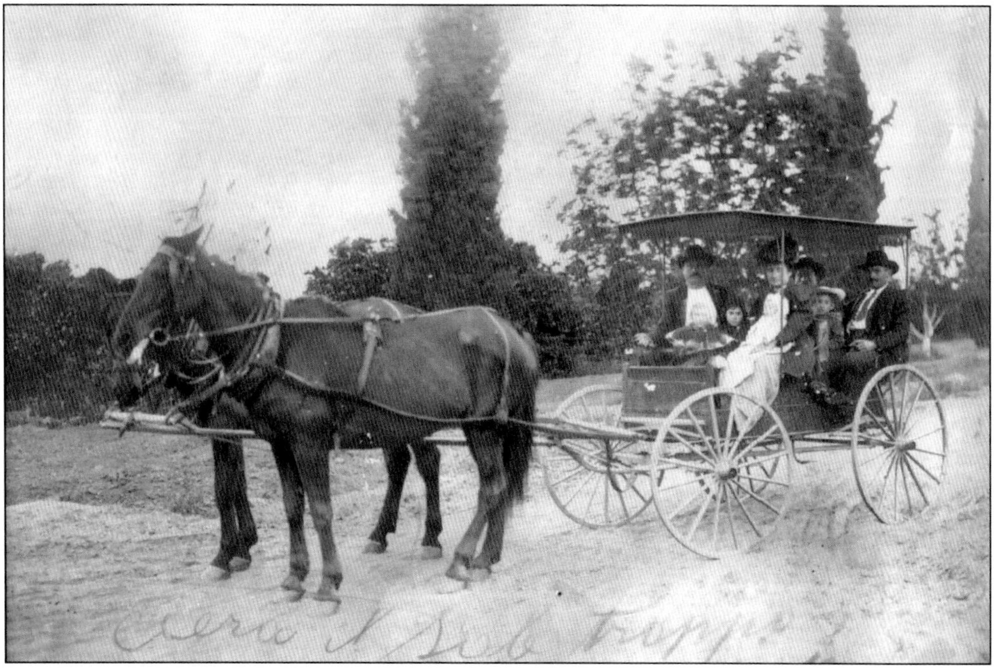

Joseph and Margaret Pagliuso, their children, and Joseph's two brothers ride to Sunday morning mass at St. Thomas the Apostle Catholic Church, located at the corner of Magnolia Avenue and Jackson Street, about 1900. They regularly arrived in their large buggy pulled by two horses. (Courtesy Marian Maxwell Pagliuso.)

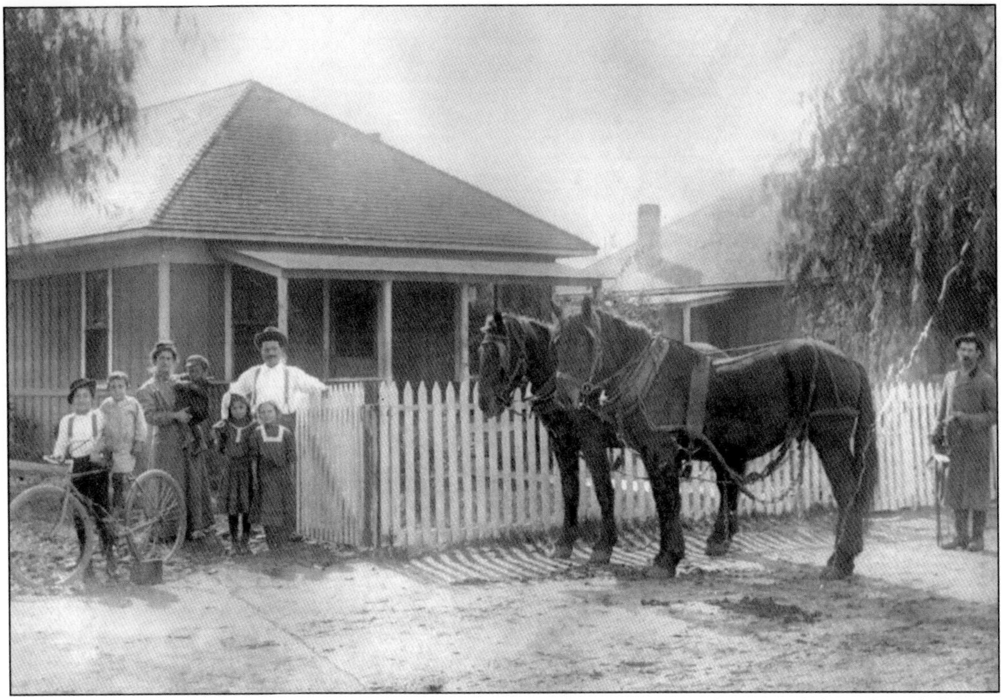

Posing around 1911 at their ranch home are Joseph and Margaret Pagliuso and their five children. One of the boys holds onto his bicycle while another sits atop the seat, and Margaret holds the youngest. Joseph always had a team of horses nearby. (Courtesy Marian Maxwell Pagliuso.)

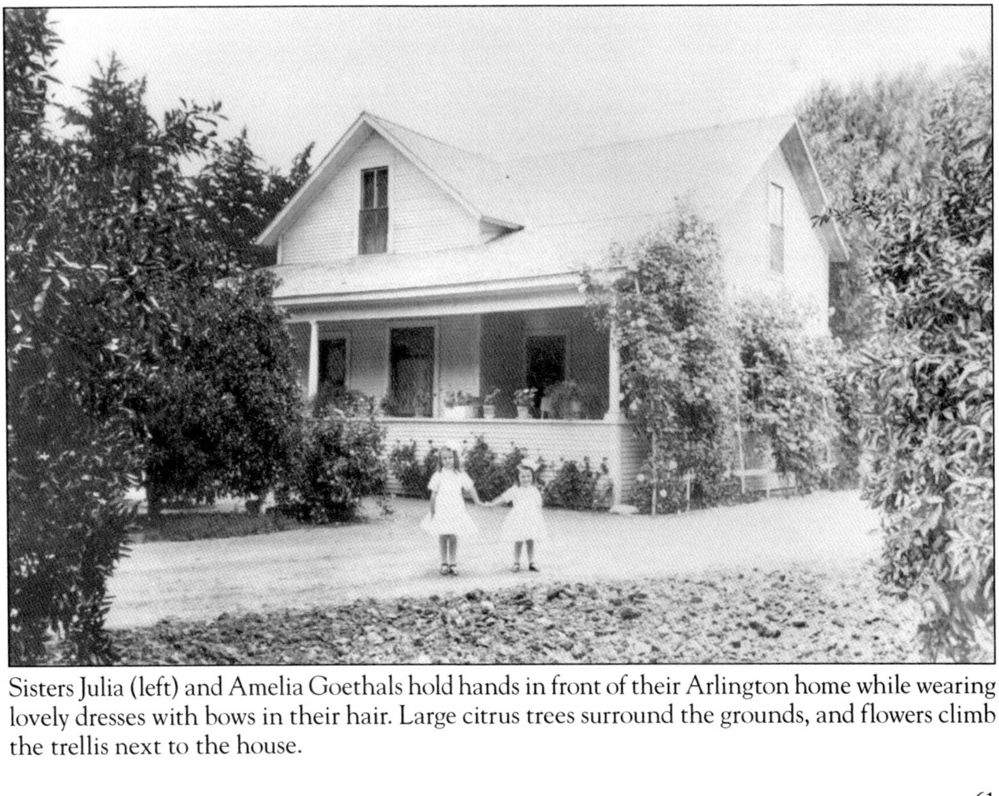

Sisters Julia (left) and Amelia Goethals hold hands in front of their Arlington home while wearing lovely dresses with bows in their hair. Large citrus trees surround the grounds, and flowers climb the trellis next to the house.

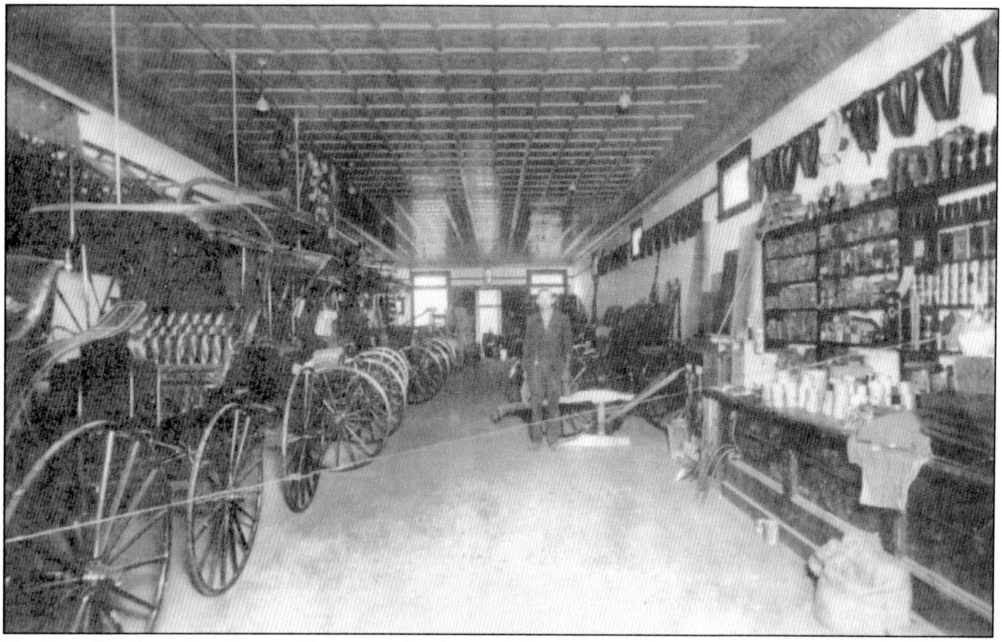

Carlson Brothers Implement Store was built in 1910 on Magnolia Avenue in the first block west of Van Buren Boulevard. Sharing the building with Isaac and Mac Carlson was Sam Gurley, who had a grocery, a predecessor to the A. M. Lewis and Davenport markets. Isaac Carlton is pictured here with his line of horseless carriages, farm implements, wagons, and saddle equipment.

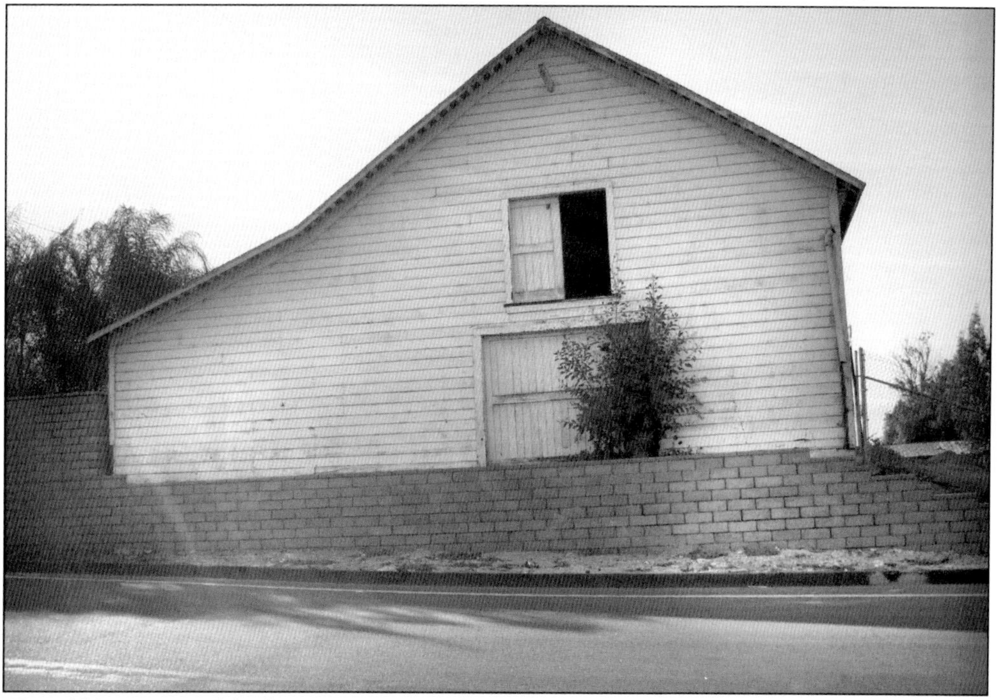

This old barn, one of the last remaining in the area, is located on Dufferin Street and was used to store farm equipment. The surrounding land has been taken, so a brick wall has been put in place to hold the dirt. The road formerly stopped at the barn but now passes by.

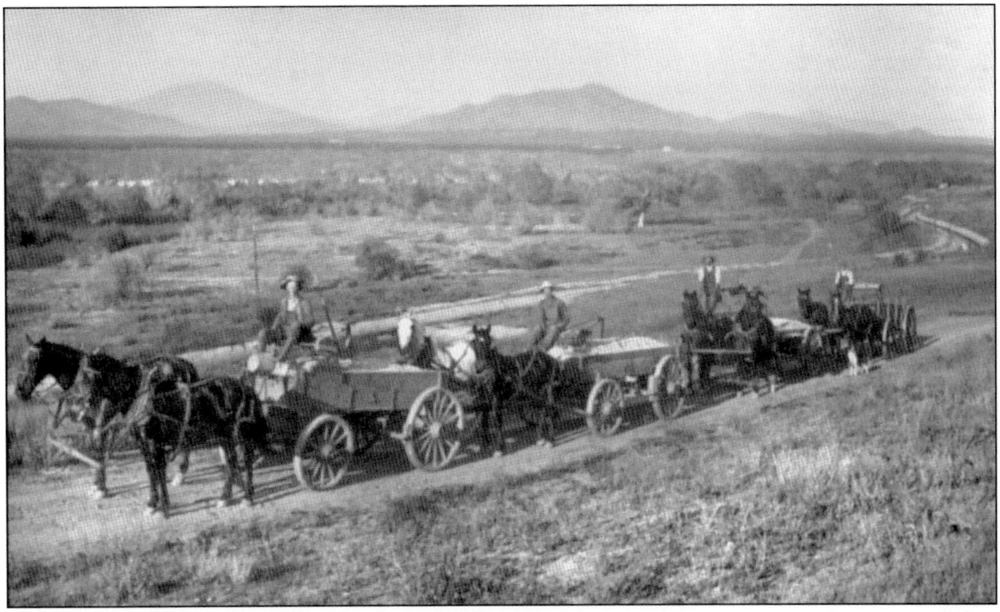

Pictured here in the 1890s, local men haul wagonloads of sand from the river bottom to fill in roads and use for new development. The area was filled with sagebrush, and the whole valley and mountains can be seen in the background. (Courtesy Bud and Lois Abraham.)

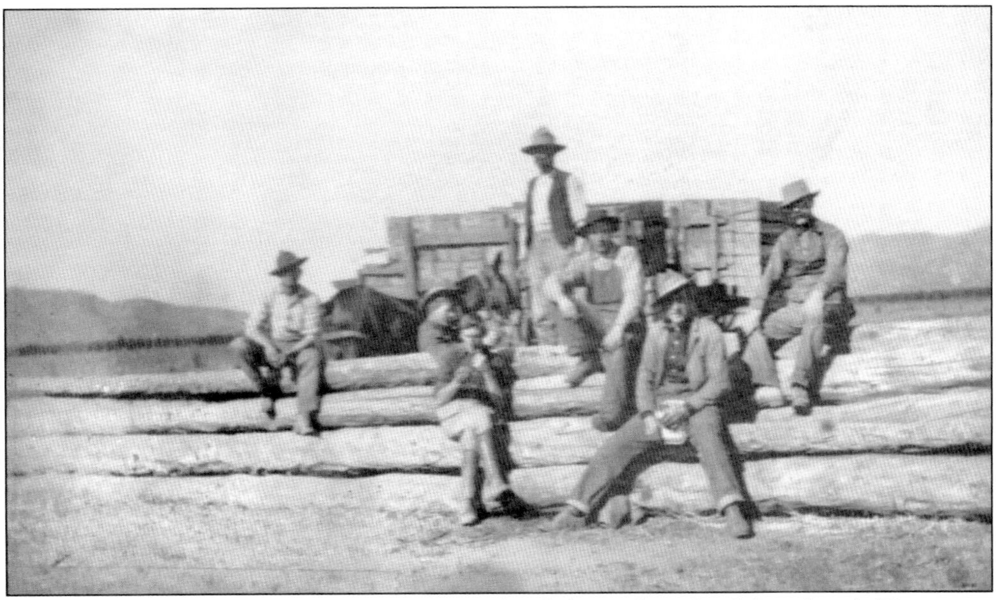

Seated on this wall of logs are six men taking a break from a long, hard day of work. The wagon is likely filled with wooden boxes for transporting citrus. (Courtesy Bud and Lois Abraham.)

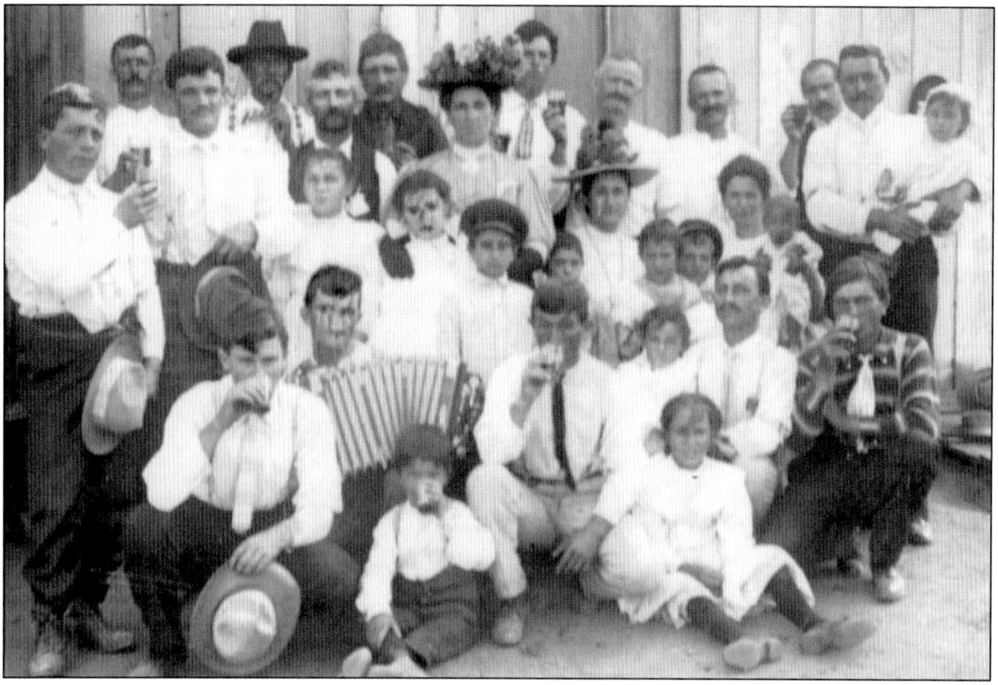

The German and Italian people of Arlington enjoyed gathering for a big party at the annual Beer Bust. From the youngest to the oldest, all would join in and toast with their beers. (Courtesy Bud and Lois Abraham.)

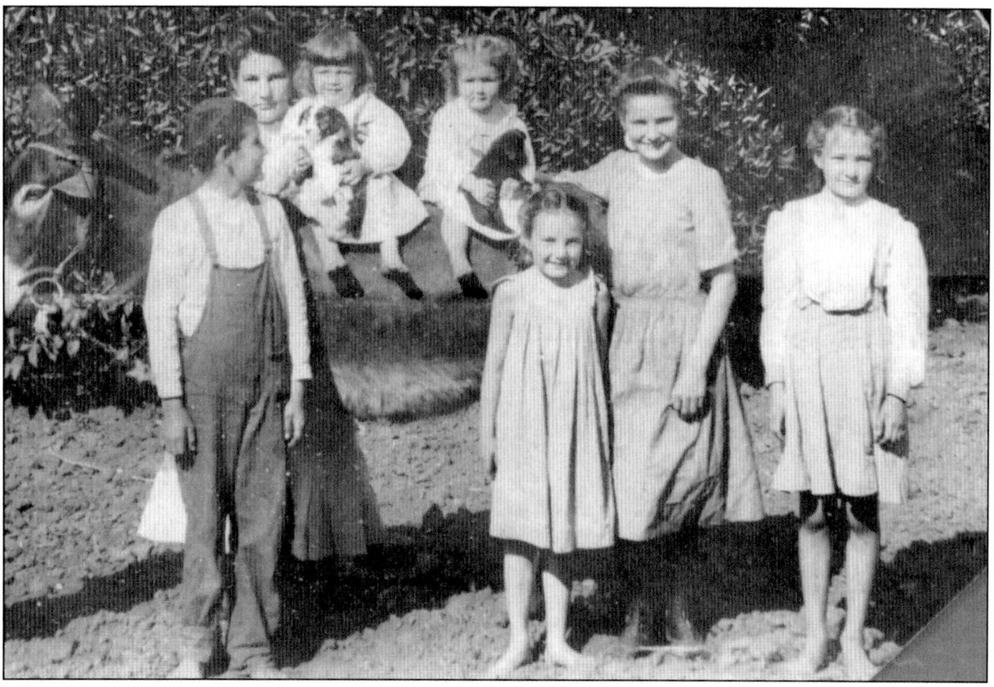

From left to right, Alberie, Marie, Agnes, Cecilia, Nathalie, Celina, and Helen Goethals play with their puppies and donkey around 1910. The season must be summer, as the children's feet are bare. They lived at 10174 Magnolia Avenue with their parents, Peter and Amelia Goethals.

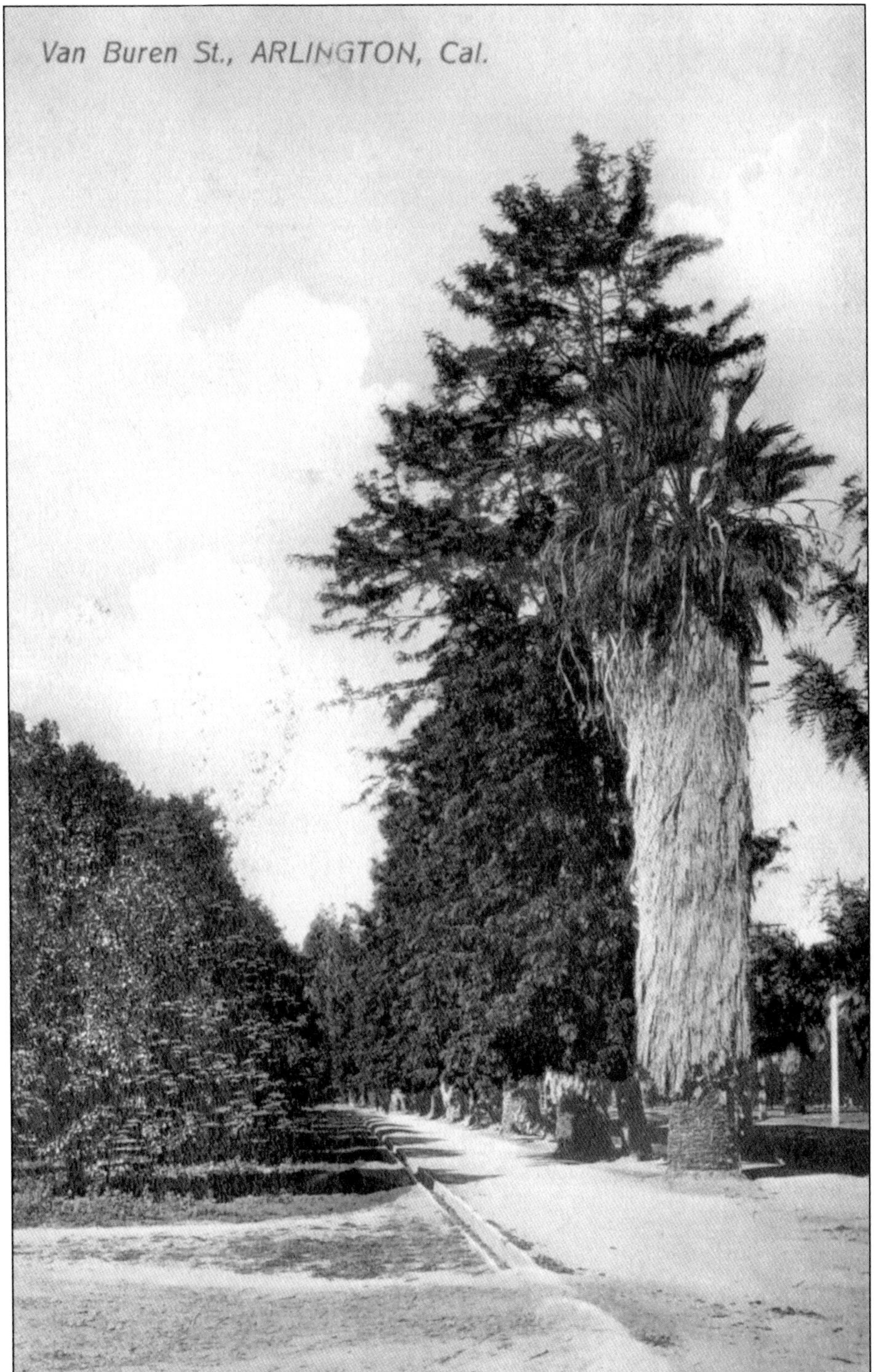

Trees always lined the busy Van Buren Boulevard, with palms on one side and oranges on the other. Travelers coming from old Highway 395 to Arlington enjoyed a long but beautiful and relaxing ride. (Courtesy Steve Lech.)

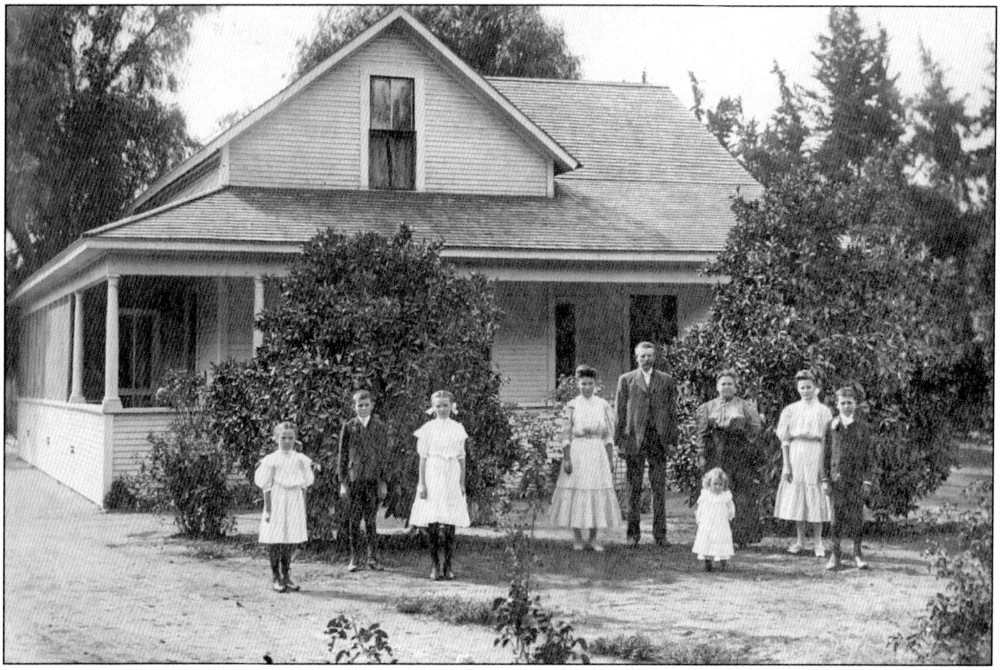

Goethals family members are dressed in their Sunday best in front of their beautiful home on Magnolia Avenue. Shown from left to right are Nathalie, Alberie, Helen, Marie, Peter, Amelia, Celina, Amandus, and Cecilia (in front).

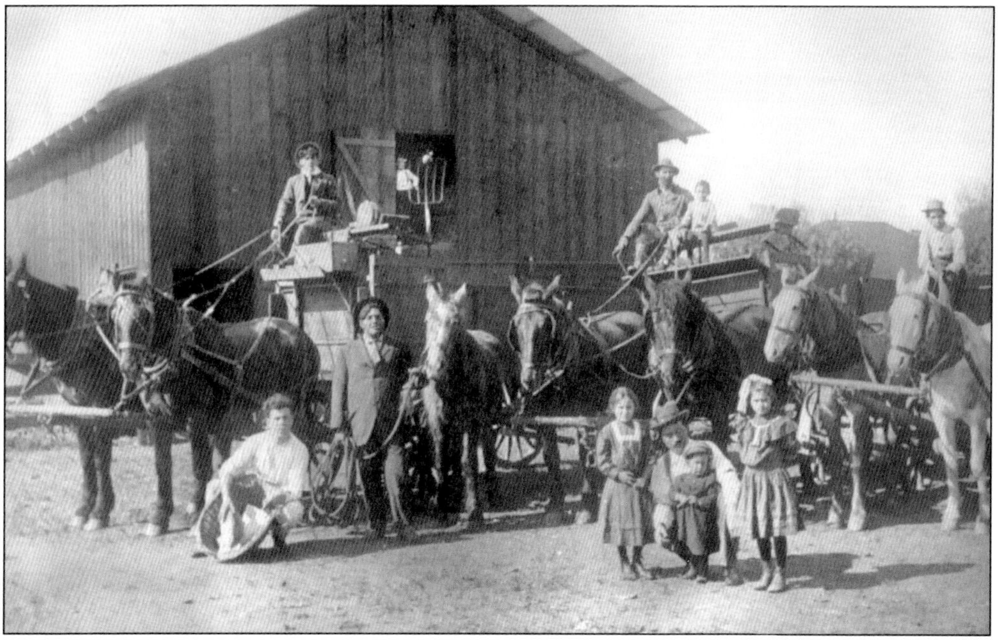

Along with his team of horses, Joseph Pagliuso and a workman are on their way out to the field to bring in a load of hay to be stored in the loft. On the far right is Joseph Pagliuso with his children Virginia, Carmel, and John. Joseph's oldest brother Frank is up in the hayloft. Seated on the wagon with the workman is Joseph's son Ernest, and at left is a friend who delivered French bread to the neighborhood. (Courtesy Marian Maxwell Pagliuso.)

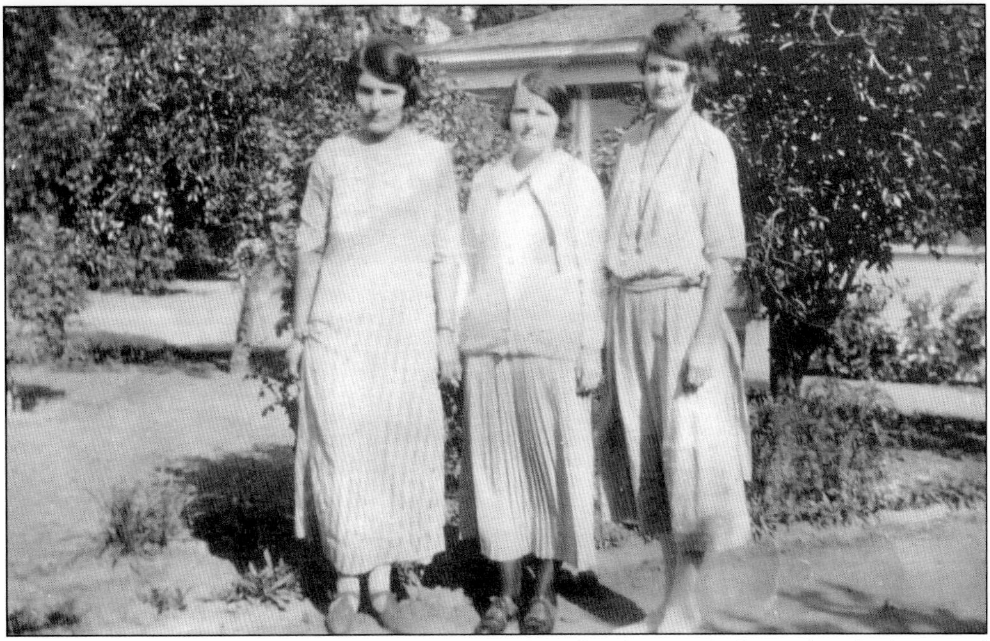

In the summer of 1924, Marie (left), Cecilia (center), and Helen Goethals stand in the front yard of their Magnolia Avenue homestead, where all three were born. The sisters sport the same short hairstyle popular during the 1920s.

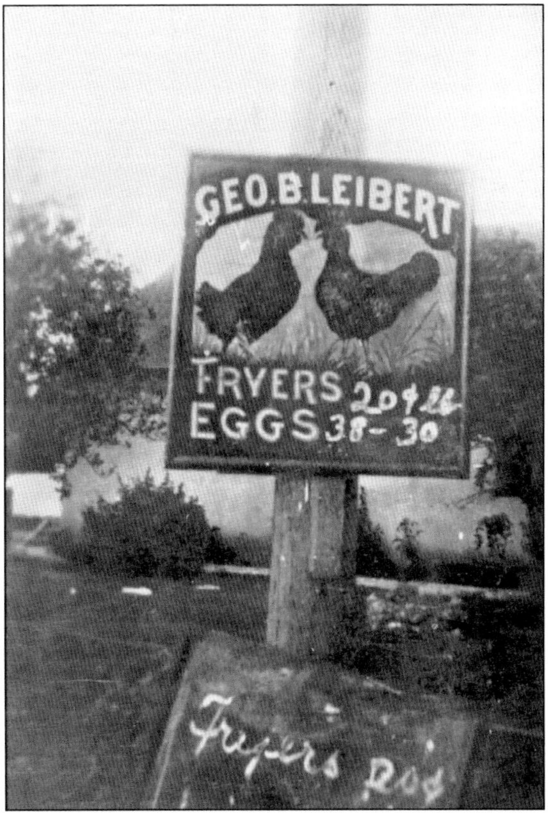

George Leibert posted his sign out front so passersby could see that he sold fryers—for 20¢ a pound. Many of his regular customers liked to come to his back door, where they knew that they could get George's freshest fryers and eggs.

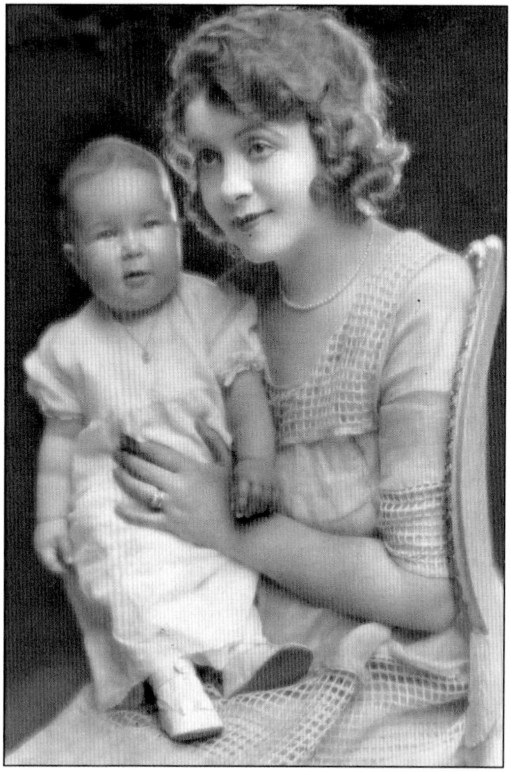

Baby Betty Dunlap, held by her mother, looks to be about six months old and is wearing a necklace with a locket. Betty's dress and shoes are in the style of the 1920s. Mrs. Dunlap has short, wavy hair.

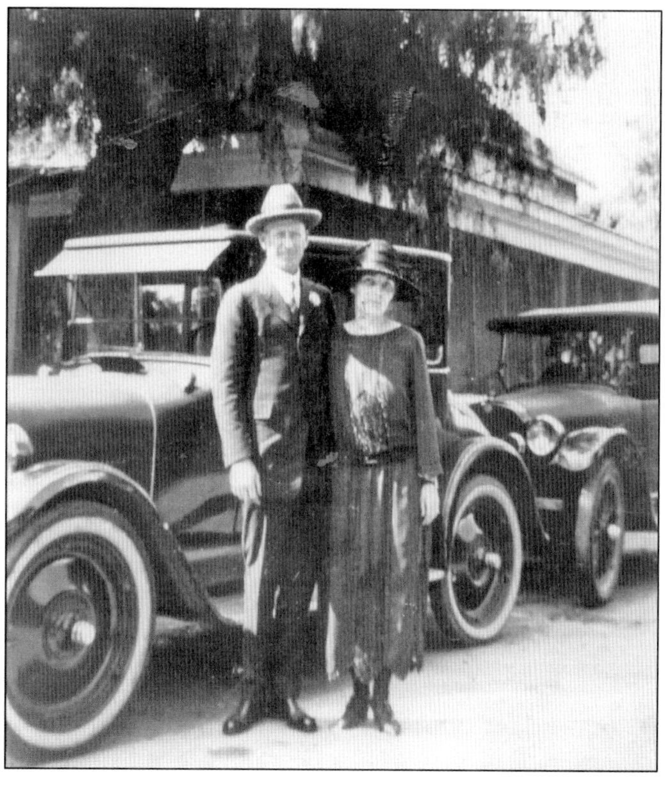

George and Marie Leibert were married on October 8, 1923, at St. Thomas Church with a reception at the bride's family home, located on Magnolia Avenue. Marie was born here in 1892 and later became a teacher in Arlington. Notice the old cars in the driveway.

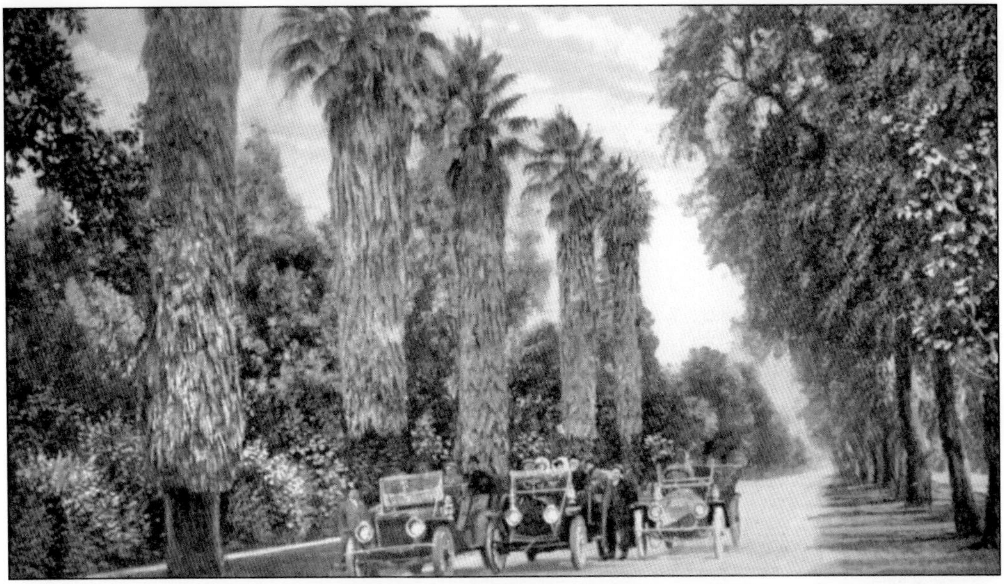

Magnolia Avenue is one of the most beautiful drives in town, flanked by tall palms and large shaded tress. These men and ladies with large hats embark on a ride sometime in the 1920s. (Courtesy JoAnne Pease-Simpson.)

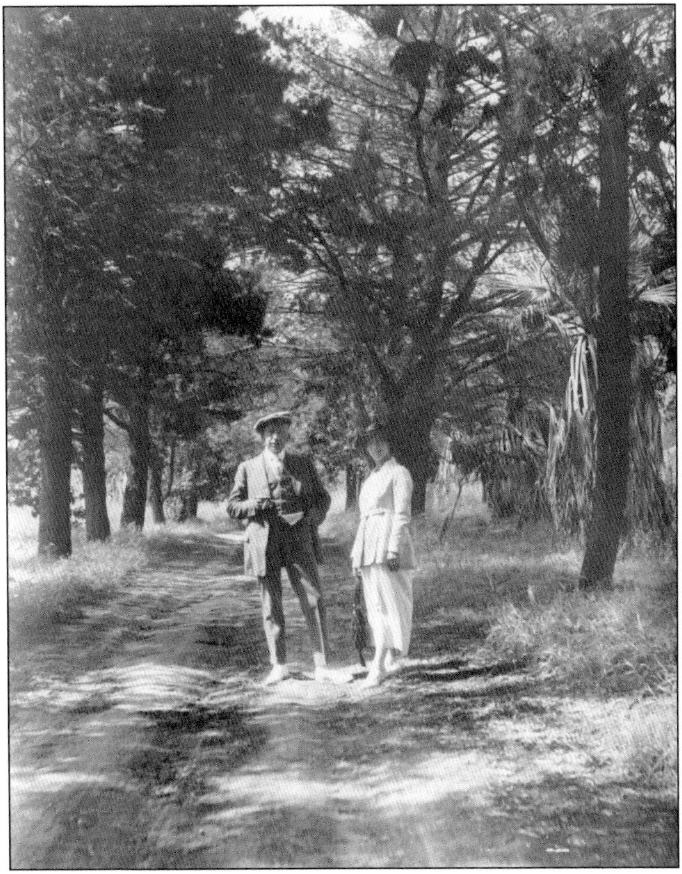

A couple takes an afternoon walk on a dirt road, lined with full shade trees.

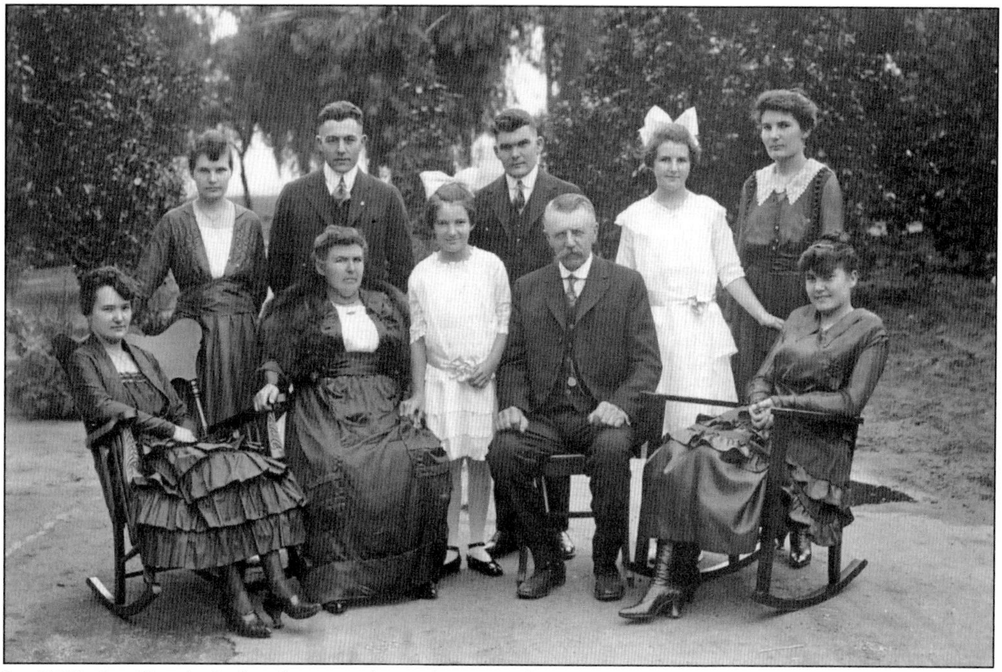

In 1915, the Goethals family poses for a photograph sitting in old rocking chairs. Pictured from left to right are the following: (first row) Helen, Amelia, Agnes, Peter, and Nathalie; (second row) Celina, Alberie, Amandus, Cecilia, and Marie. The clothing is very dashing; from Peter's vest hangs an old pocket watch.

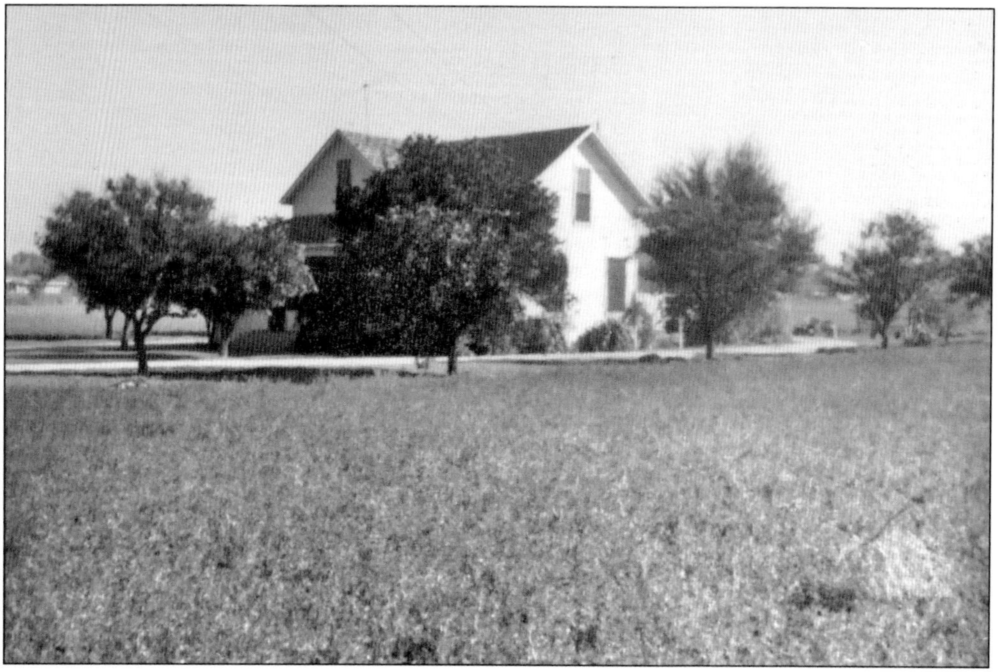

The old Goethals homestead was situated on Magnolia Avenue in Arlington. The children were born and raised here at the family home, which was demolished in 1966 to allow for a shopping mall. Gone are the days of homes surrounded by lots of land and trees.

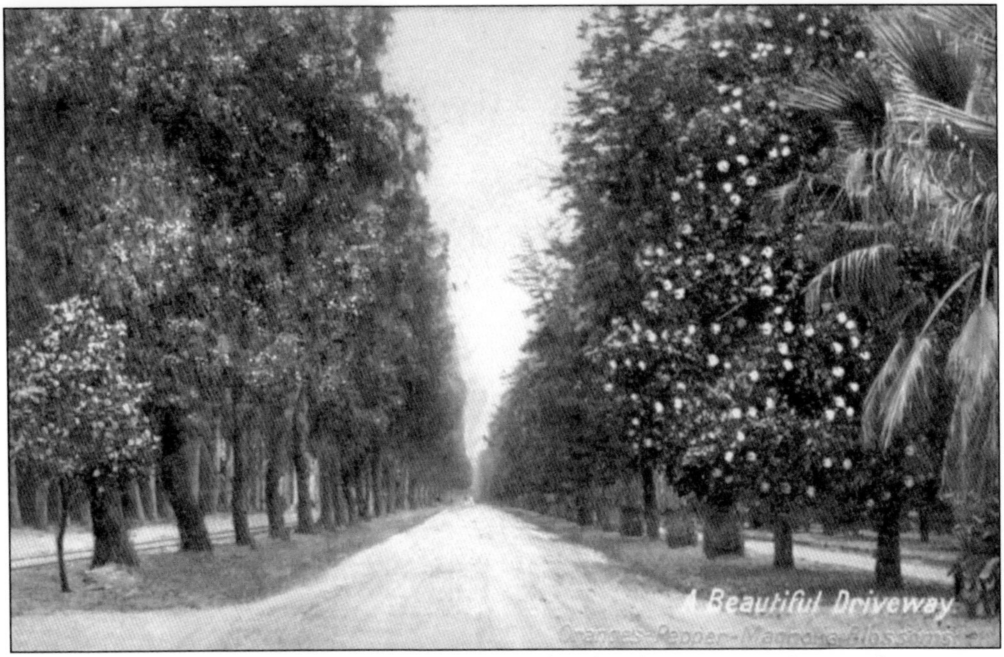

Shown in the 1920s, this long, beautiful driveway is lined with orange trees bearing fruit, pepper trees with red berries, and magnolia trees filled with white flowers. The long driveways were formed to aid in finding the home, and the trees were planted as landmarks. (Courtesy JoAnne Pease-Simpson.)

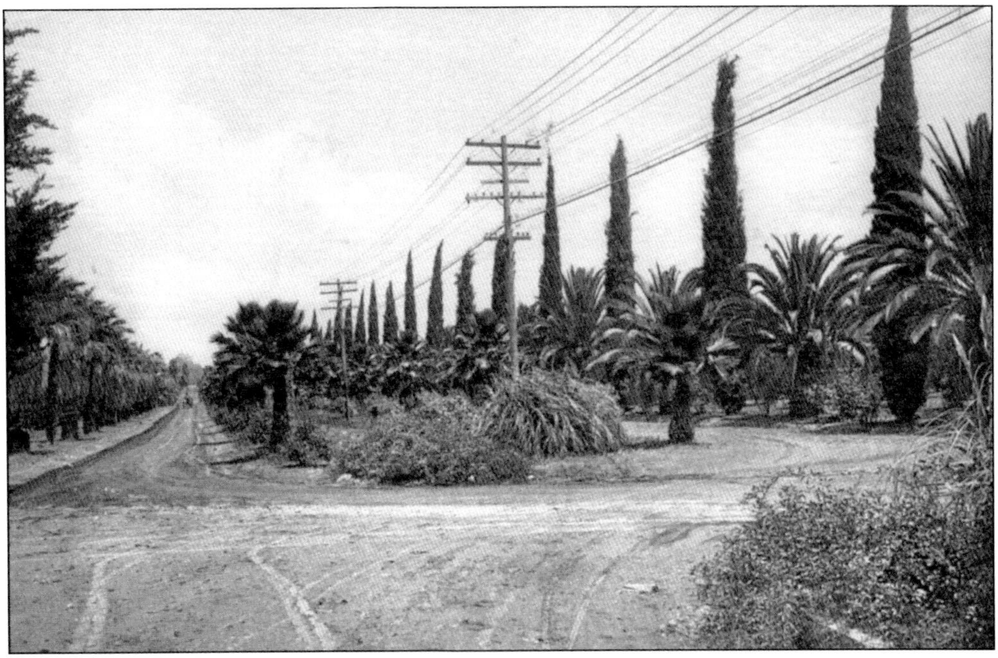

Victoria Avenue, known all around for its beauty, was a two-sided road separated by elegant palms, roses, and shrubbery. Cypress and palm trees formed the outer sides. Pictured here in the 1920s is the end, where a driver could easily turn around. (Courtesy JoAnne Pease-Simpson.)

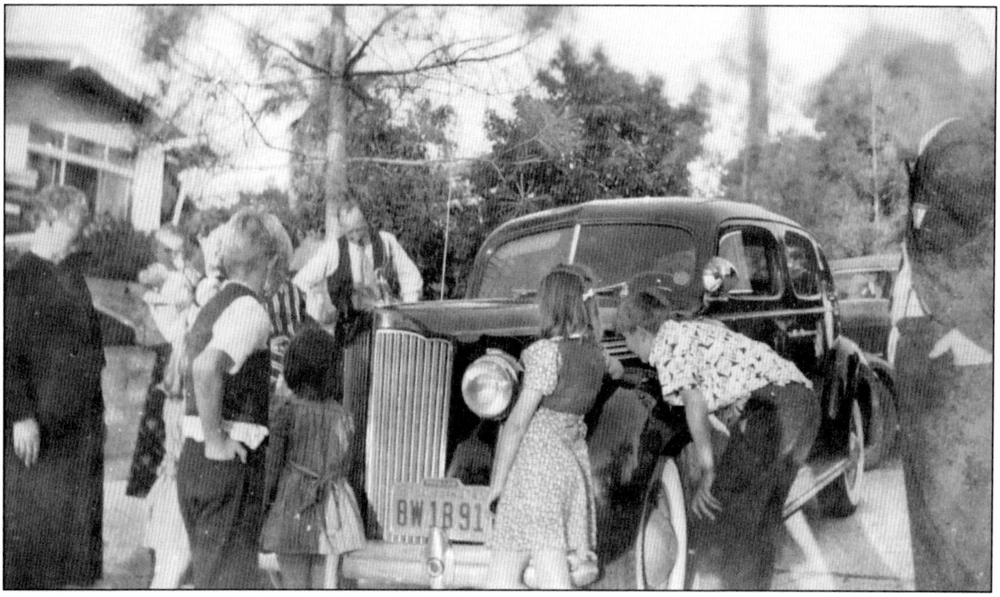

It was a special day when Uncle Bill Haney bought his 1938 Packard. The entire family, including cousins and adults, gathered around to "ooh and ahh" over every detail of his new shiny car.

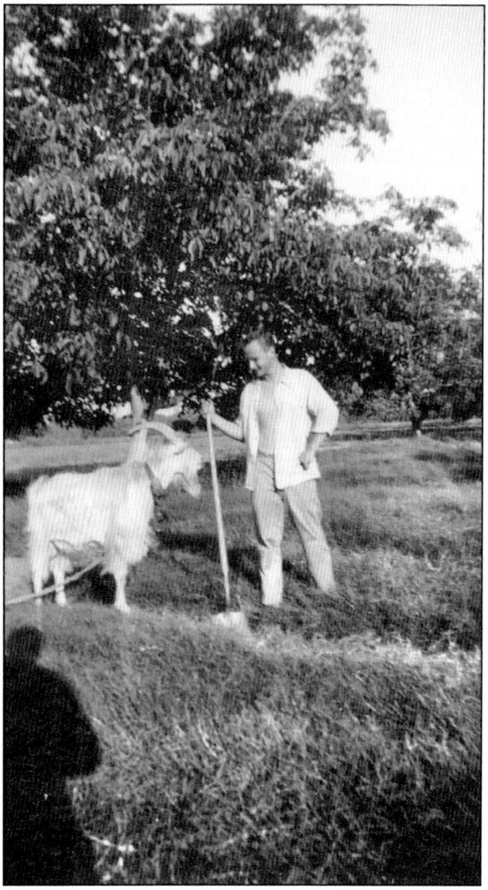

With his shovel in hand, Harry Morgan prepares for a day of work. His goat will rest in the shade of the large trees while keeping Harry company.

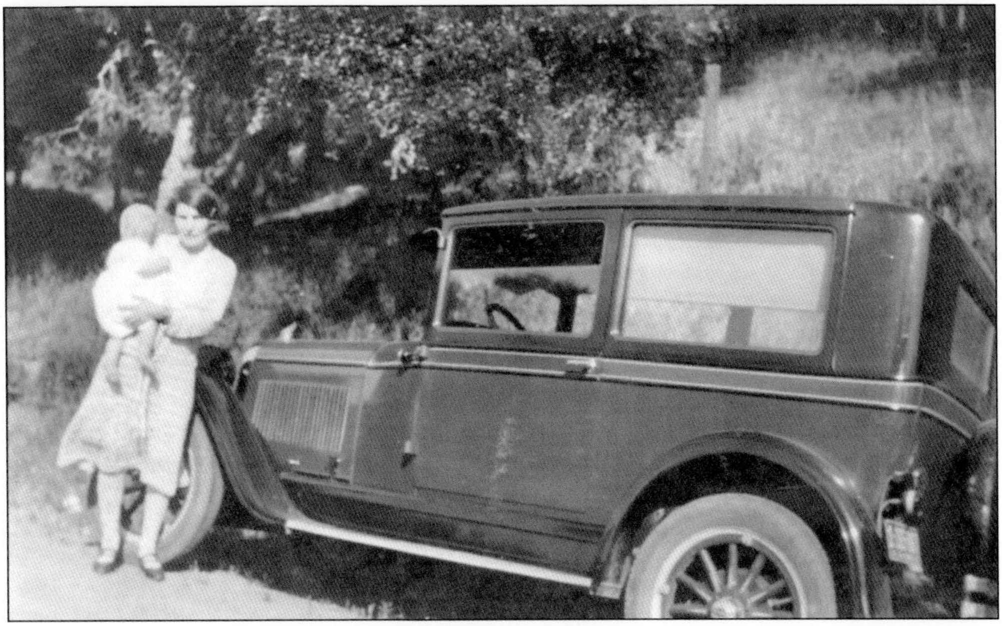

Marie Leibert and baby Theresa, out for a Sunday ride in this 1927 Pontiac, have stopped for a break and a walk around. There is also a lovely tree where they could sit and relax.

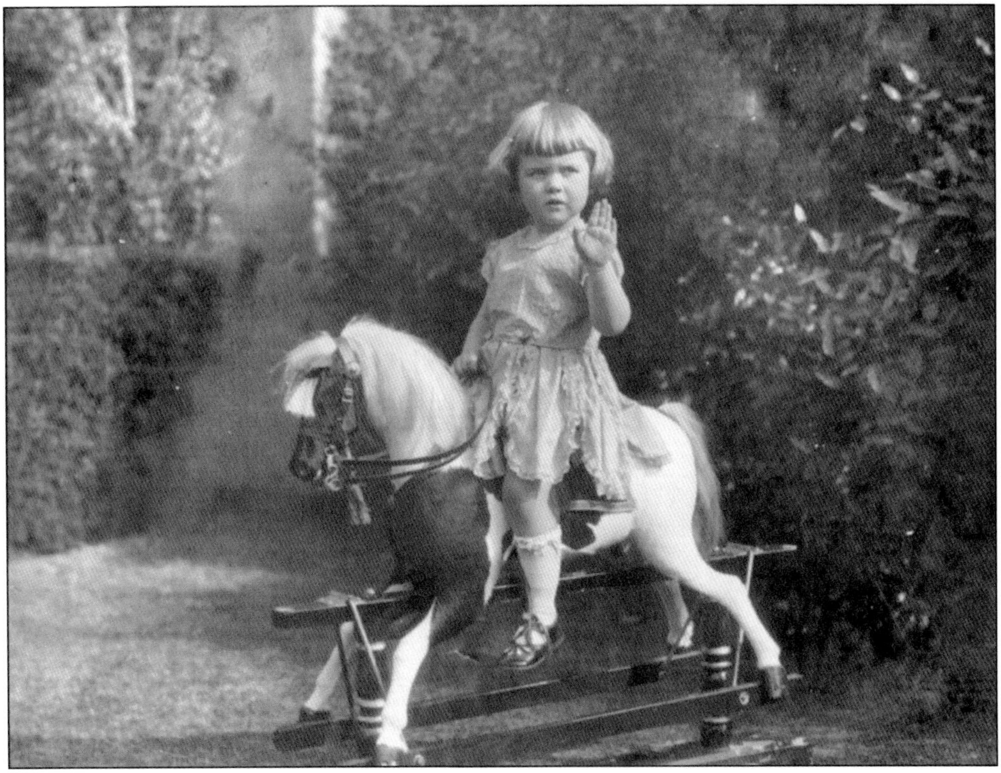

Jane Schultz, at about two years old, sits on her play horse in the yard. The horse jumps up and down as Jane holds onto the reins and waves to everyone. It is just her size, as her shoes fit perfectly in the stirrups.

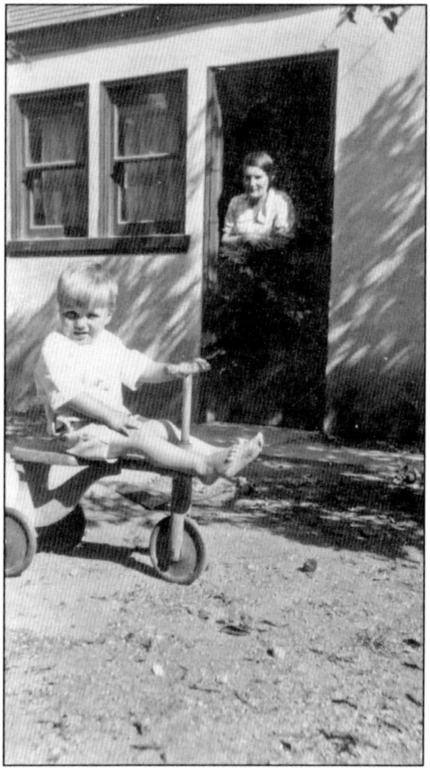

Around 1930, little John rides his tricycle with his feet straight out, playing in the back yard and looking for the other kids. His mother, Marie Leibert, gazes out of the garage as she prepares the laundry with the old ringer washer.

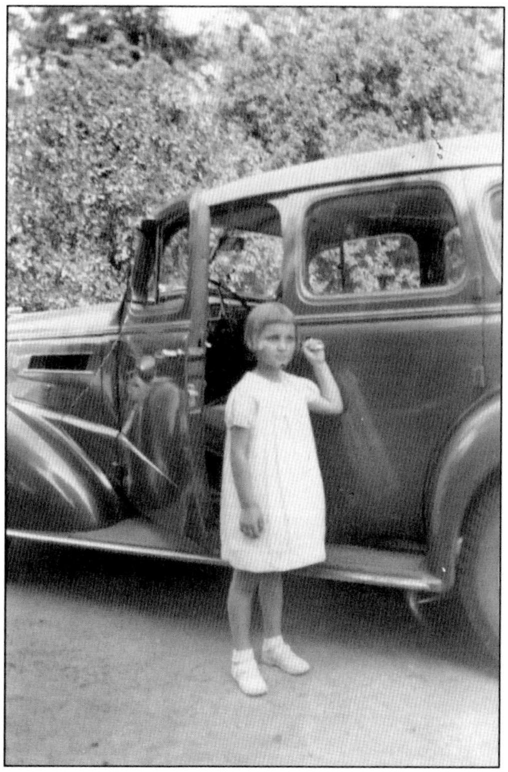

Nathalie Leibert, at Grandma Goethals's house, stands by the car with the door open waiting patiently to go home in 1939.

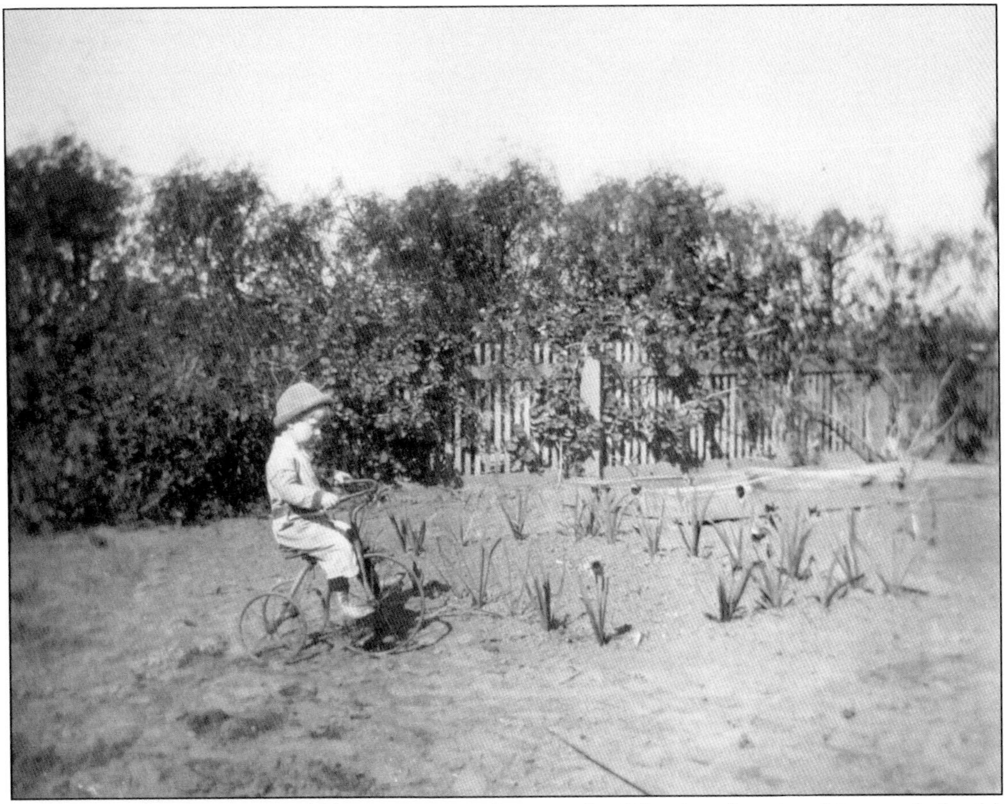

Jack Burns, a local two-year-old boy, maneuvers his tricycle of the time (bearing thin metal wheels) right through Grandma Helen's flower garden. She was not real happy at the sight.

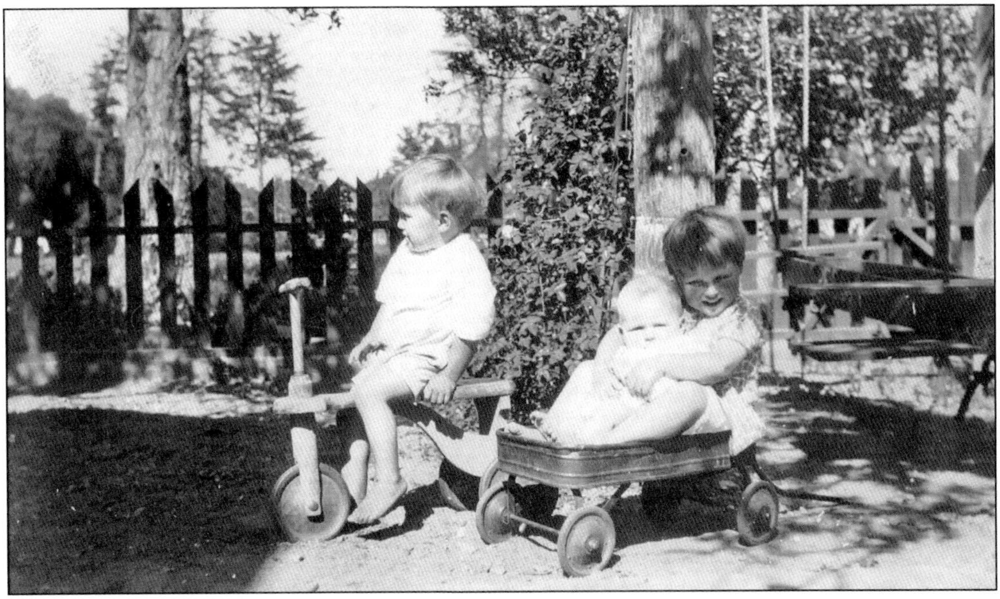

John sits on his tricycle while his sister Theresa holds baby Peter in this 1930 photograph. They wait patiently in a wagon, hoping someone will come along and pull them for a ride. Hanging from the tree like a swing is their homemade airplane Speedo created by their father.

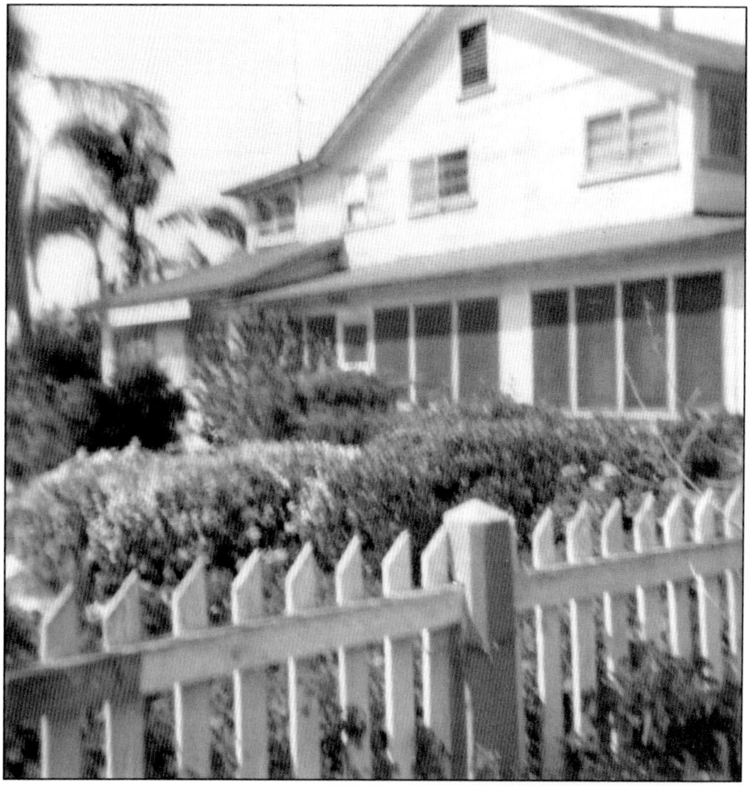

The Greiner house (left), located on Magnolia Avenue in Arlington, operated as a boarding school with dormitories for boys and girls. Children were placed there when they had no other place to go or when their parents just wanted to send them off to school. Years later, the home was divided into apartments with plenty of add-ons and lots of room (below). In the late 1970s, it was sold and demolished to make room for a new strip mall.

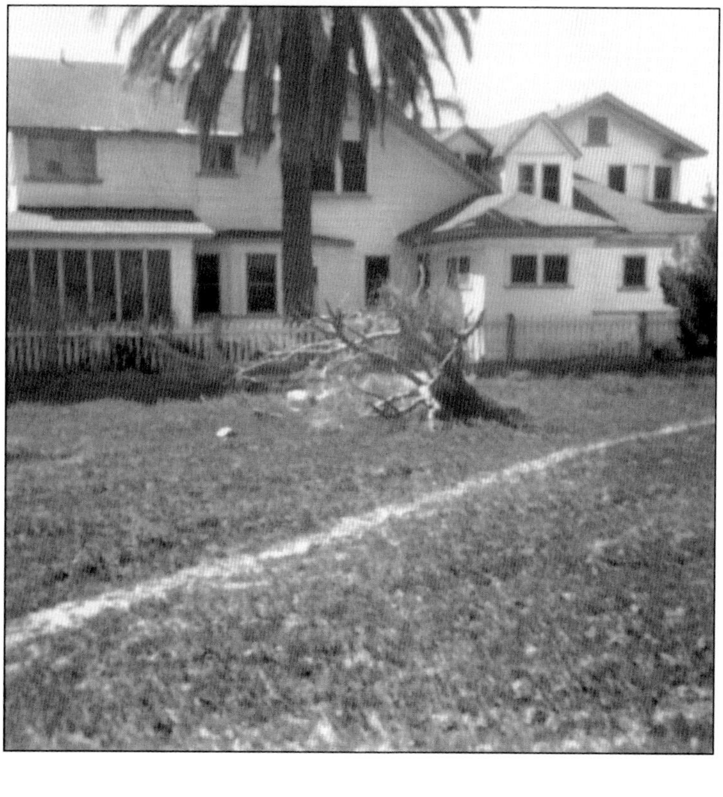

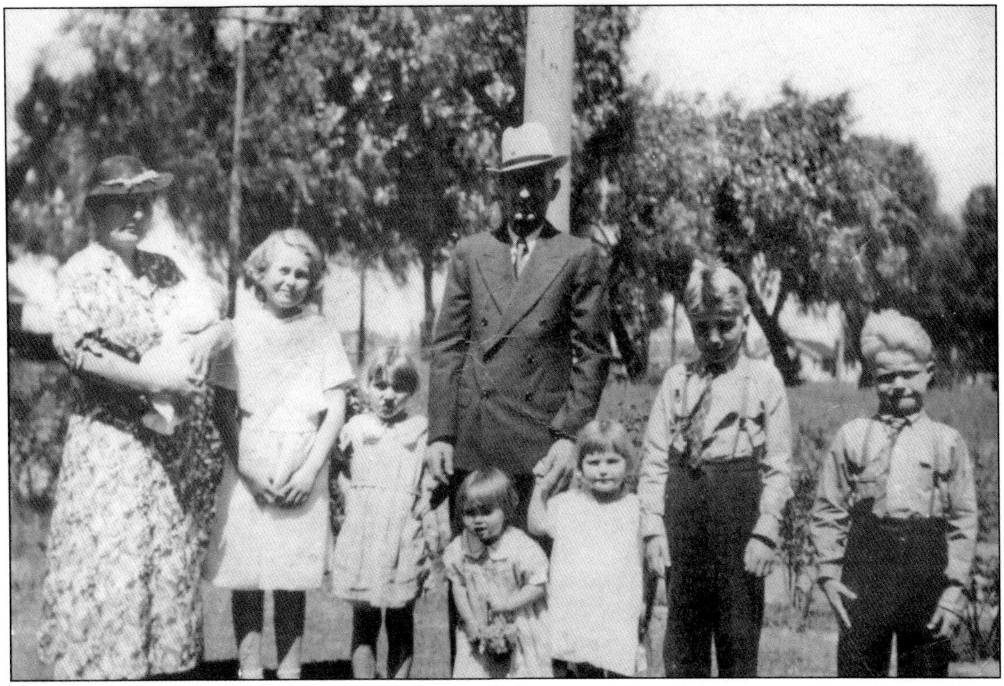

All the Leibert children were raised in the family home on Magnolia Avenue. Gathered on Easter Sunday in 1937 are, from left to right, Marie (mother), holding baby David; Theresa; Nathalie; George (father); Agnes, in front of her dad; Patsy; John; and Peter.

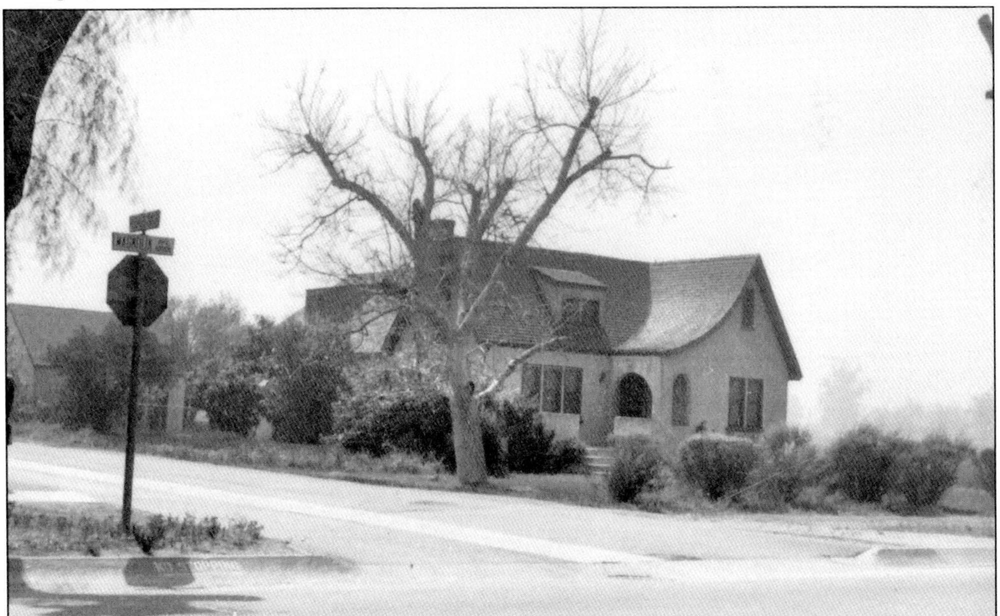

The intersection of Hughes Alley and Magnolia Avenue was the site of the George and Marie Leibert home. They raised their seven children in this structure, which was built in the late 1920s and demolished in 1966 to allow for the new Tyler Mall construction. Hughes Alley was a narrow street also known as Lovers Lane.

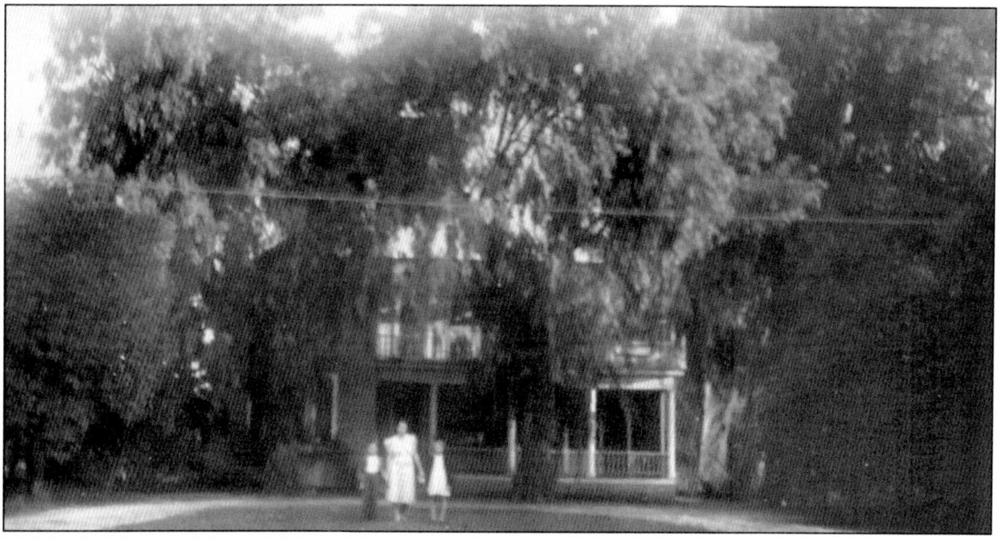

Mildred Kelley and her children Norman and Lovanna are on their way out for the day. They lived in a beautiful home on Magnolia Avenue with a large front porch and a circular driveway surrounded by trees. (Courtesy Norman and Velda Kelley.)

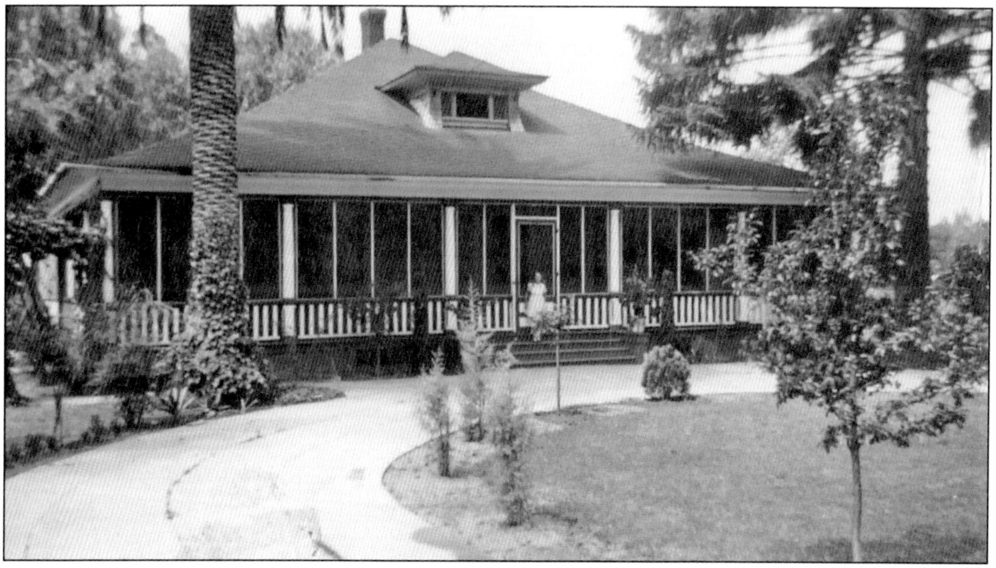

Houses once had large screen porches like this one, wrapping around the front and sometimes along the sides. The Alessio home is pictured during the late 1930s on the corner of Van Buren Boulevard and Hoag Street (now Primrose Drive). Barbara Miller stands at the front door. (Courtesy Barbara Miller Trujillo.)

Mischievous Norman Kelley and his sister Lovanna play with the garden hose in the front yard of their home in Arlington. The little girl has her hand over her mouth in an expression saying, "Oh no! What are you doing?" (Courtesy Norman and Velda Kelley.)

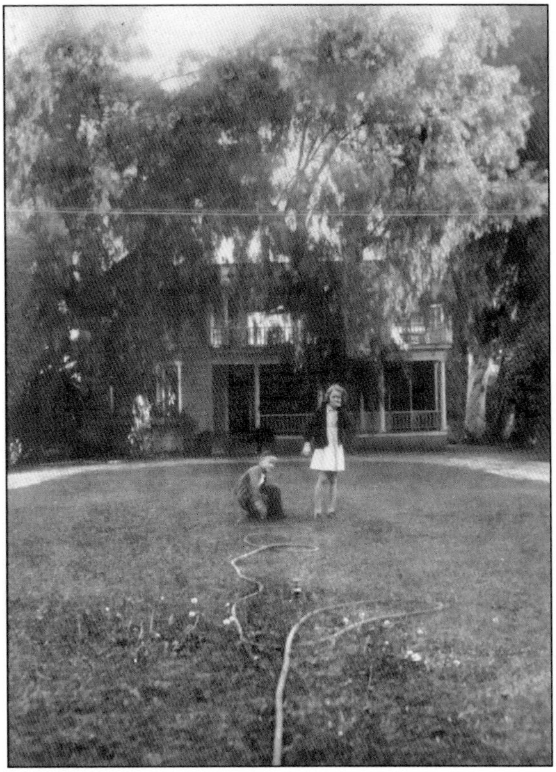

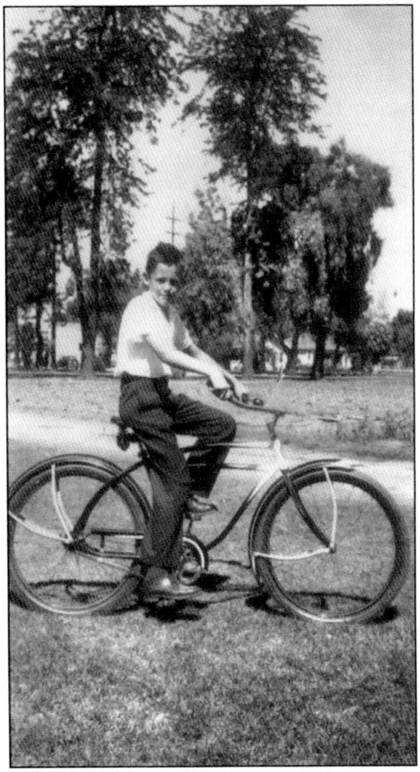

Norman Kelley is out for a trial run on the brand-new bicycle he purchased from Montgomery Ward. He has plenty of room to ride, as his home stands in the far back of the yard. He still owns this bicycle today. (Courtesy Norman and Velda Kelley.)

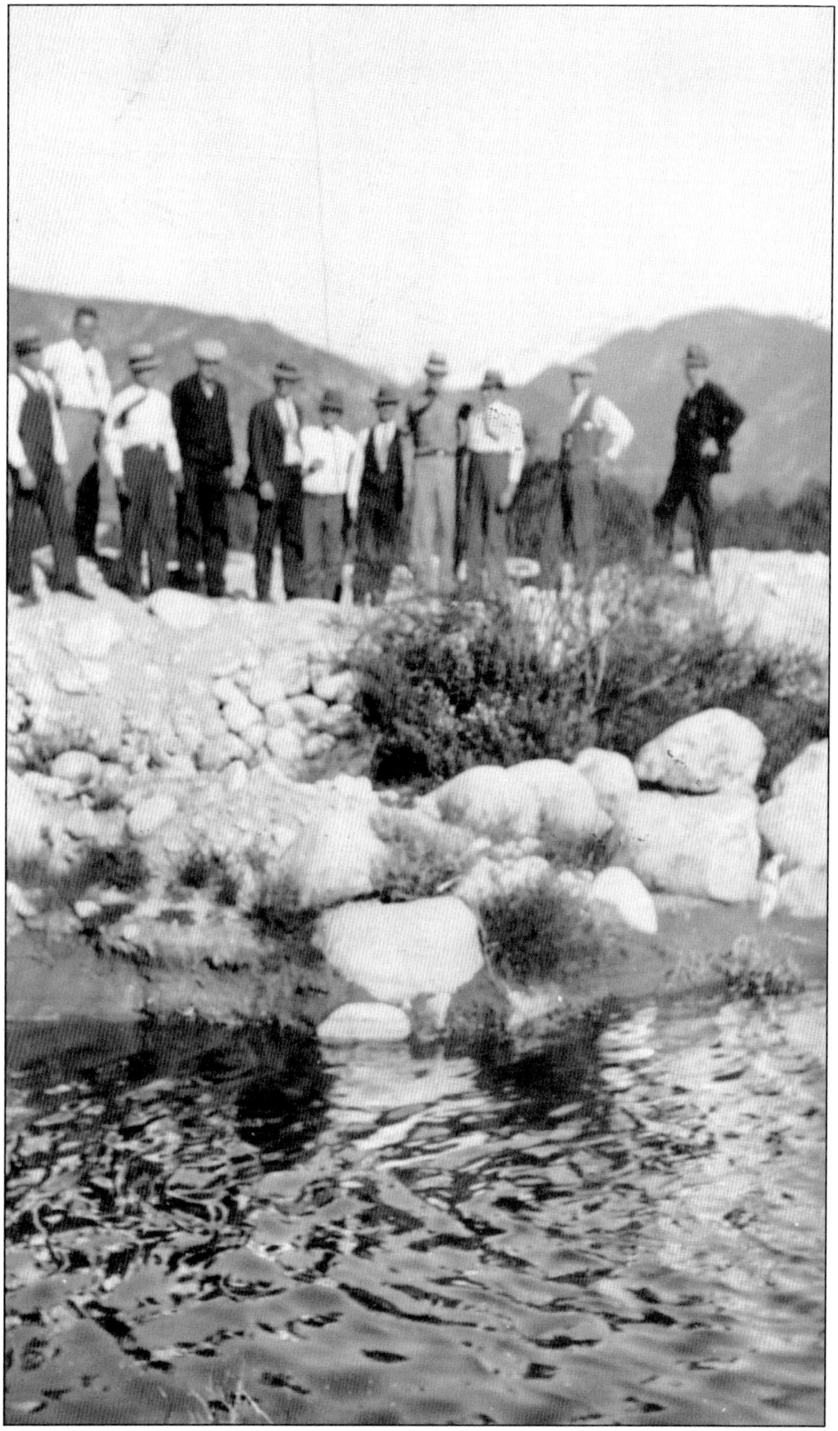

Samuel C. Evans Sr. and associates financed the building of what was known as the lower canal in order to place water on the Hartshorn tract (Arlington). The Evans' interests soon acquired the upper canal, merging the interests of the Southern California Colony Association with a new company called Riverside Land Irrigating. This photograph was taken around 1930.

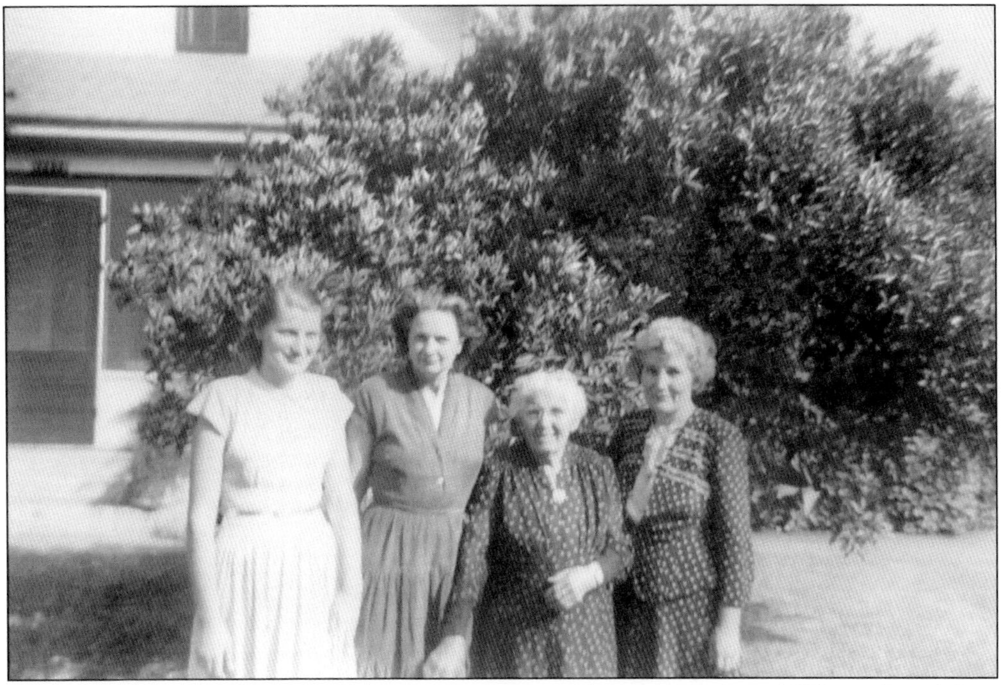

These four ladies represent three family generations. Shown here about 1950 are, from left to right, Nathalie Leibert, Gladys Goethals, Amelia Goethals, and Marie Leibert.

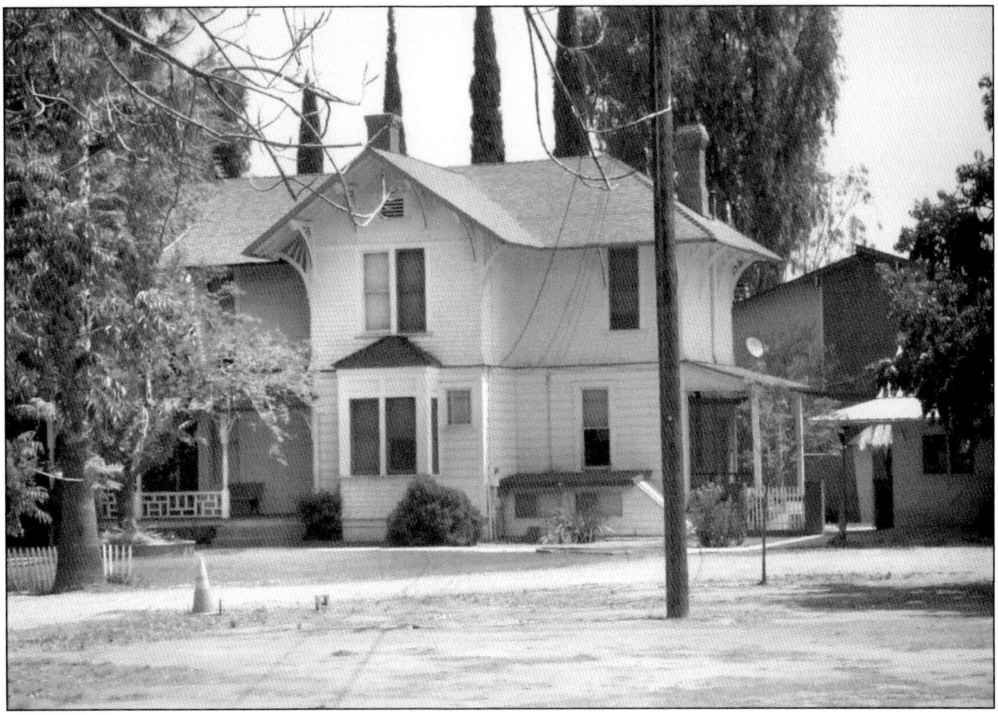

This old farmhouse, set back from Monroe Street, remains today with its surrounding land and fruit and shade trees. It includes two stories with a basement, two fireplaces, porches in front and back, and a large overhang.

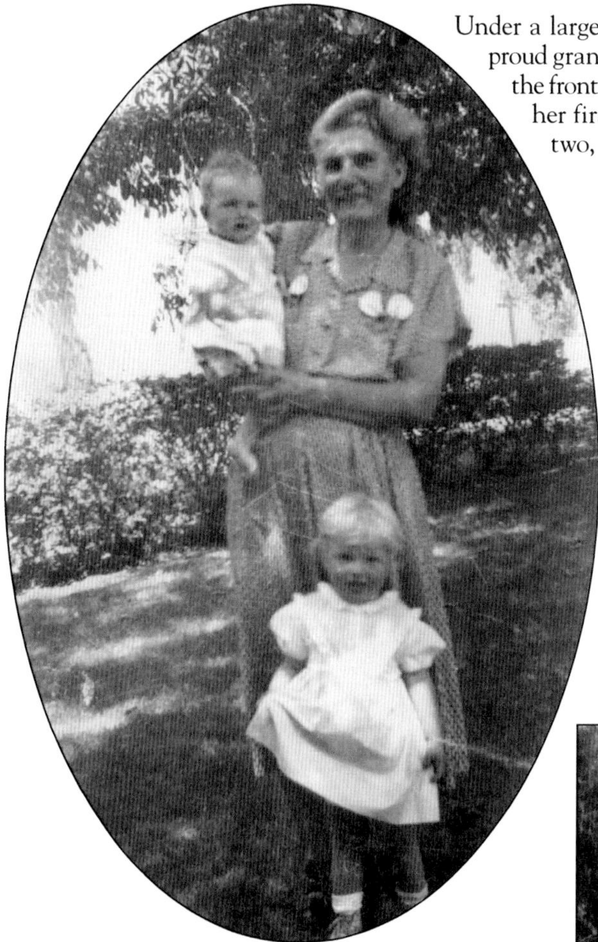

Under a large walnut tree on a spring day in 1948, proud grandmother Marie Leibert enjoys a visit in the front yard of her Magnolia Avenue home with her first grandchildren: Sandra Gordon, age two, and Georgia Gordon, four months.

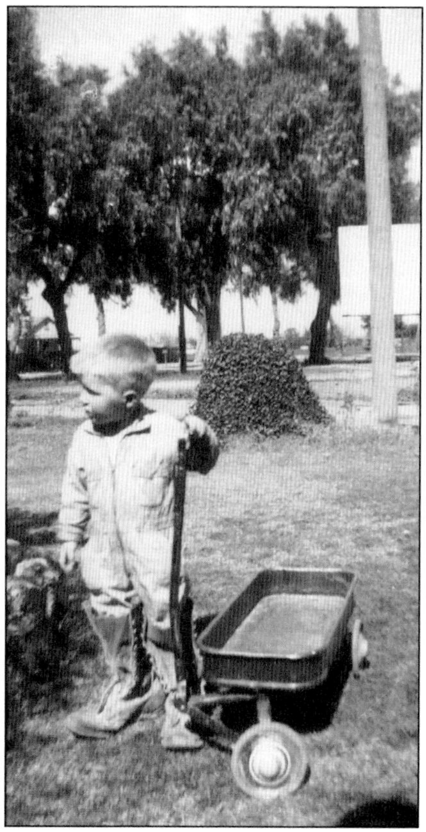

A two-year-old David Leibert wears his coveralls with his father's boots and appears to be looking for something to put into his little red wagon. He has a big area to cover in his search of the yard.

From left to right, Ray Hulbert and his cousins Peter and David Leibert pose for a photograph while Ray is on leave from the U.S. Marine Corps around 1944. The Leibert family lived at the corner of Magnolia Avenue and Hughes Alley.

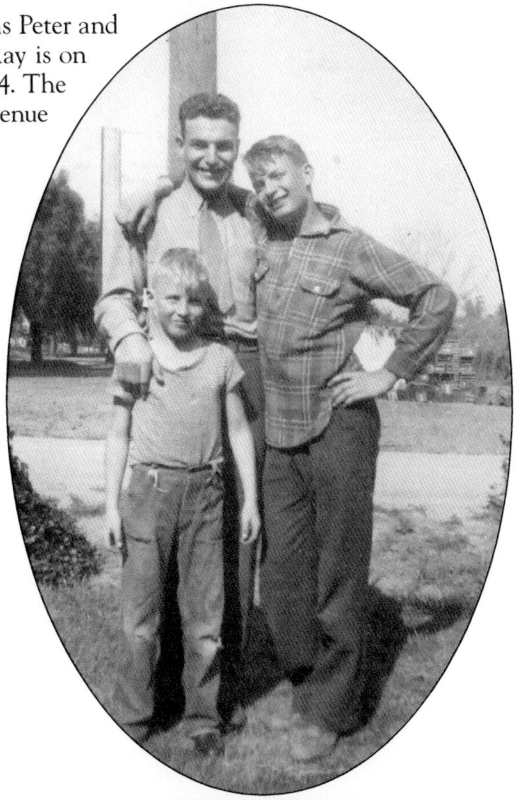

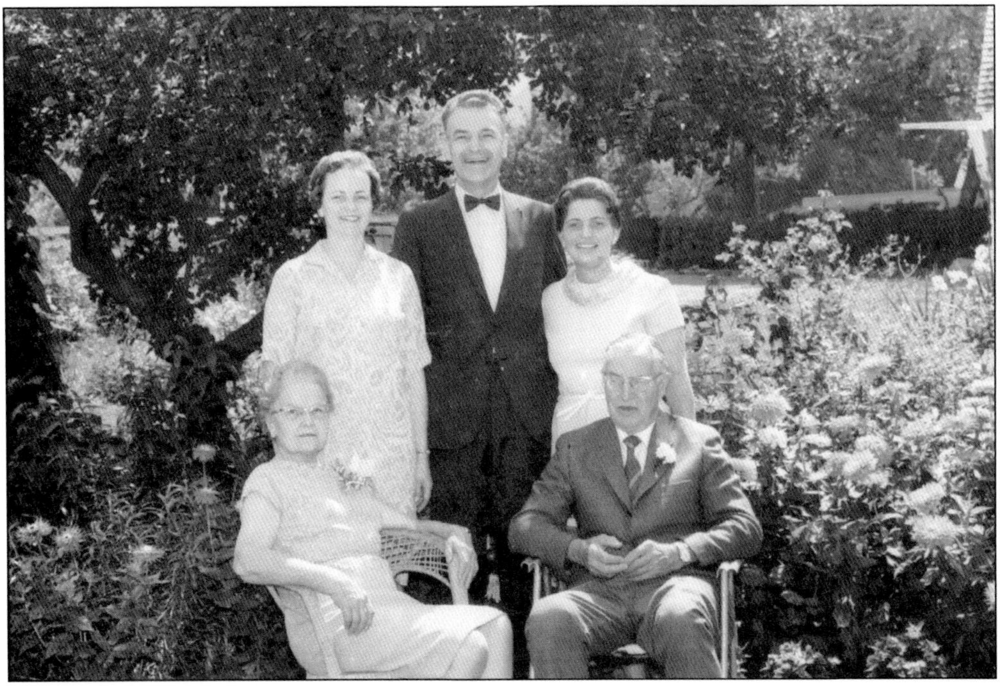

The Hulbert family celebrates Celine and Harold's 50th wedding anniversary. The couple's children are Helen (left), Ray (center), and little Celine.

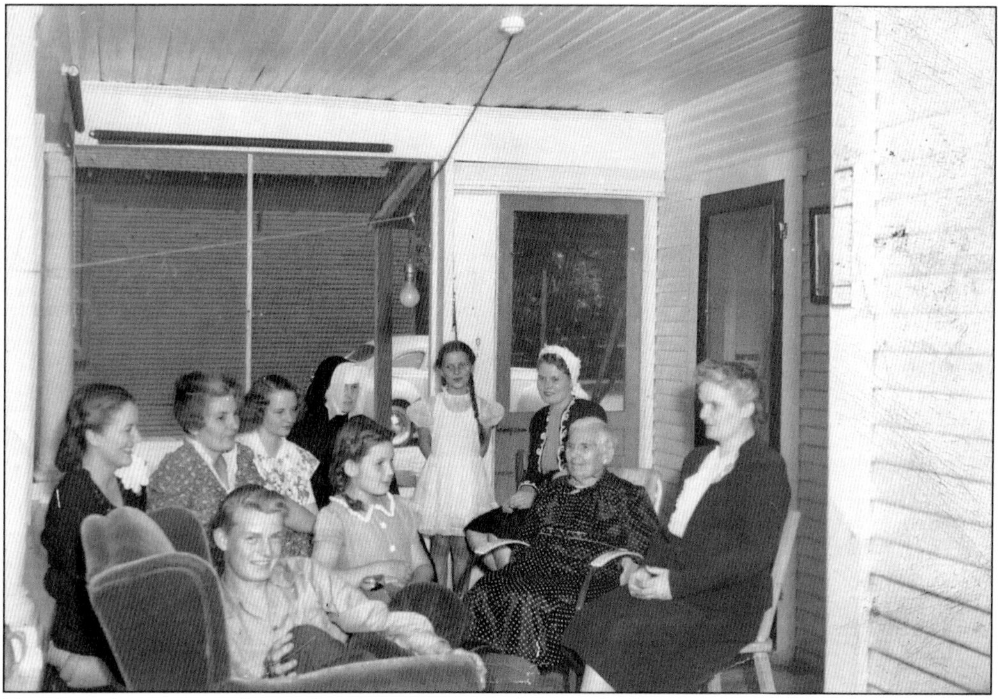

Family gatherings involving three generations often took place on the screened porch at the Goethals home. Pictured here from left to right are the following: (first row) Peter Leibert and Agnes Leibert; (second row) Agnes Watson, Marie Leibert, Helen Hulbert, Sr. Amelia Marie, little Celine Hulbert with braids, Theresa Leibert, Amelia Goethals, and Celine Hulbert.

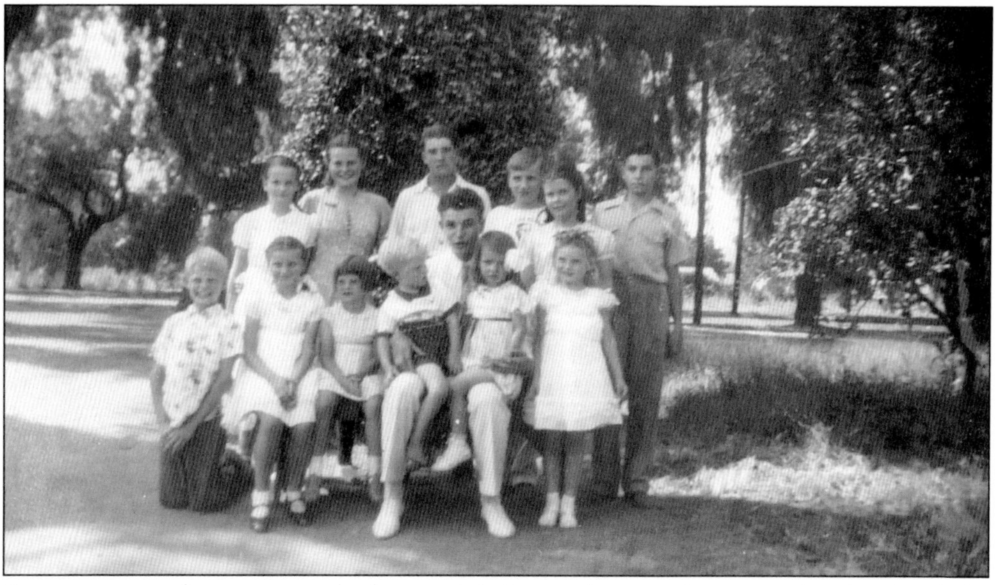

Cousins met each summer at the home of their grandparents Peter and Amelia Goethals. Arlington was where their parents grew up and their grandparents lived, and half of them were also raised in the town. The 13 grandchildren include the following, from left to right: (first row) Peter, Nathalie, Agnes, Ray, David and Celine (on Ray's knees), and Patsy; (second row) Helen, Theresa, Clarence, John, Mary Helen, and Dick.

Oscar McNicholl poses with his wife, Bertha, daughter Laura, and son Loren at their home on Indiana Avenue in the 1940s. On the property was a natural sulfur spring that often smelled like rotten eggs; after about a week, the odor would go away.

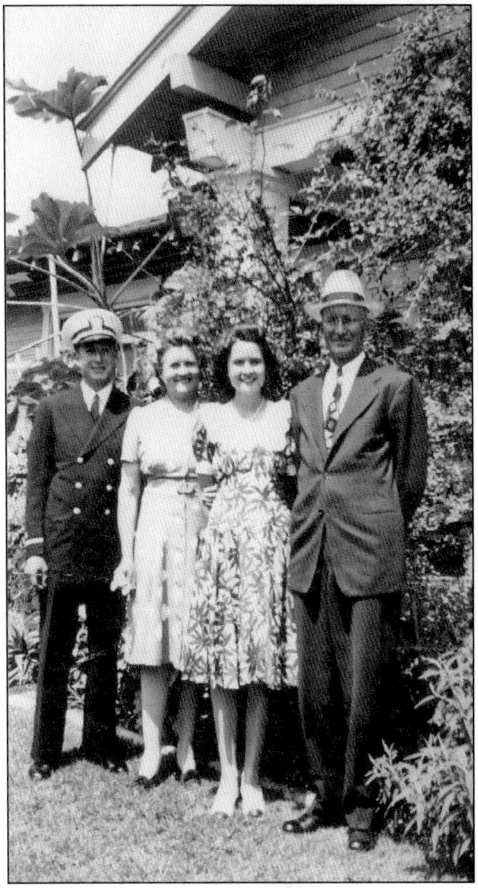

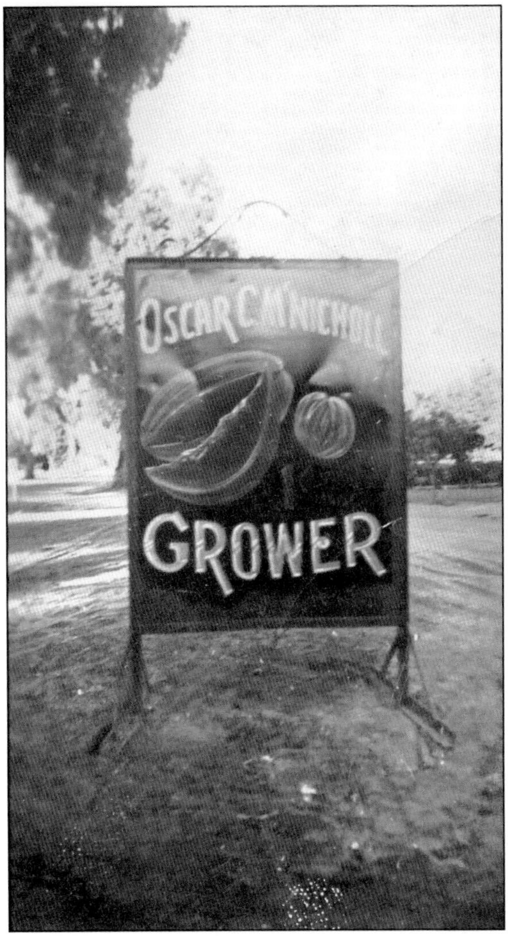

Oscar McNicholl and Peter Goethals made a business of planting watermelons. Oscar posted a sign in front of his Indiana Avenue property reading "Oscar McNicholl, Grower," which displayed an image of the fruit. Peter had large harvests of melons and hauled wagonloads of his bounty to Riverside and Corona.

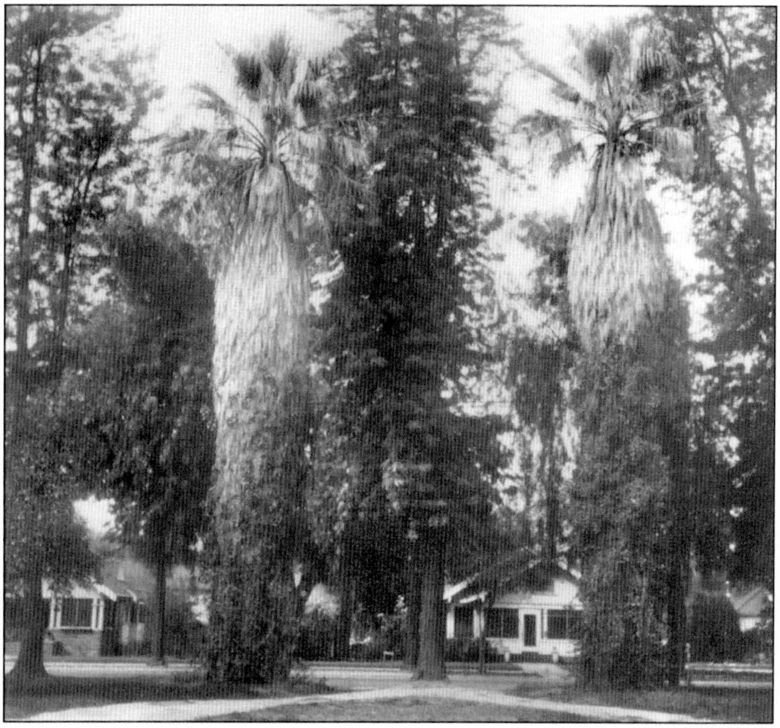

These homes stood on Magnolia Avenue in the heart of Arlington. In their yards were wonderful shade trees that provided respite from the town's hot summer days. The old Arlington Post Office was located on the same block. (Courtesy Norman and Velda Kelley.)

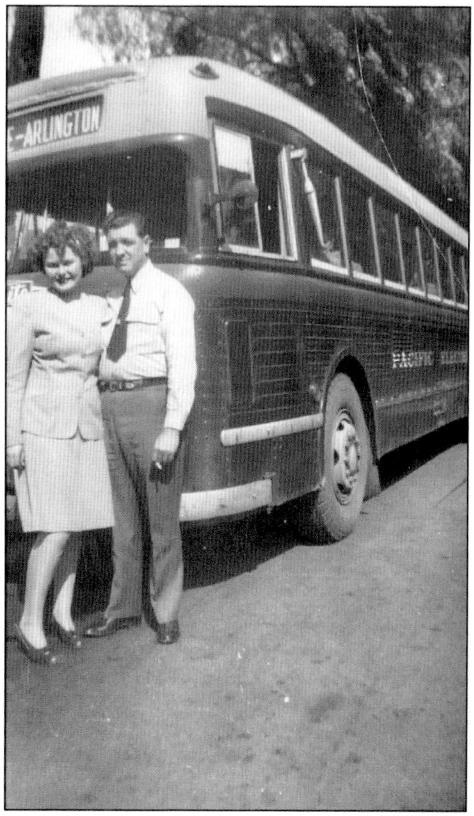

Longtime resident Theresa Leibert waits to board the Riverside-Arlington bus, whose main route was down Magnolia Avenue, around 1945.

Poppy Hill, known for its big, beautiful homes, is situated on Tyler Street just south of the Tyler Mall, over the railroad tracks and up the hill. In the spring, the hill fills with brilliantly orange wild poppies, the California state flower.

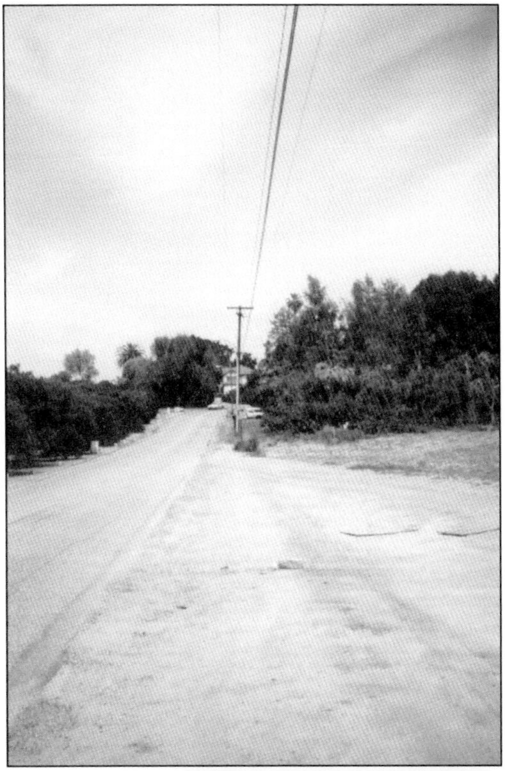

In the 1960s, Victoria Avenue remained the most beautiful and scenic drive in town. The area includes tall palms, thriving orange groves, and lovely colorful red roses in the middle divider. The road is two-sided, with one way in each direction. (Courtesy JoAnne Pease-Simpson.)

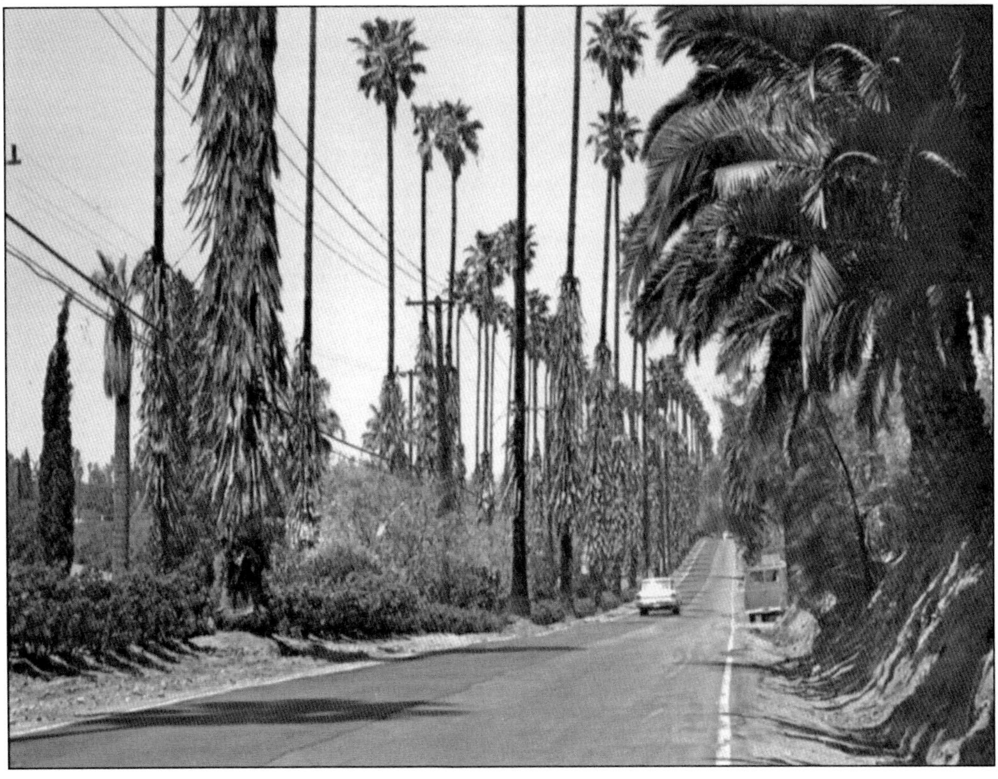

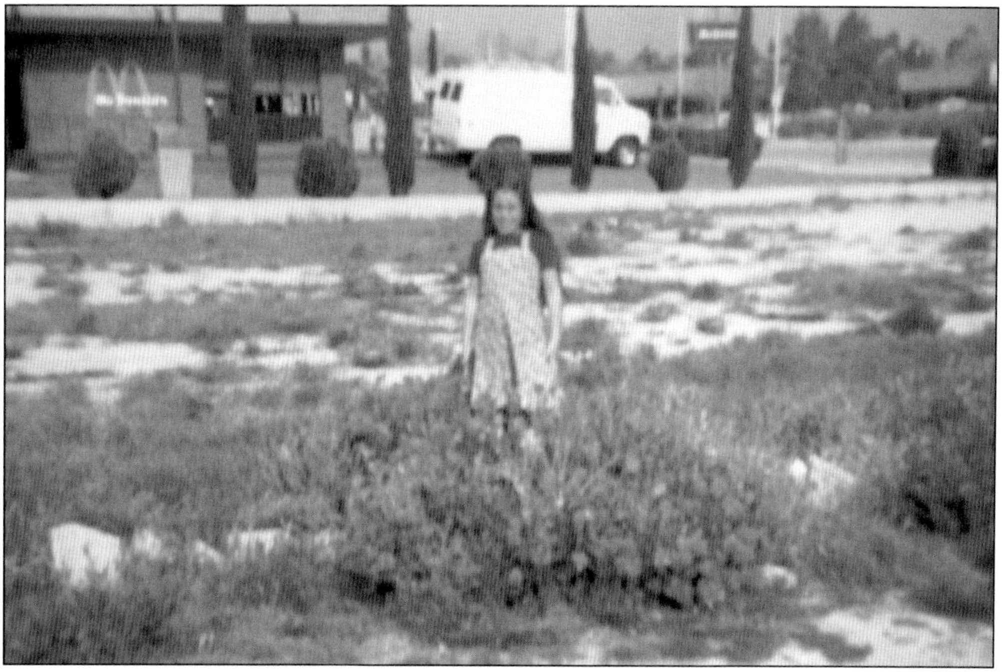

Tammy Sercl stands in the middle of her great-great-aunt Helen's poppy field on Magnolia Avenue in March 1979. Helen was known all around as "the lady with the poppy field of Arlington."

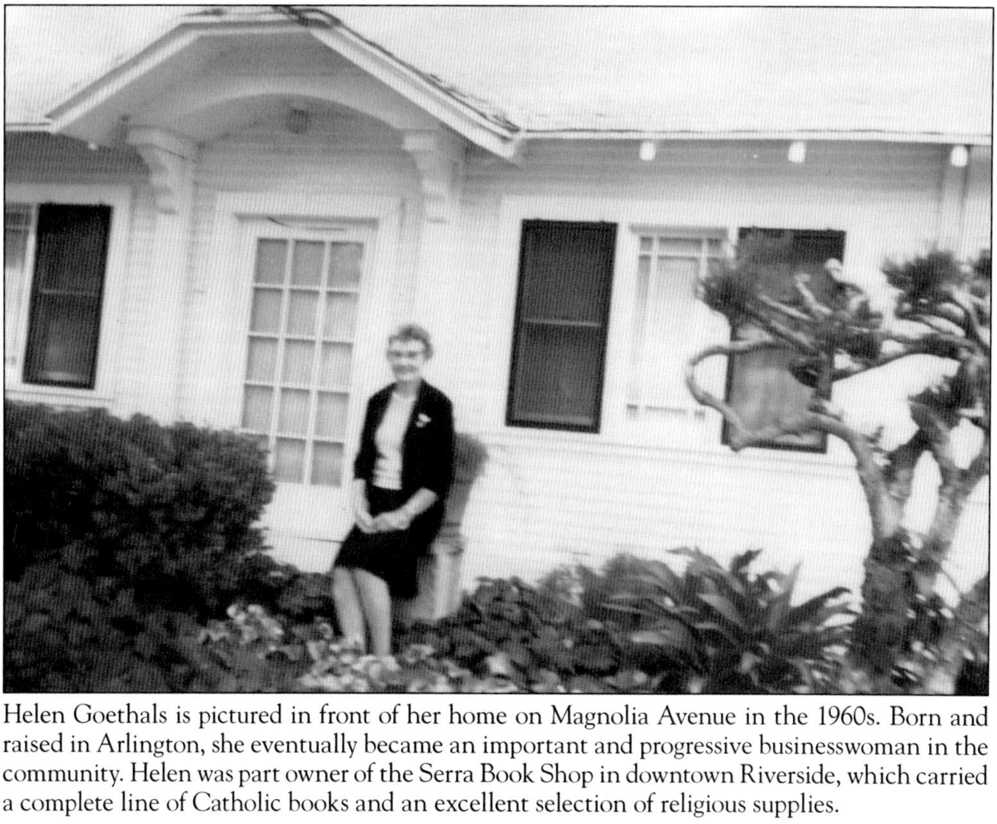

Helen Goethals is pictured in front of her home on Magnolia Avenue in the 1960s. Born and raised in Arlington, she eventually became an important and progressive businesswoman in the community. Helen was part owner of the Serra Book Shop in downtown Riverside, which carried a complete line of Catholic books and an excellent selection of religious supplies.

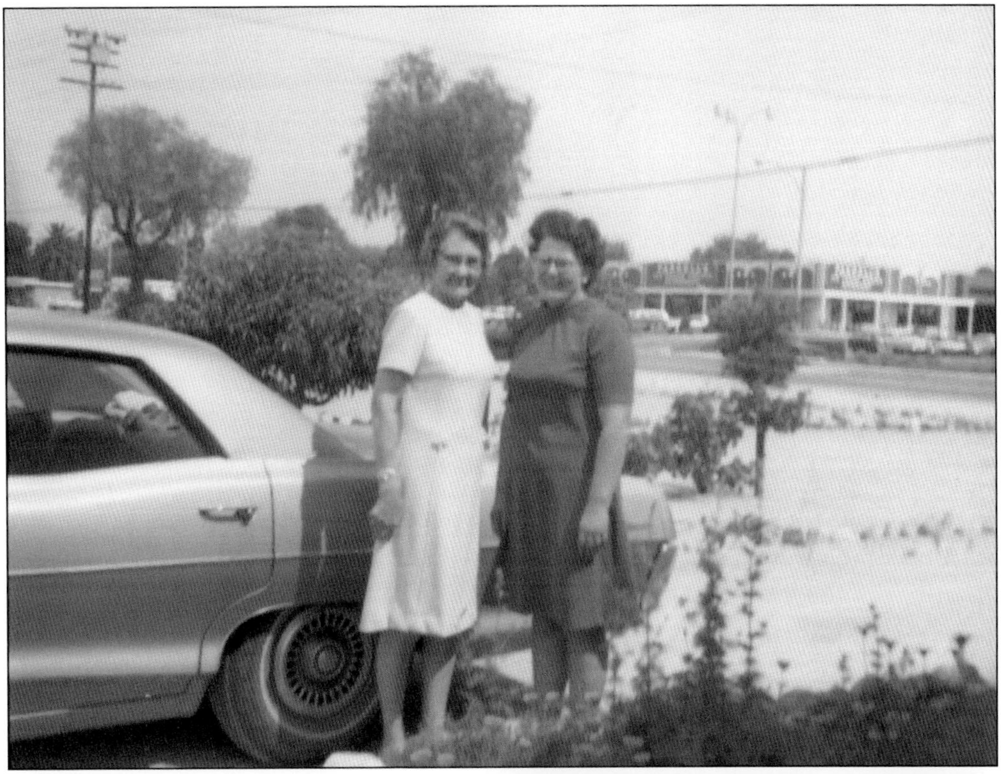

Helen Goethals (left) and Theresa Gordon stand on Magnolia Avenue with Hughes Alley in the background. At that corner about 1967 was Farrell's Ice Cream Parlor, where a featured menu item was a "trough" filled with ice cream. The shop had quite a lively atmosphere.

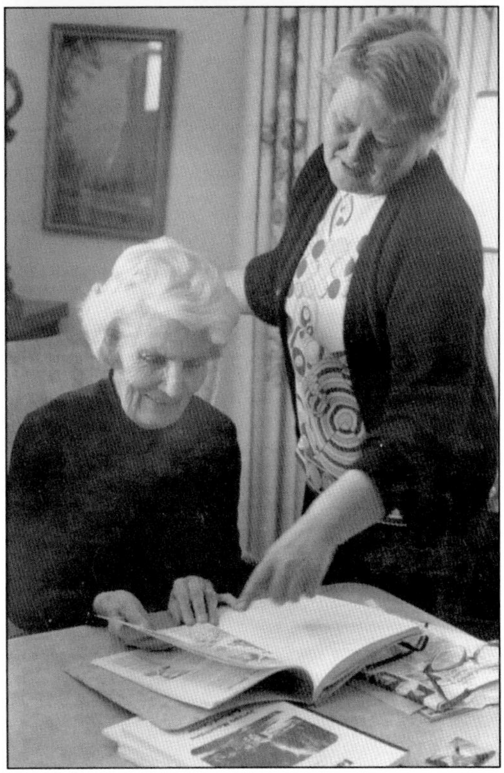

Marie Leibert (left) and her daughter Theresa Leibert Gordon were quite accomplished local historians, as each had written several books about the town. Here Marie peruses one of her books with Theresa around 1970. Since both were locals of Arlington, they each had firsthand knowledge of area history.

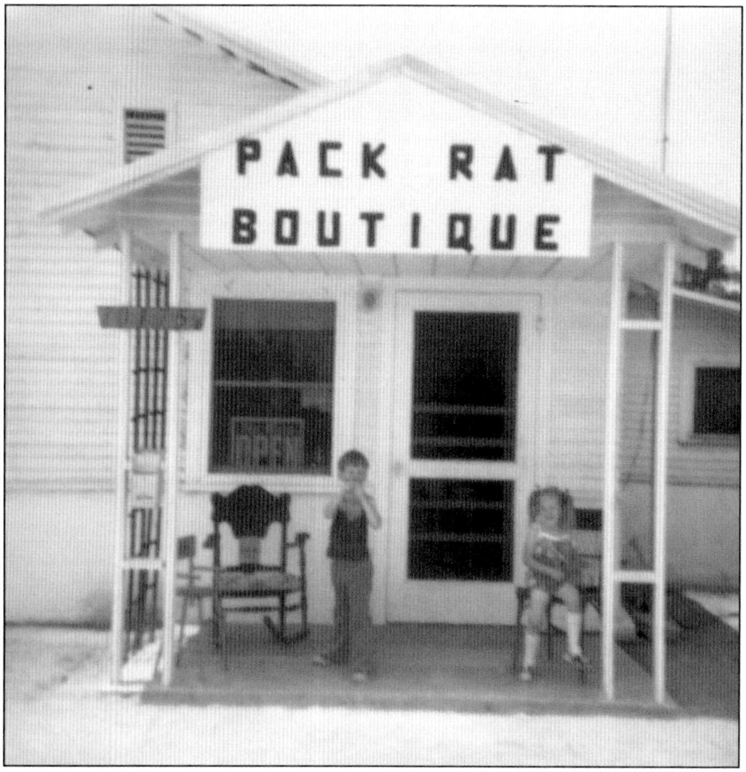

This storefront was once a business specializing in antiques and collectibles situated on Magnolia Avenue across from the Tyler Mall. It was typical for businesses to be there one day and gone the next. Mike Sercl stands while Jenny Hall sits in a chair on the porch next to the front entrance.

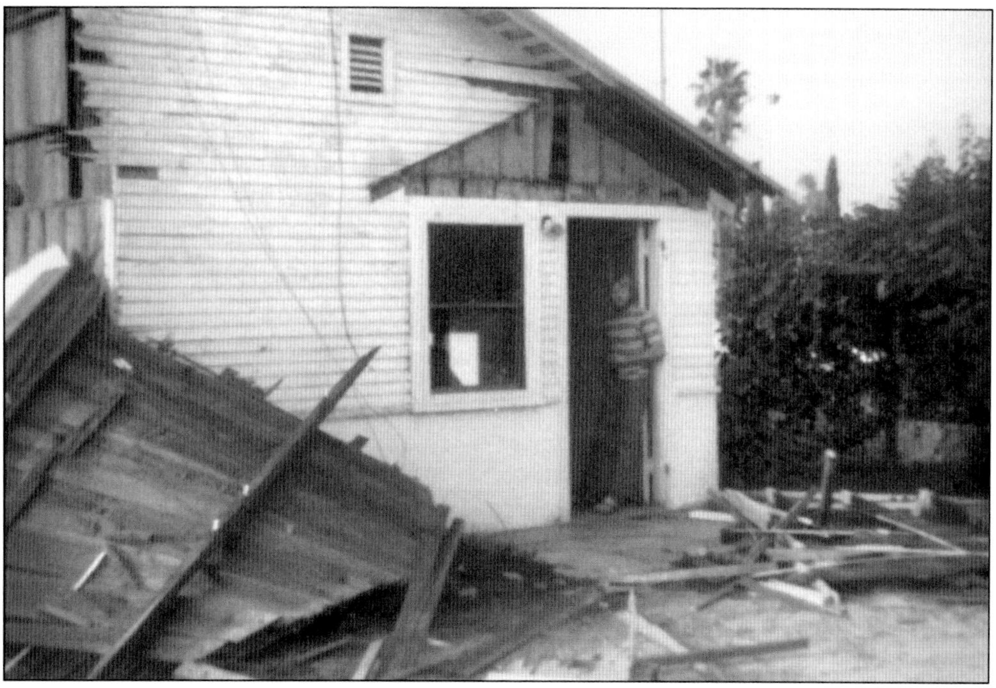

Progress is in motion as the old barn is replaced with a brand-new shopping center. Mike Gordon stands in the doorway as the structure comes down board by board. The days of big barns are now gone in the town of Arlington.

Arlington Park is located at 3860 Van Buren Boulevard in Arlington, one block north of Magnolia Avenue. Victoria and Nicholas Williams, the author's grandchildren and fifth-generation Arlingtonians, sit on the sign made of concrete with some kind of a beautiful finish. The property was the site of the old Magnolia School, built in 1891, which was later renamed Arlington School.

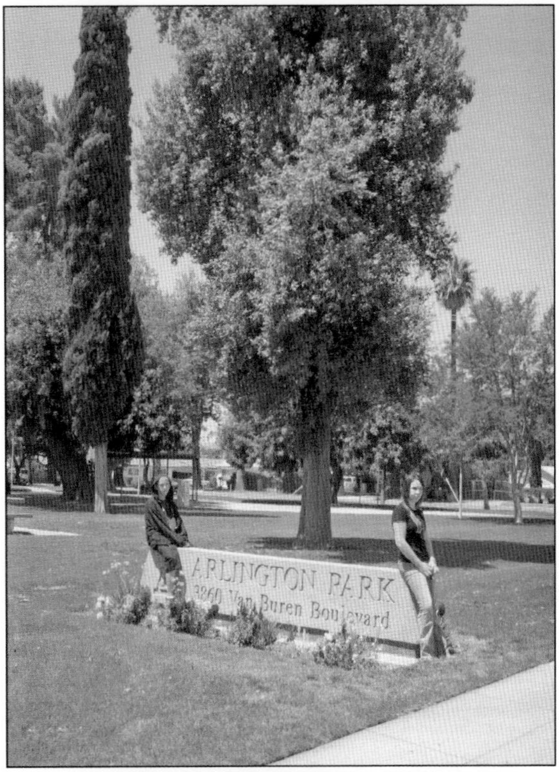

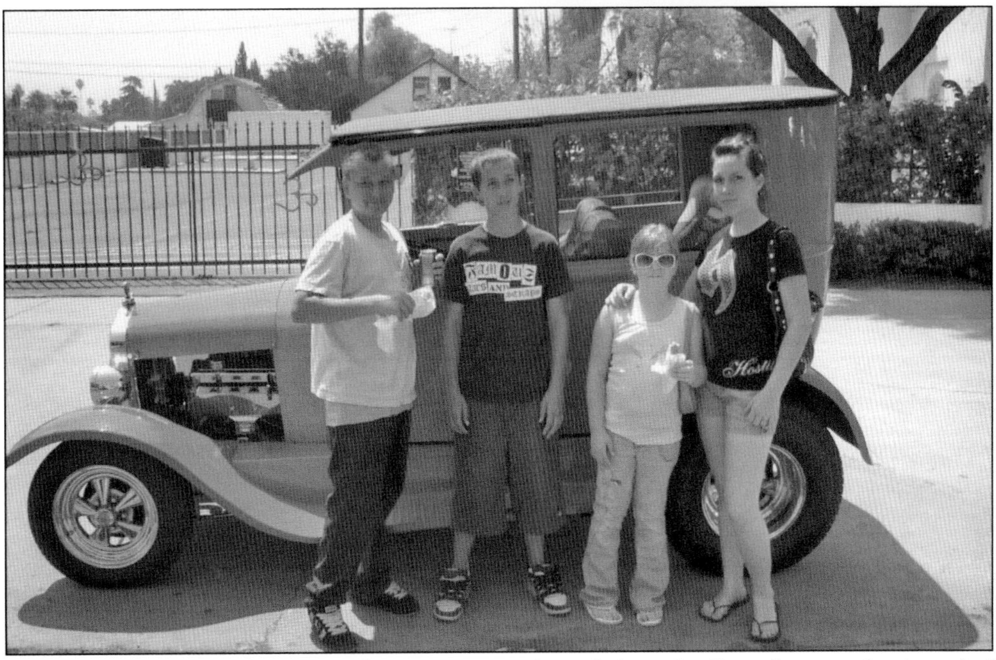

The townspeople of Arlington gather once a year for a chili cook-off on the main boulevard of Magnolia, which is blocked off from Van Buren to Jackson. The event attracts many vendors and a grand display of old cars. In front of this vintage car, from left to right, are Robby Kurowshi, Nick Williams, Jamie Sercl, and Tori Williams.

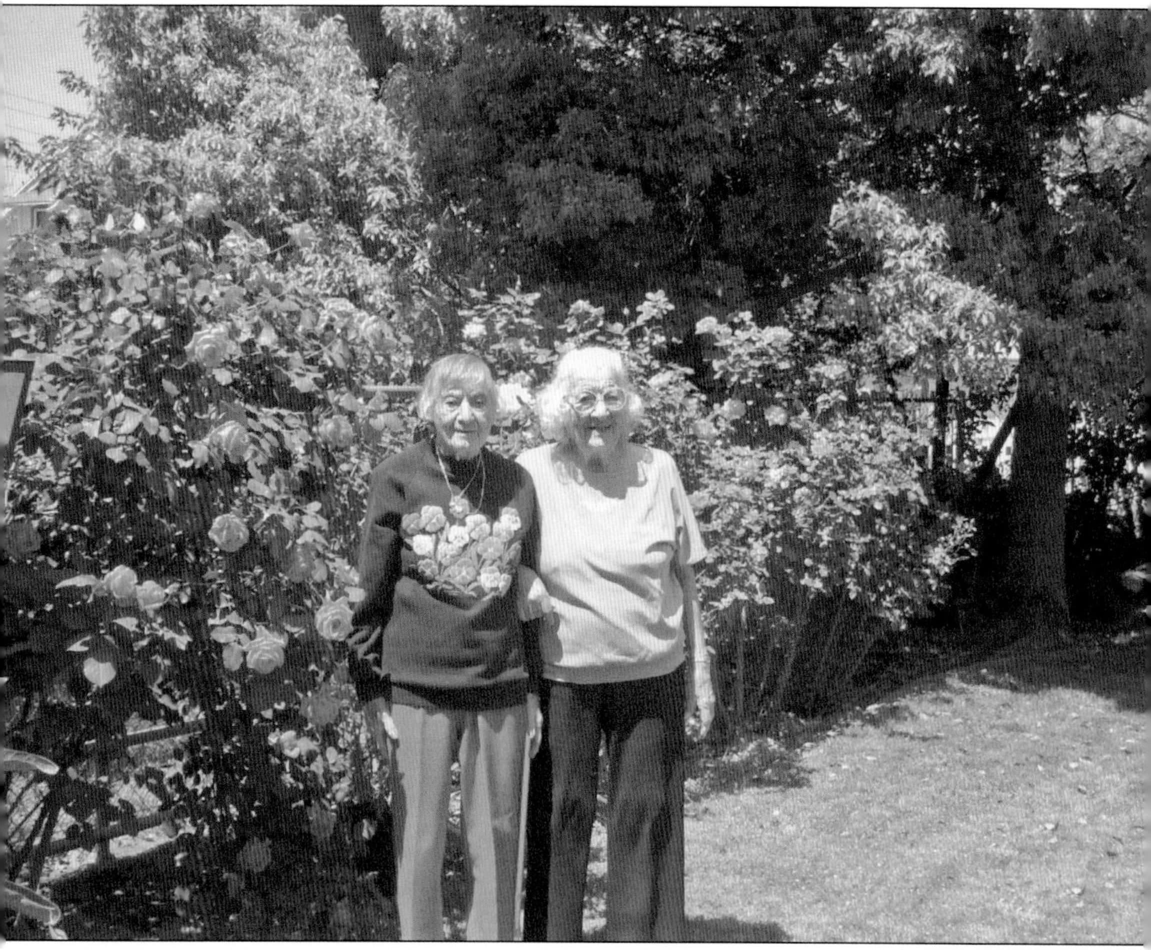

The longest living resident of Arlington is 104-year-old Virginia Pagliuso (left), seen here with her sister Marian Pagliuso Maxwell, 96 years old. They both still live in Arlington and love to tell their stories. Their brother Albert also resides in town. (Photograph by author; courtesy Virginia and Marian Pagliuso.)

Five

The Arlington Green Belt

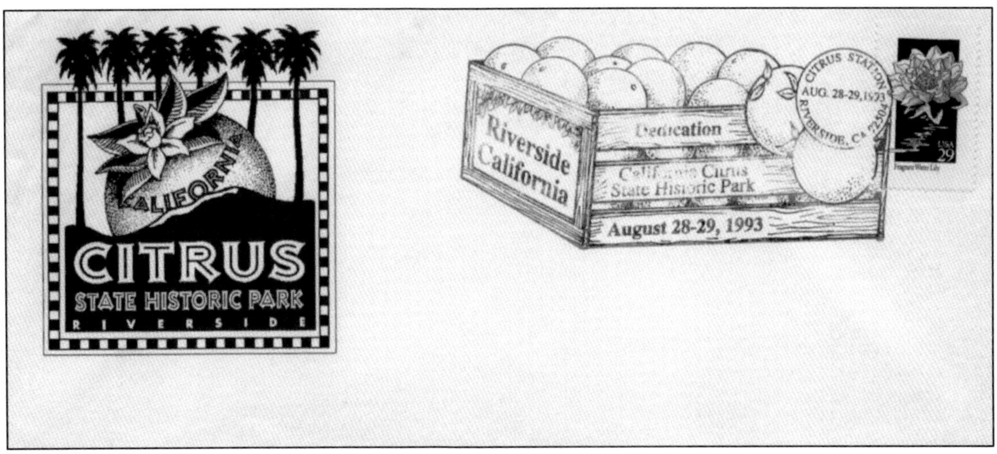

California Citrus State Historic Park opened on August 28, 1993, at the corner of Van Buren Boulevard and Dufferin Avenue. This stamp was produced by the U.S. Post Office in commemoration of the grand opening. The only way to get one of these precious stamps was to attend.

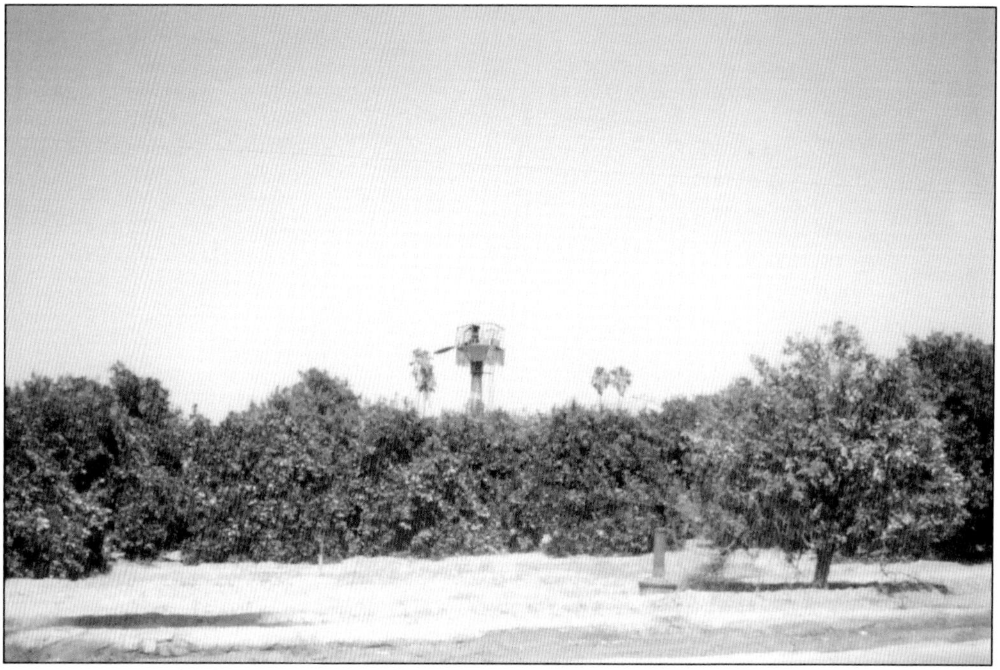

Citrus was one of Arlington's main industries. A smudge pot sits to the left side of the citrus tree in front; in the far back stands a wind machine that moved the air to protect the oranges from freezing in the cold weather.

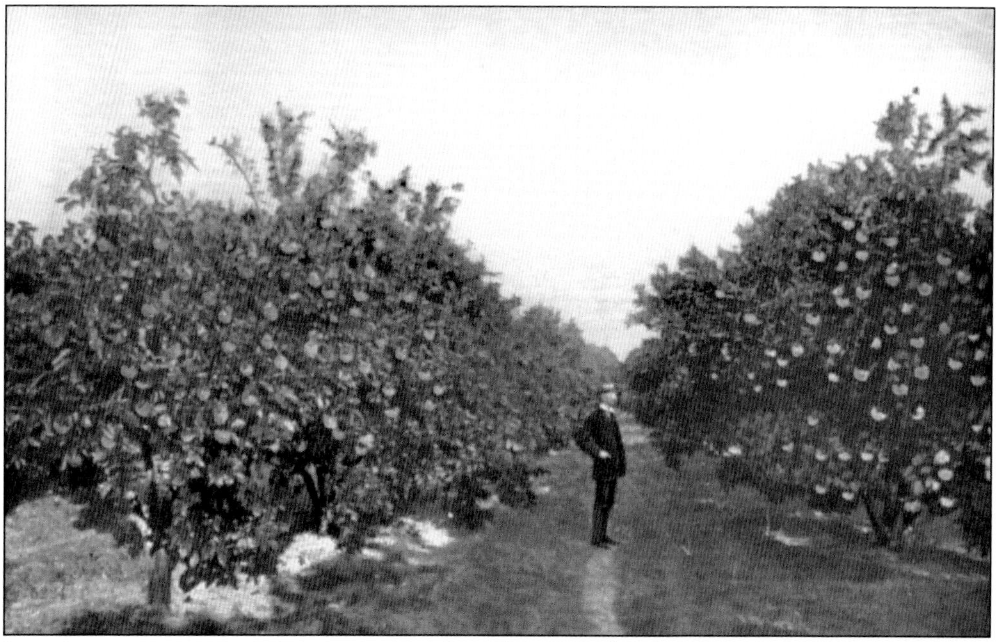

Irrigating citrus groves in Arlington was a big job, especially since farmers were always fighting the gophers. They had a tendency to divert the stream by burrowing and creating mounds of dirt that would change the water's course. Workers would repeatedly check that the water was moving in the right direction.

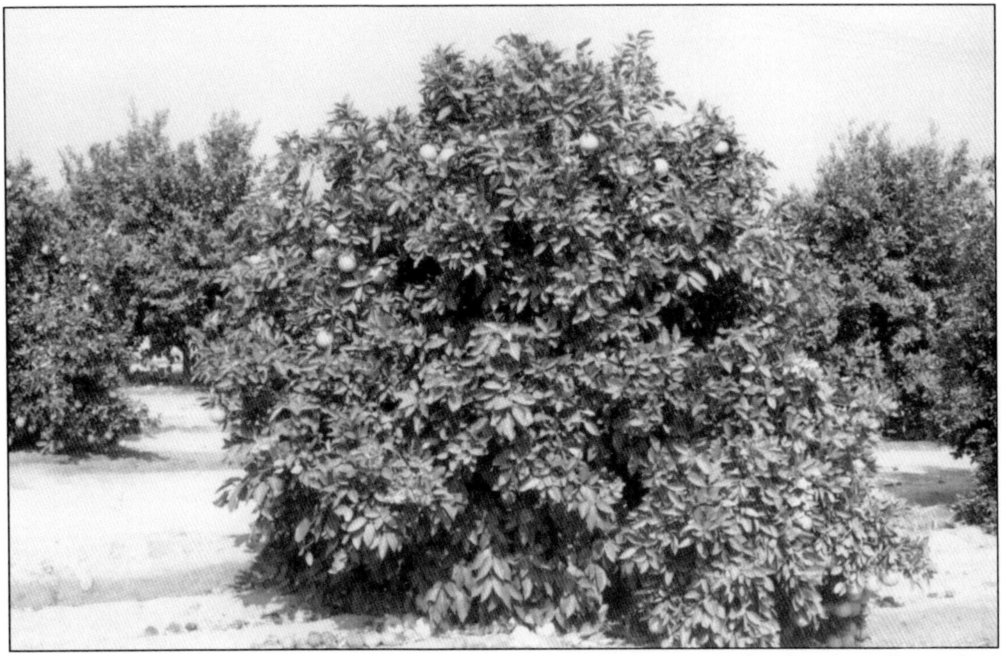

The orange industry provided a reliable source of work for many people. One big job was fruit picking. To make it less tedious, picking sacks opened up from the bottom, allowing the oranges to fall right into shipping boxes. Chinese, Japanese, and Hispanic people made up the bulk of the fruit pickers.

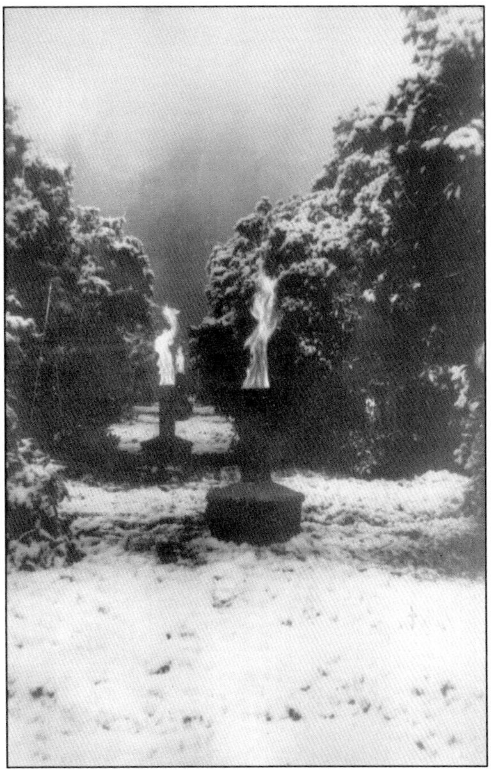

In the early years, most of the heating in the citrus groves was accomplished by burning oil in pots. Although this process provided warmth and protected the groves against frost damage, it also created an unpleasant black smoke, or "smudge," that filled the air for miles. In 1938, the wind machine was introduced, which stopped the need for smudging because circulated air created the same effect. The winter of 1949 was a particularly bad one, and the pots burned nonstop. (Courtesy Norman and Velda Kelley.)

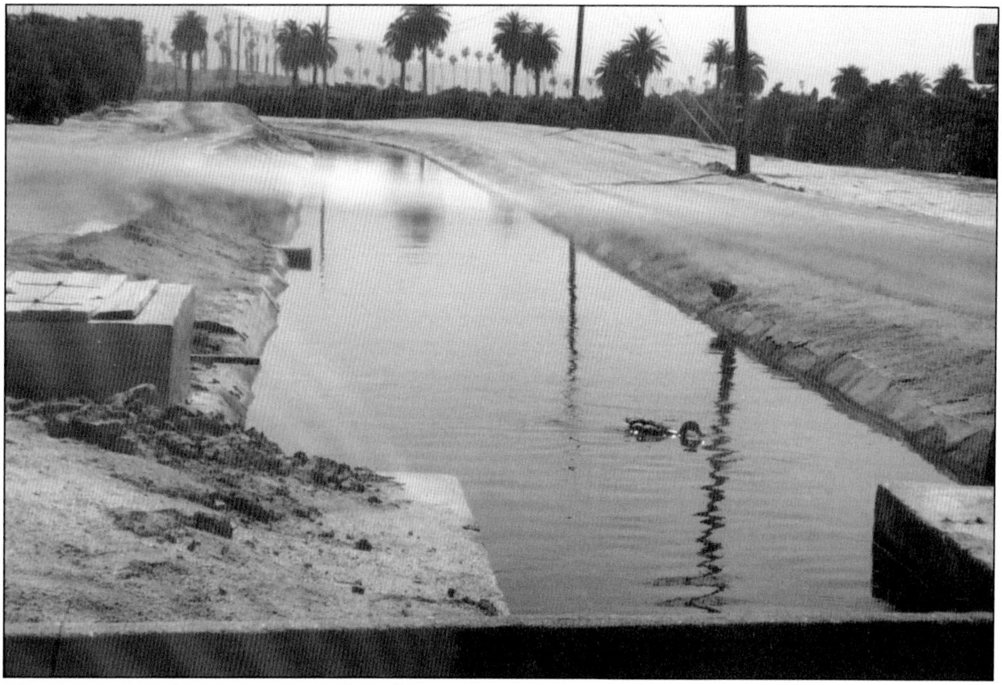

The Gage Canal was constructed in the 1880s as an irrigation system for thousands of acres of orange groves. Though Matthew Gage built the canal, the Riverside Trust Company purchased it and all associated stock in 1889 because Gage could not meet his deadline.

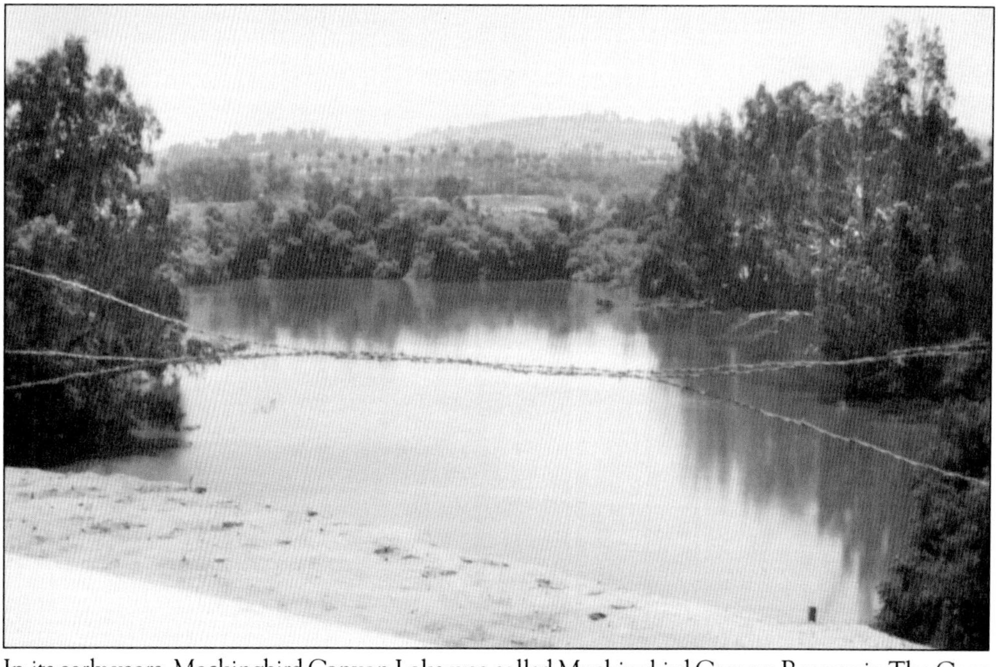

In its early years, Mockingbird Canyon Lake was called Mockingbird Canyon Reservoir. The Gage Canal would run water into the reservoir during the day, and at night the water was let out. The lake is located between Van Buren Boulevard and Jackson Street and Dufferin and Firethorn Avenues, south of the California Citrus State Historic Park.

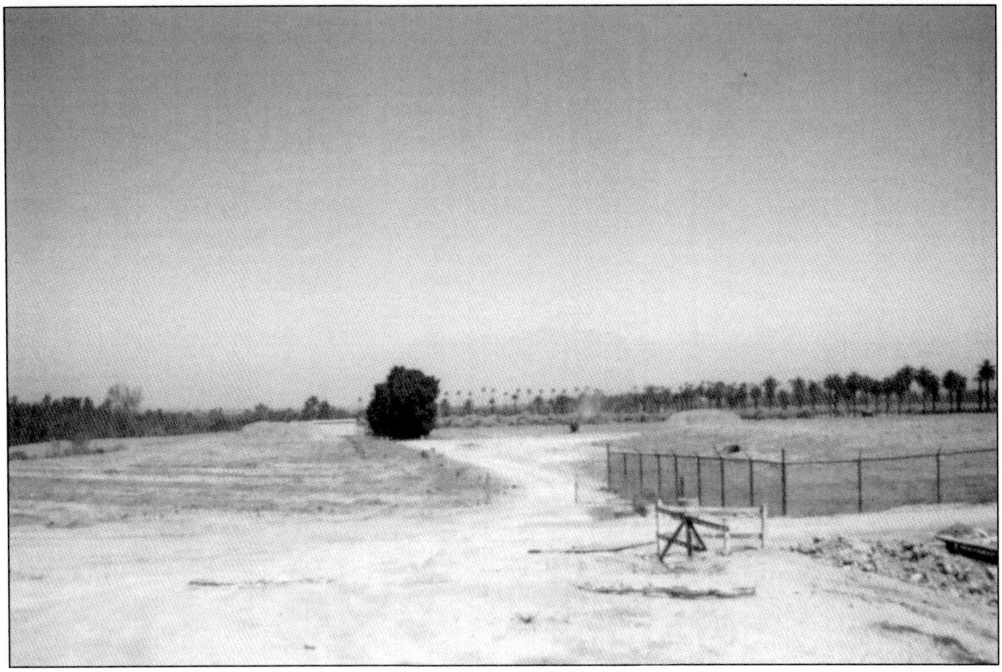

Older trees are culled out of the groves at the California Citrus State Historic Park. They are mulched and replaced by new trees, which will produce far better citrus.

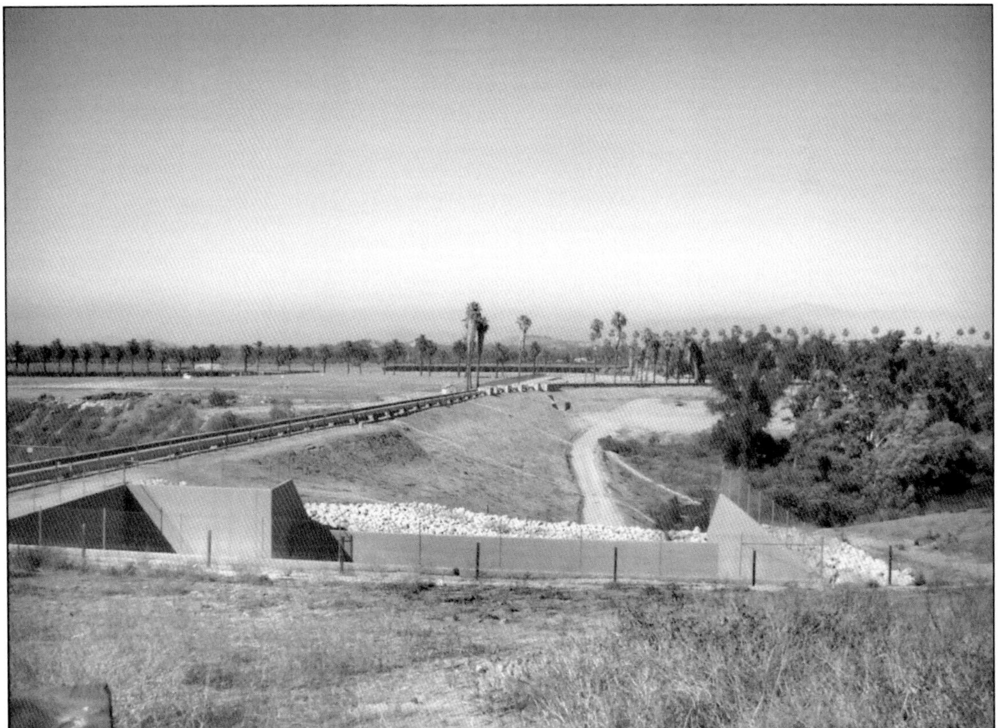

The half-mile-long concrete spillway for Mockingbird Reservoir was erected by order of the California State Division of Dams in 1932. A plaque is placed in its middle.

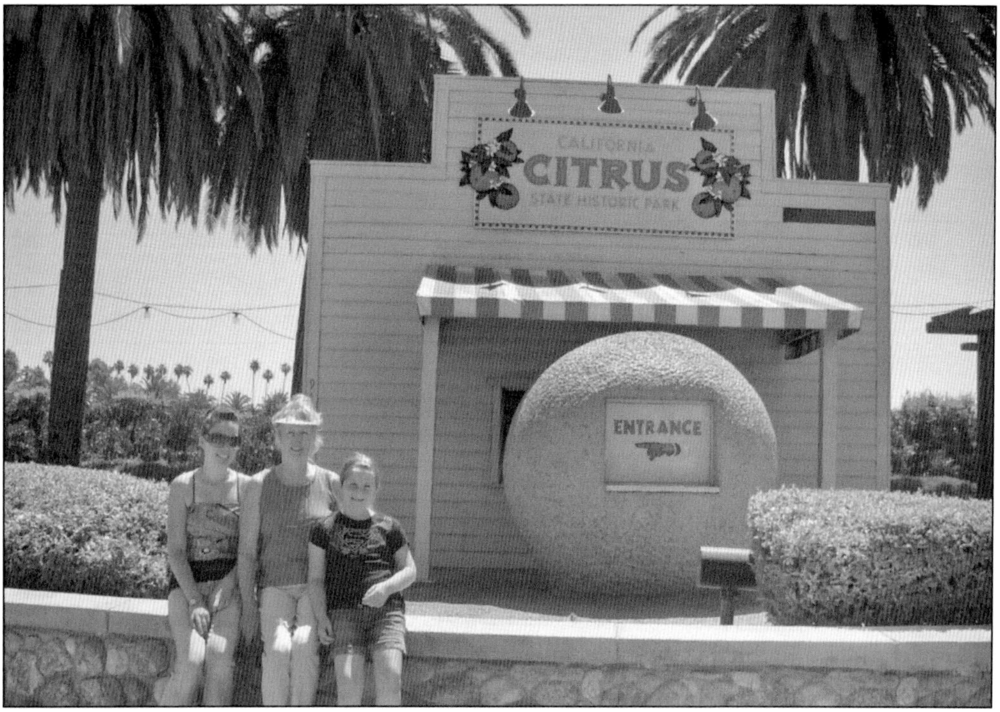

The large orange with the hand points the way to the entrance of the California Citrus State Historic Park. Sitting on the wall next to the sign are author Georgia Sercl (center) and her two granddaughters, Victoria Williams (left) and Jamie Sercl.

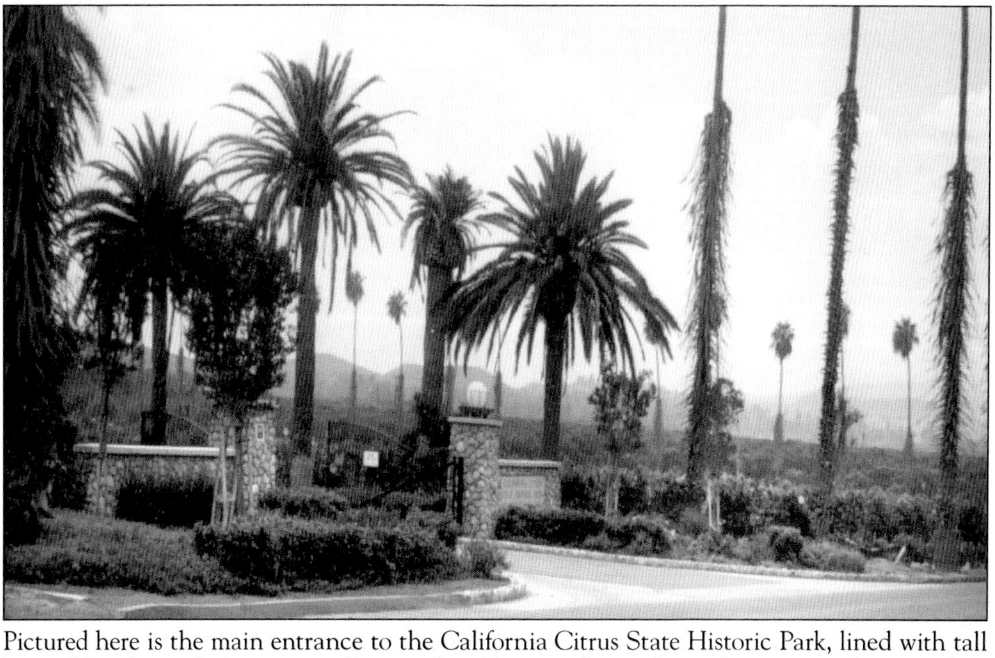

Pictured here is the main entrance to the California Citrus State Historic Park, lined with tall beautiful palm and citrus trees all around it. One can learn about the citrus industry and its preservation and take a guided or self-guided tour at the park. The museum takes visitors back to the time of the citrus industry.

Six

PUBLIC SERVICES AND ENTERTAINMENT

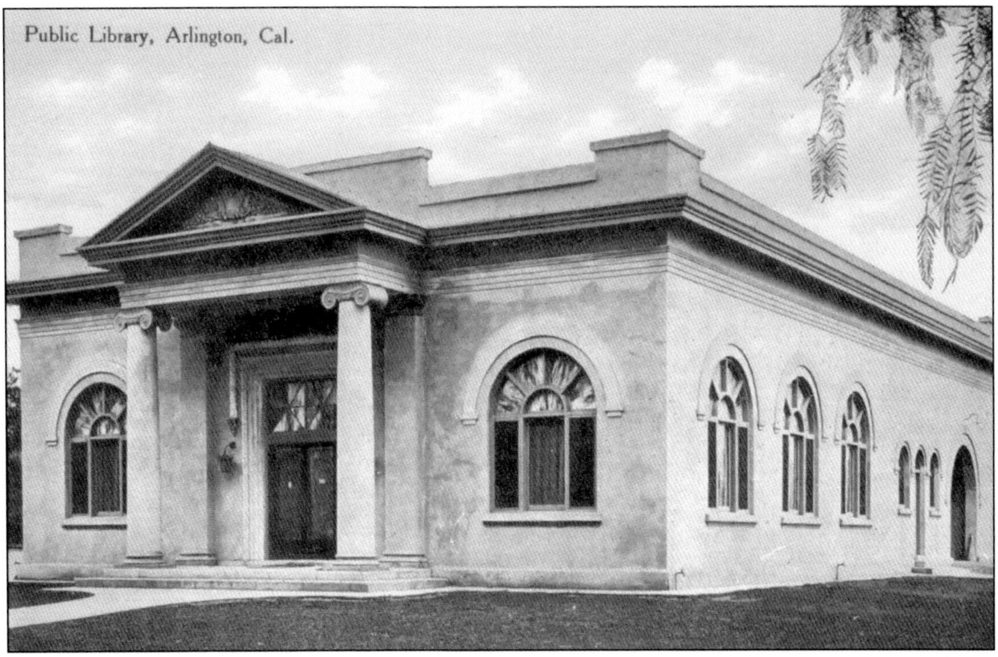

The Arlington Library, at 9556 Magnolia Avenue, west of Van Buren Boulevard, celebrated its grand opening in 1909 with festive ceremonies. At the time, Andrew Carnegie donated funds for libraries to be built across the country, and Arlington was a recipient. Local resident Mrs. Frank Pedley donated many books to the library, which is now a designated historic building. (Courtesy Steve Lech.)

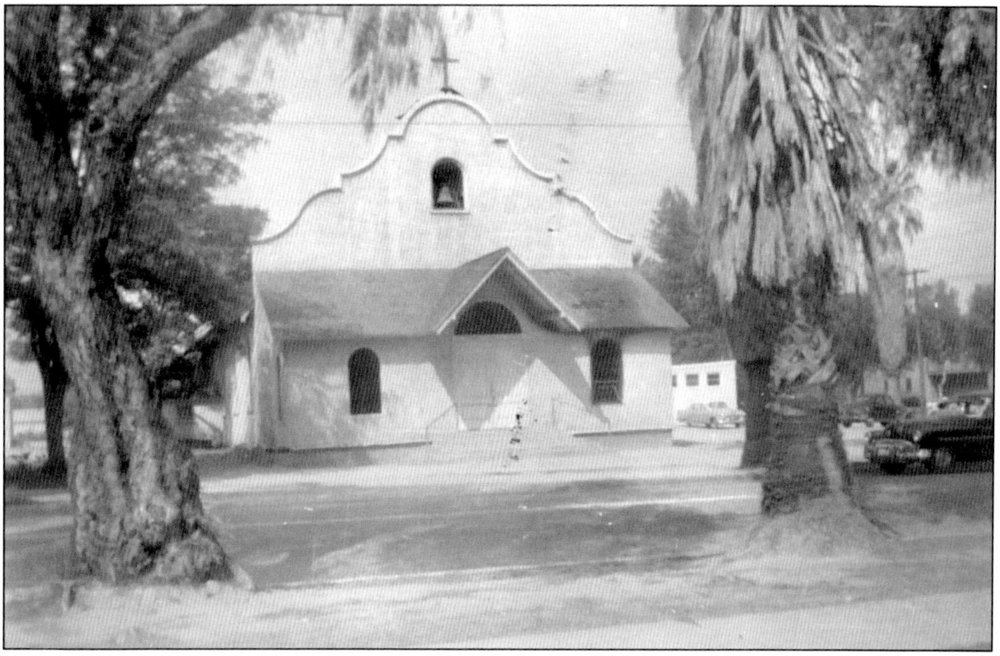

St. Thomas the Apostle Chapel was originally founded in 1904 as a Native American mission and became a full parish in 1914. Peter Goethals and Father Conneally were instrumental in the Native Americans' spiritual learning at the church. The structure was built at the corner of Magnolia Avenue and Jackson Street by J. W. Carroll.

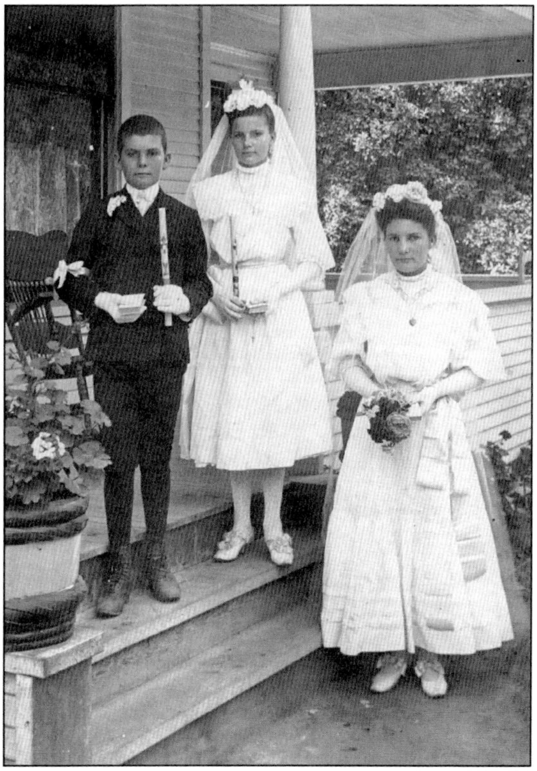

It is a special day for Alberie (left), Celine (center), and Marie Goethals, as it is their confirmation with the Catholic Church. The children stand on the front steps of the family home on Magnolia Avenue around 1906.

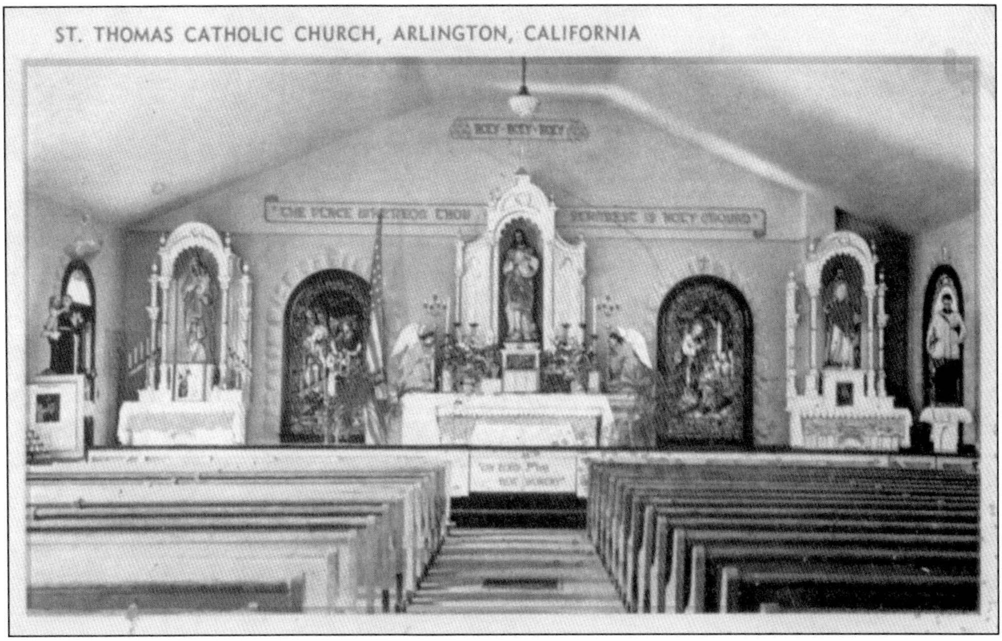

This beautiful altar at St. Thomas the Apostle Church burned in a fire in April 1957. A new church was built at the same site—on Magnolia Avenue at the corner of Jackson Street.

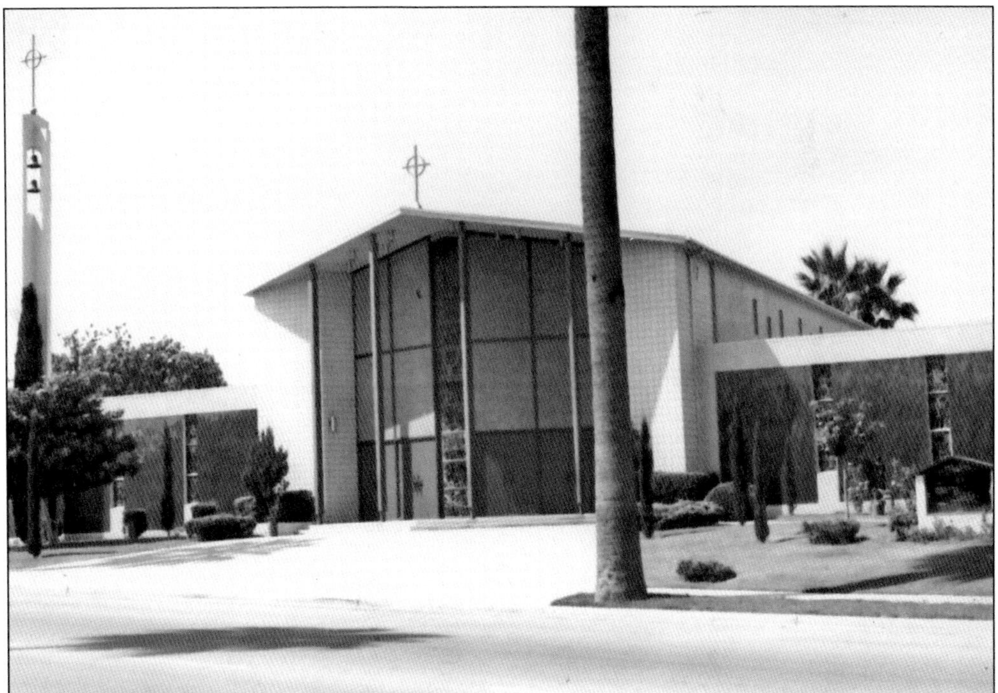

In 1967, St. Thomas the Apostle Catholic Church celebrated a groundbreaking for the new church. The first mass was held on Christmas day in 1968. On June 15, 1969, the church was dedicated by Auxiliary Bishop John Quinn of San Diego, a native of Riverside.

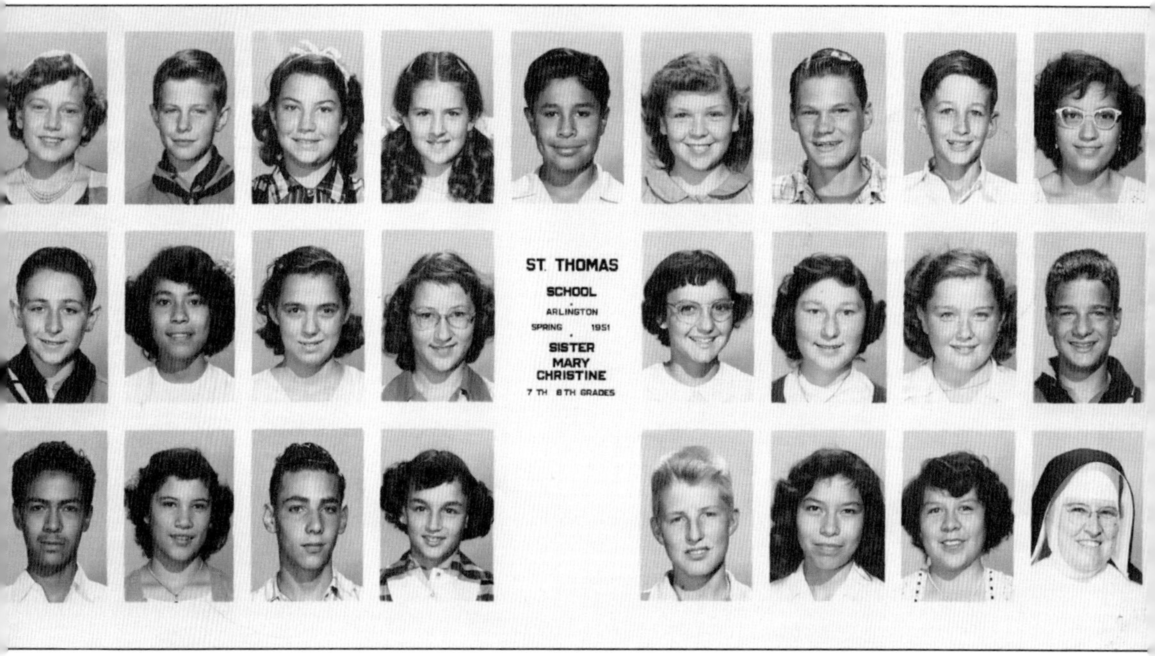

St. Thomas the Apostle Catholic School, a part of the church, was located at the corner of Magnolia Avenue and Jackson Street in Arlington. Sr. Mary Christine poses with her seventh- and eighth-grade class in the spring of 1951. David Leibert appears in the first row, fifth from the left.

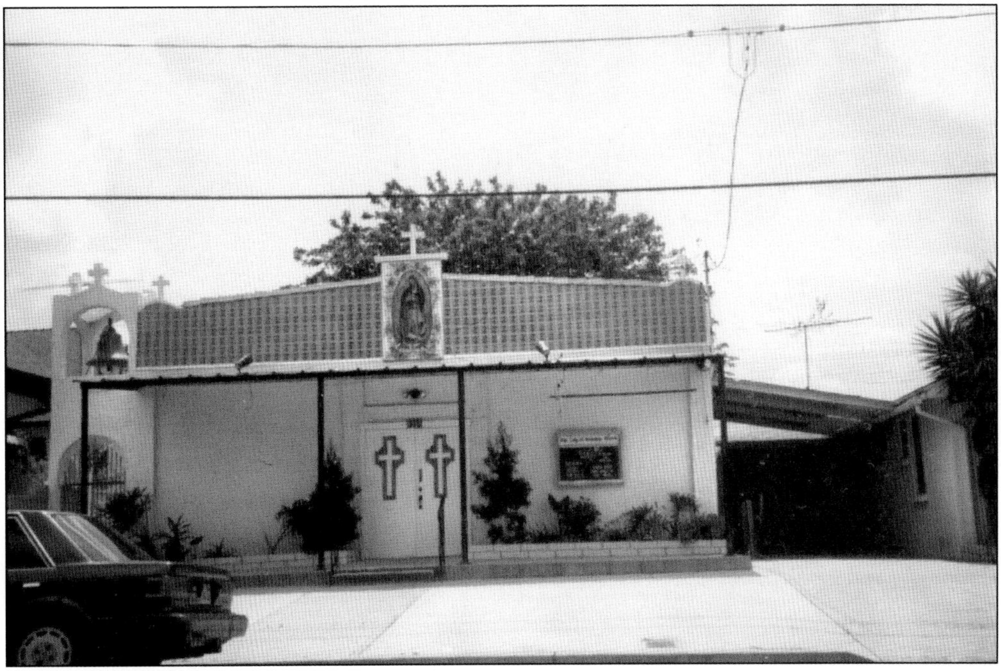

Our Lady of Guadalupe Catholic Church, founded in 1949, stood at 9398 Indiana Avenue near Van Buren Boulevard. The parish was predominately Hispanic, and the masses were all in Spanish.

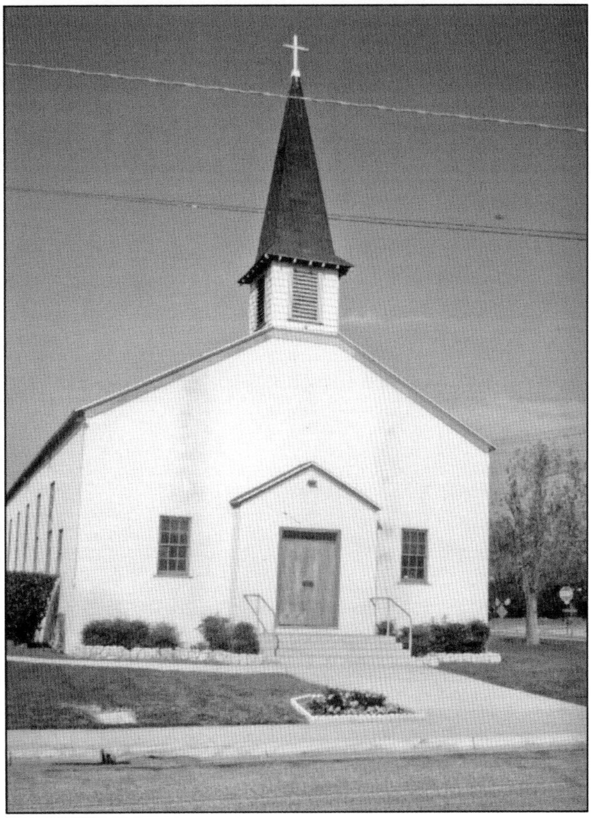

In the 1940s, the old Army Camp Chapel was located at the corner of Chapel Street and Cypress Avenue. The army base, called Camp Anza, occupied a space on Van Buren Boulevard and Arlington Avenue. Now this area is known as Arlanza, and the building is still used as a church.

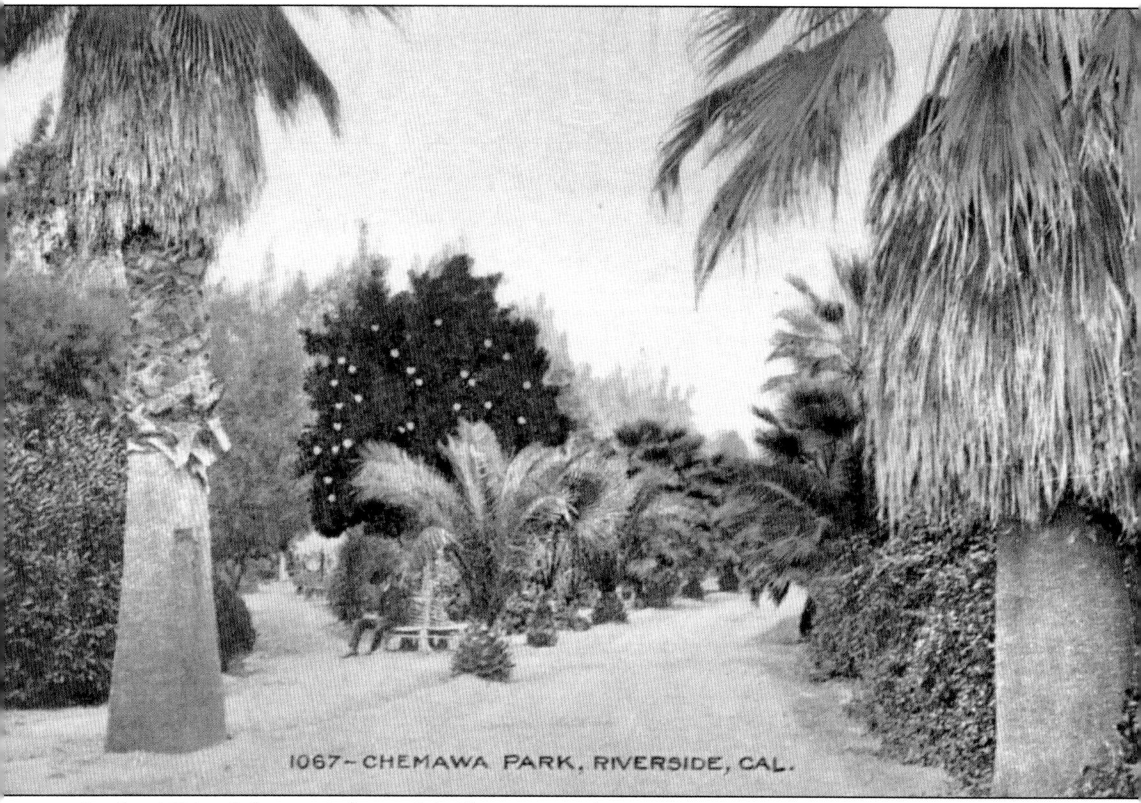

In the 1890s, Arlington's beautiful Chemawa Park was a 23-acre site owned by Pacific Electric Railway and filled with big, beautiful trees and plants. The park also included a small zoo with monkeys, tropical birds, bears, and a few other animals. Brow's ostrich farm was across the street. Picnics were frequently held at Chemawa Park. (Courtesy Steve Lech.)

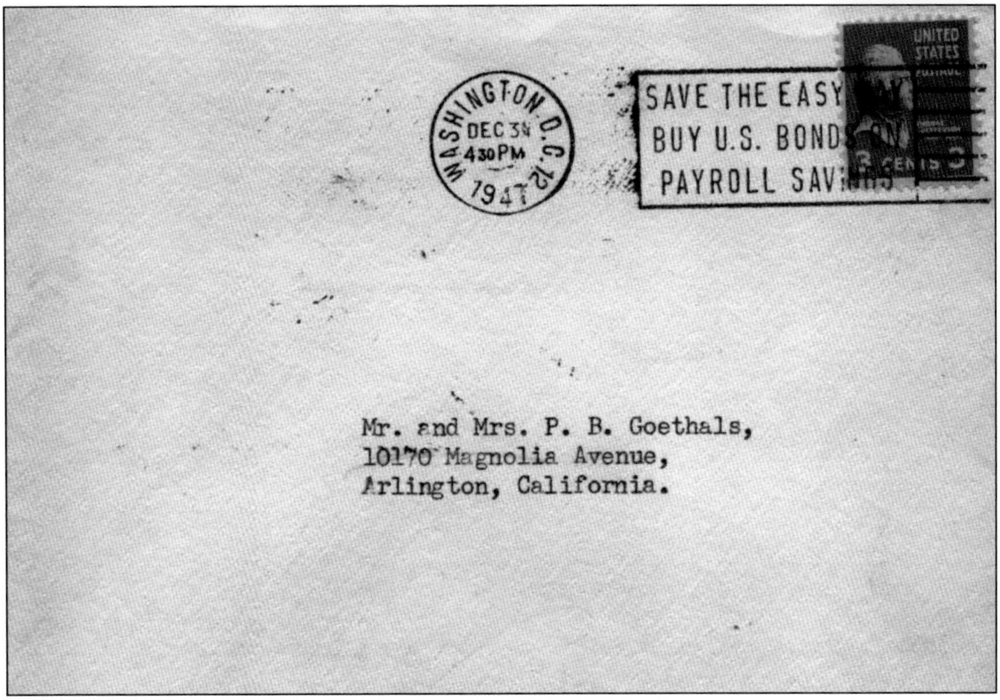

Addressed to Mr. and Mrs. P. B. Goethals, 10170 Magnolia Avenue, Arlington, California, this letter is postmarked December 31, 1947, at 4:30 p.m. from Washington, D.C. The envelope is 60 years old and still holds the original card. It bears a 3¢ Thomas Jefferson stamp and an ink message reading, "Save the easy way. Buy U.S. bond on payroll savings."

This postcard is addressed to Mr. and Mrs. G. B. Leibert of Arlington and dated July 13, 1938. At that time, there were no listings for post office box number or physical house address, just "Arlington, Calif.," which would suffice. The mail was delivered with a 1¢ stamp. Somehow letters always found their way to the people of Arlington.

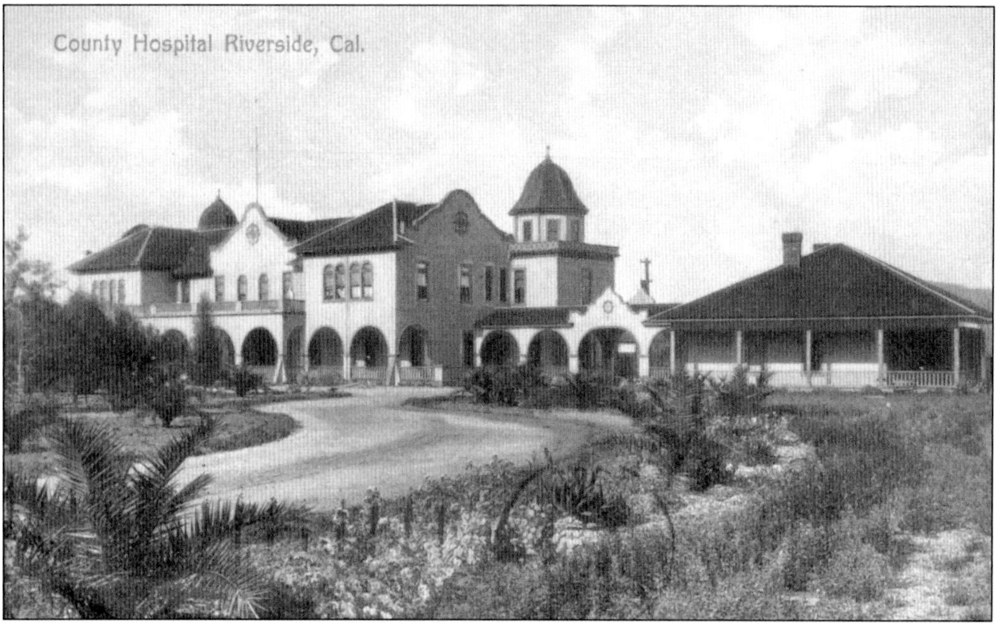

Founded in 1893, Riverside General Hospital burned to the ground in 1898 and was relocated to the corner of Magnolia Avenue and Harrison Street in Arlington. It was originally constructed in 1900 as a wooden building with Spanish arches. The hospital was 100 years old before it was relocated to the city of Moreno Valley. In the 1990s, its name was changed to the Riverside County Regional Medical Center. (Courtesy Steve Lech.)

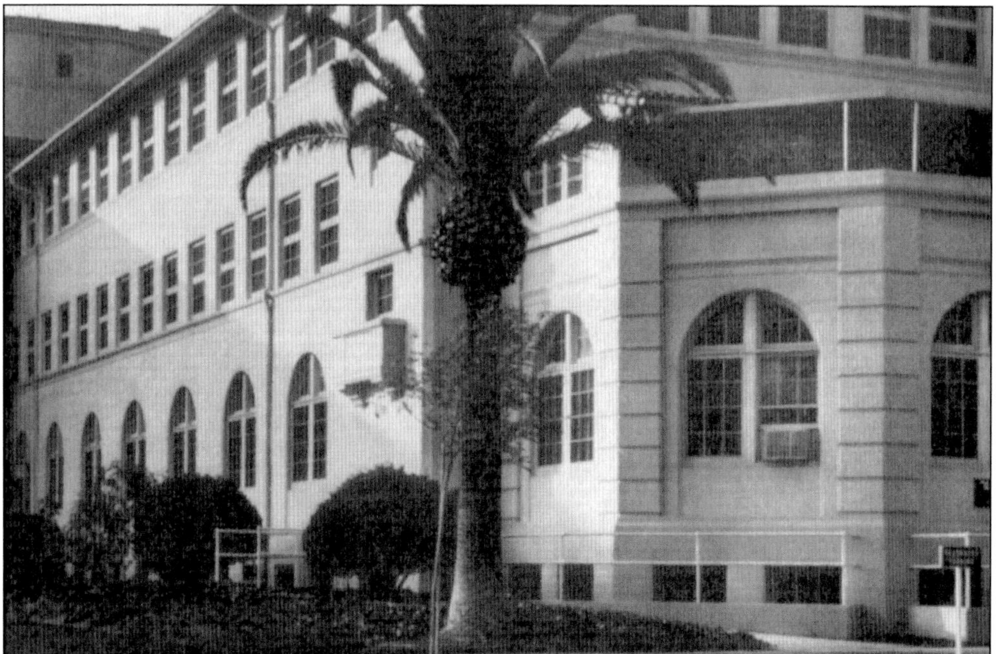

Riverside General Hospital in Arlington added a surgical wing in 1938. The structure was very modern at the time, with large windows and a covered balcony on the second floor. The hospital limited visitors, so the balcony allowed patients to go out and wave to their families waiting outside.

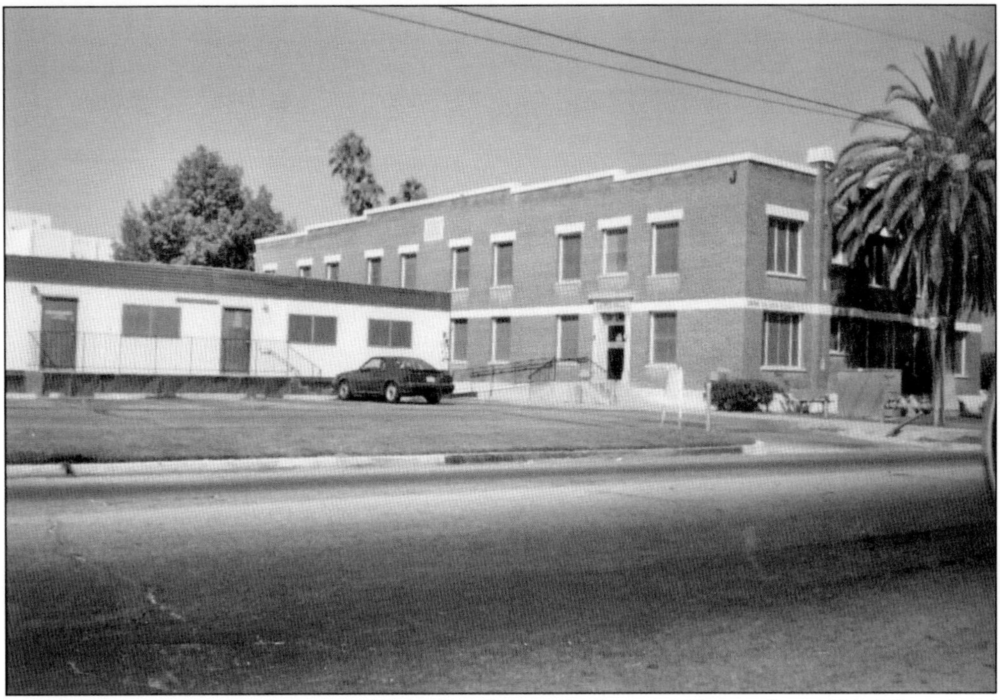

A nurses' training school was established at Riverside General Hospital in 1908. The school building faces Harrison Street. The first graduation class hit the headlines of the *Arlington Times* with four young women graduating on November 30, 1909.

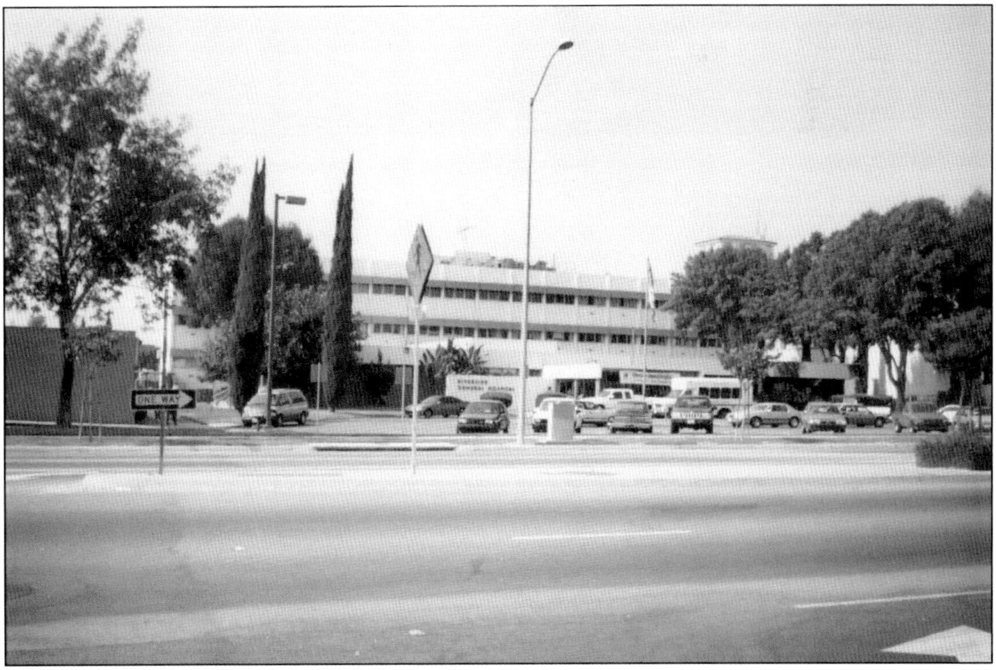

Riverside County General Hospital, located on Magnolia Avenue in Arlington, was a training school in every major field of medicine. Pictured here is one of many additions to the hospital throughout its years: a new administration building, constructed in 1960.

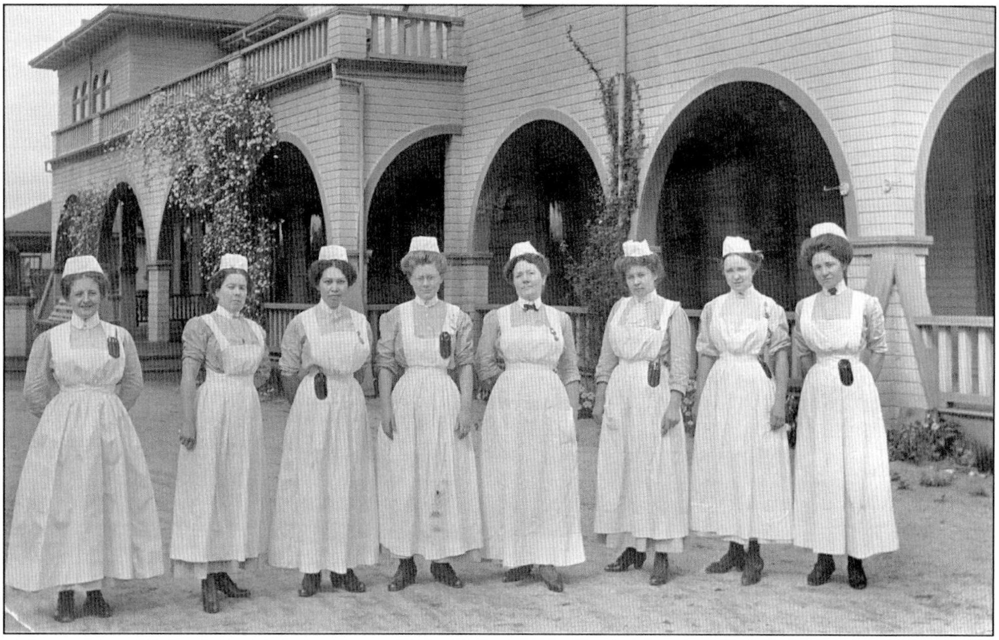

Riverside General Hospital was located on Magnolia Avenue in Arlington. There are eight nurses, pictured here around 1900, dressed in long sleeves, high collars, nurses' hats, and long aprons and ready for a day's work.

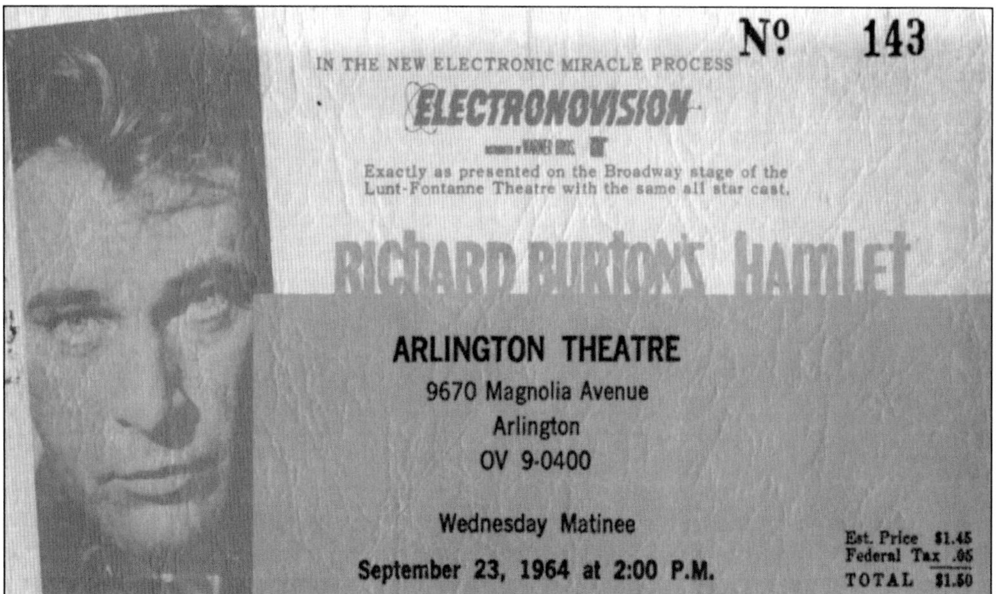

This $1.50 ticket allowed entrance to see Richard Burton in *Hamlet* at the Arlington Theatre, located at 9670 Magnolia Avenue, for the Wednesday matinee on September 23, 1964, at 2:00 p.m. The story of Hamlet is told on the back of the ticket.

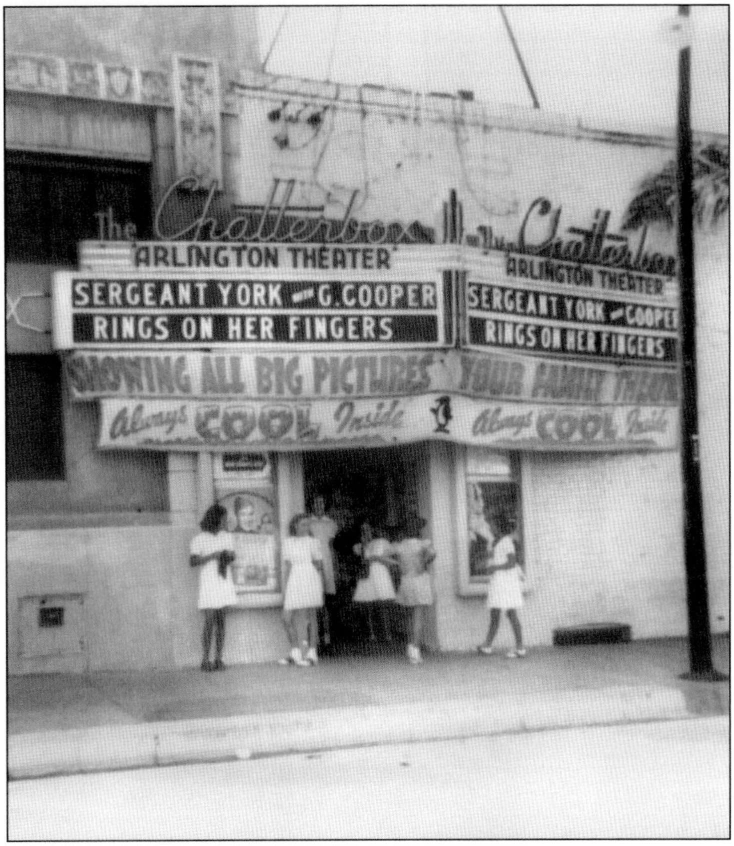

A small indoor theater called the Chatterbox opened in the early 1940s next to the bank on Van Buren Boulevard between Arlington Park and Magnolia Avenue. A large banner read, "SHOWING ALL BIG PICTURES—YOUR FAMILY THEATER." Movies playing at the time were *Sergeant York* with Gary Cooper and *Rings on Her Fingers* starring Gene Tierney. (Courtesy Riverside Metropolitan Museum.)

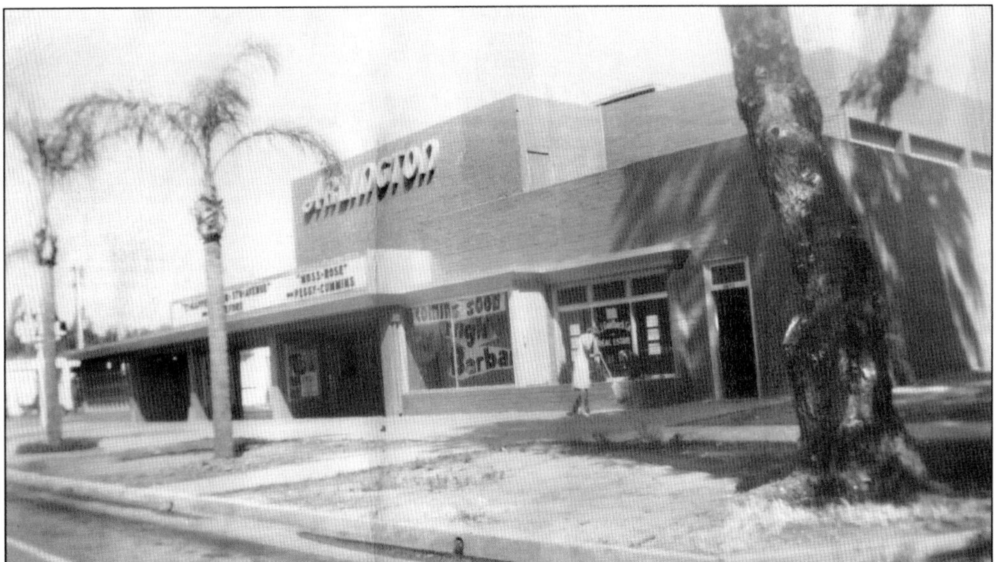

In the 1950s, Robert Elder opened the Arlington Theater. Known for "fine entertainment," it was also a treat to enjoy a movie in an air-conditioned theater with comfortable, upholstered seats. The Arlington had an upper level, but children were not allowed there unless accompanied by an adult. (Courtesy Riverside Metropolitan Museum.)

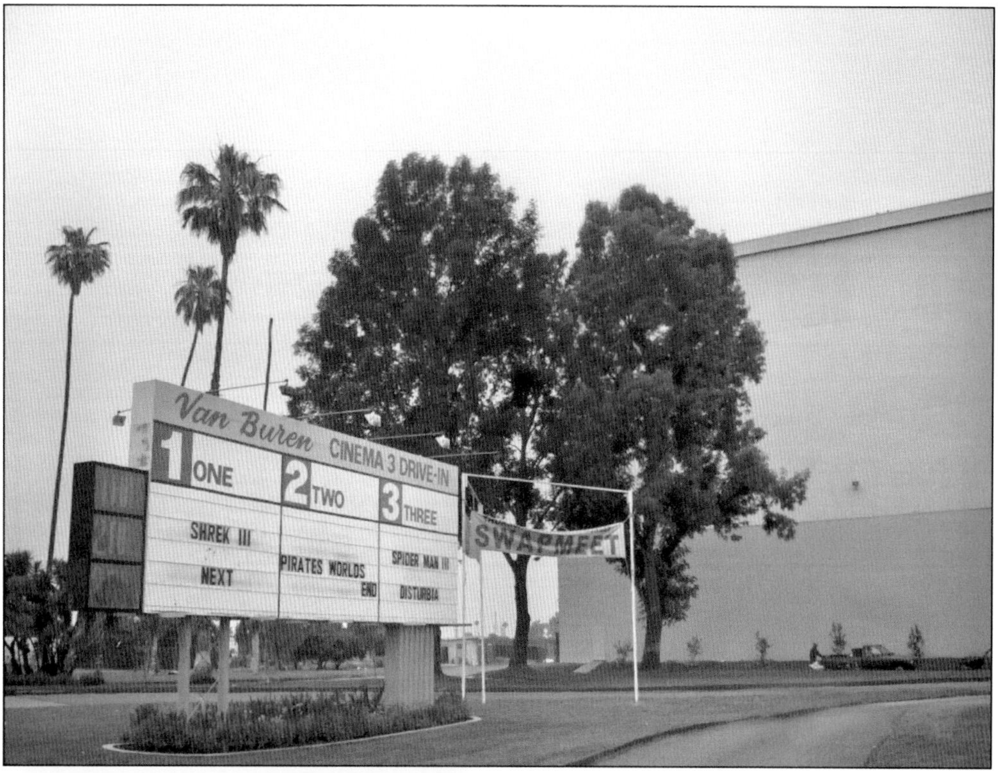

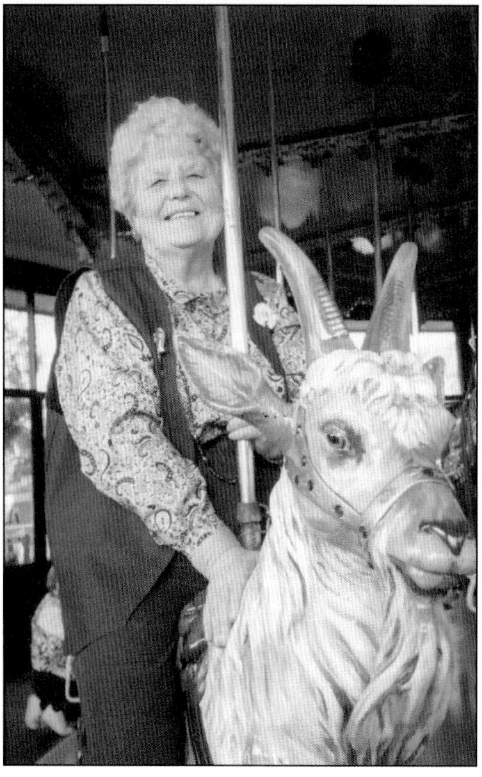

The Van Buren Drive-in was the last of its kind, a great place for family entertainment with three large screens. One price by the carload admitted the entire family. Folks would often bring their own snacks and chairs to sit outside, or they could just stay inside the car. The drive-in was located south of Magnolia Avenue, just past the 91 Freeway.

In 1984, Castle Park began providing fun for the entire family in Arlington. The facility included a carousel (made from two carousels dated 1907 and 1914) with 52 beautiful wooded animals. Here Theresa Gordon sits on the goat, which is quite appropriate as she loved goats and kept them in her youth. As an adult, Theresa became the local historian.

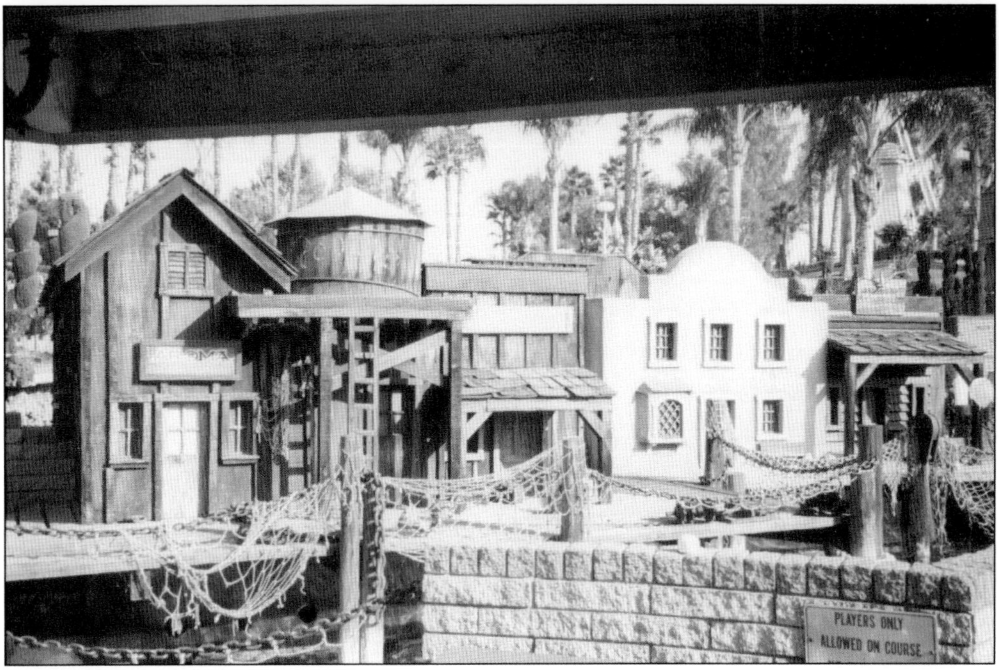

Four different miniature-golf courses are situated at Castle Park, a family fun place with an arcade for the kids. The park's other attractions include a roller coaster, a fireball, and water rides.

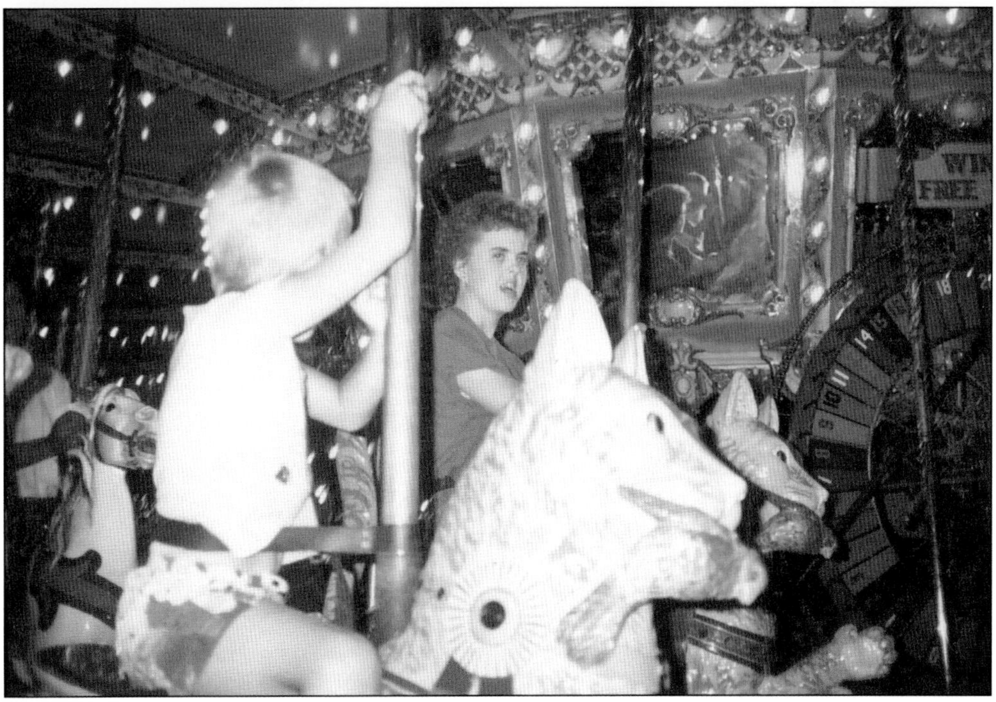

Jeramy Gordon (left) and Tina Hall ride the Castle Park carousel, whose wooden animals were all refurbished. They had giraffes, goats, horses, lions, ostriches, tigers, rabbits, and more. Some were stationary while others moved up and down. The carousel was housed in a large round building with stained-glass windows.

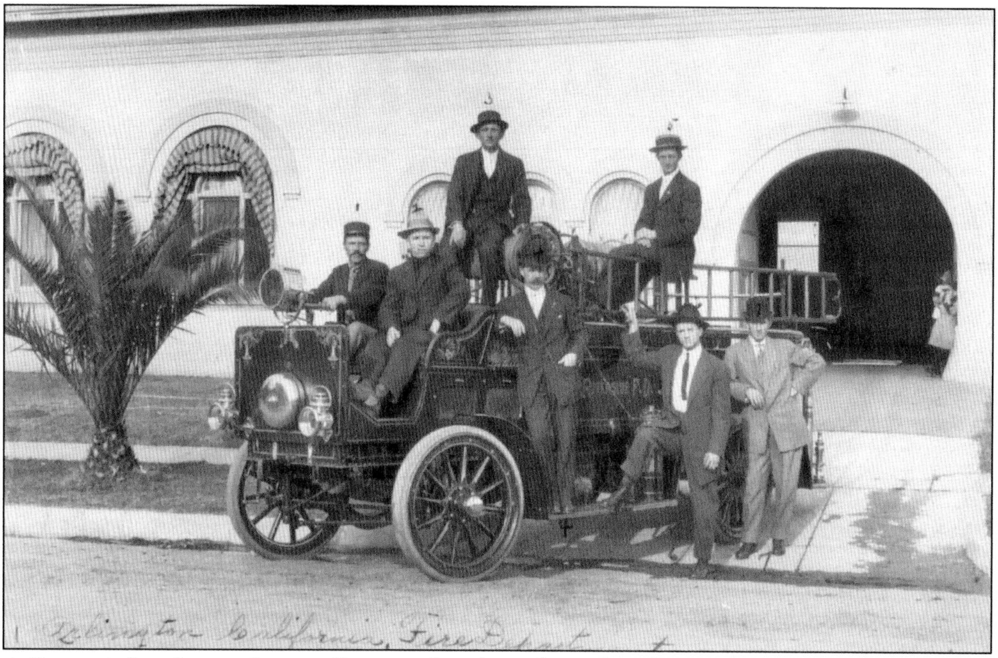

Arlington's first fire truck was a Seagrave hand-me-down from Riverside in 1913. The volunteer crew worked many fires. Chief Shelby Tabler sits in the driver's seat; beside him is H. Davidson. On top of the truck are Isaac Carlson (left) and Floyd Miller, and standing beside the Seagrave are A. C. Turner, Frank Charlton, and Samuel Gurley. (Courtesy Daniel Balboa.)

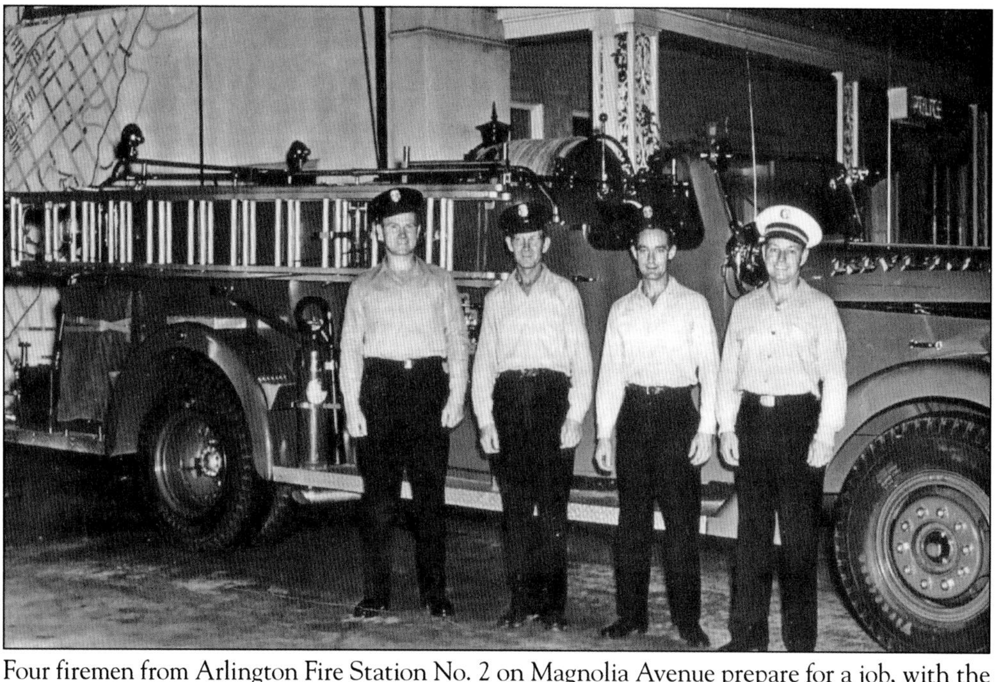

Four firemen from Arlington Fire Station No. 2 on Magnolia Avenue prepare for a job, with the big red fire truck behind them. This truck is a 105-horsepower American LaFrance unit with a triple combination pump capable of throwing 730 gallons of water per minute. It was first placed in use here in 1921. (Courtesy Daniel Balboa.)

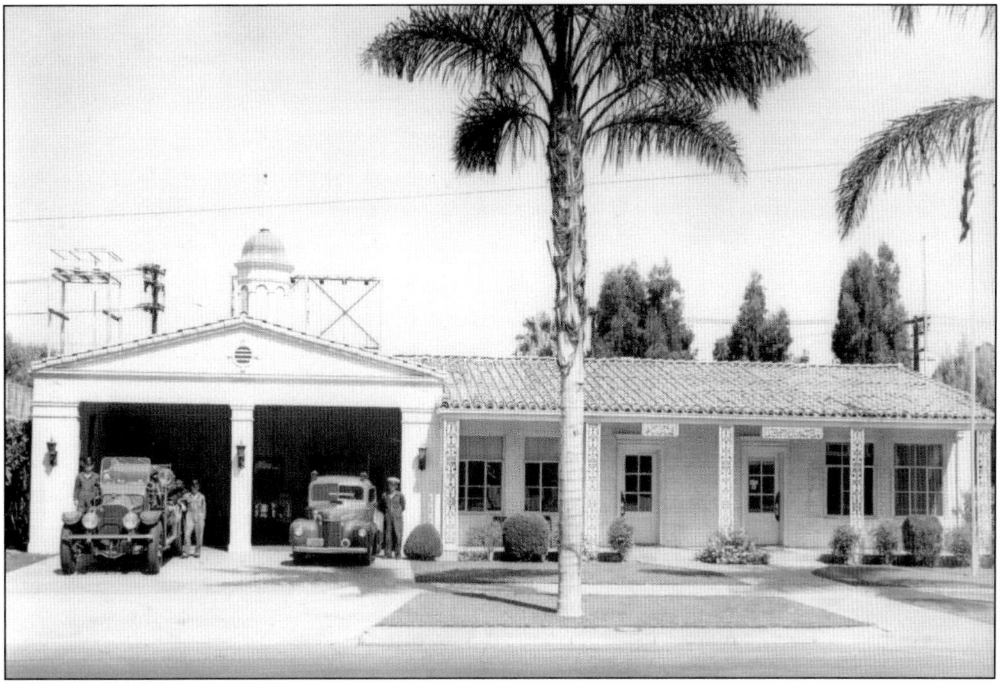

Two trucks are parked in front of the Arlington Fire Station on Magnolia Avenue. On top of the building was a metal tower that produced an alarm to alert everyone of fire. This brick building also served as headquarters for the police and utilities department. Called the Arlington Substation, the 1938 structure was dedicated by the Arlington Chamber of Commerce and still stands today. (Courtesy Daniel Balboa.)

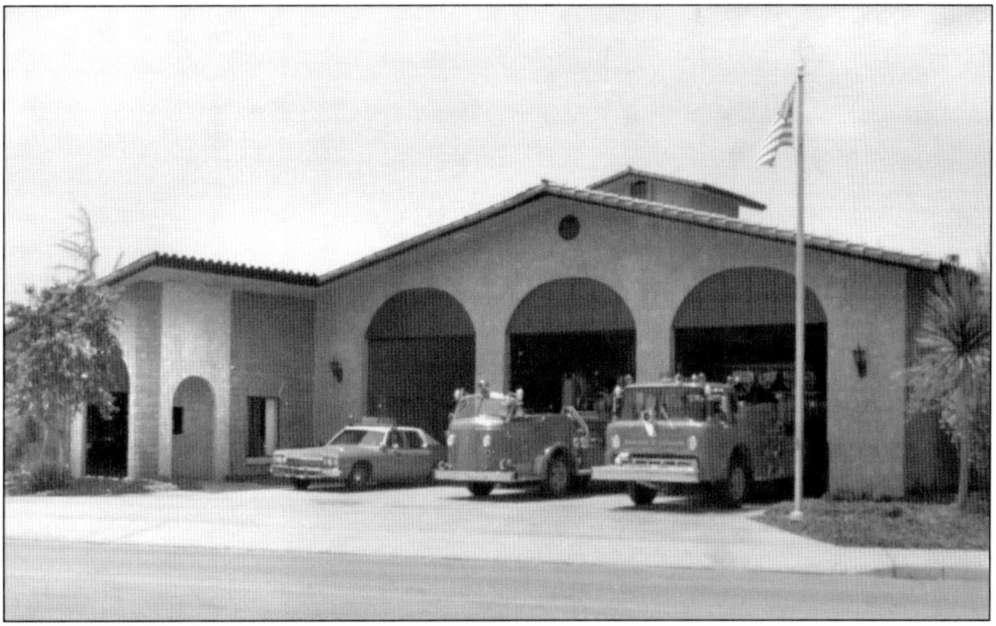

Shown in the 1950s are two fire trucks, along with chief's car, in front of Arlington Fire Station No. 2. The fire station moved from Magnolia Avenue to this new and larger building on Andrew Street. The trucks were ready to go at any time. (Courtesy Daniel Balboa.)

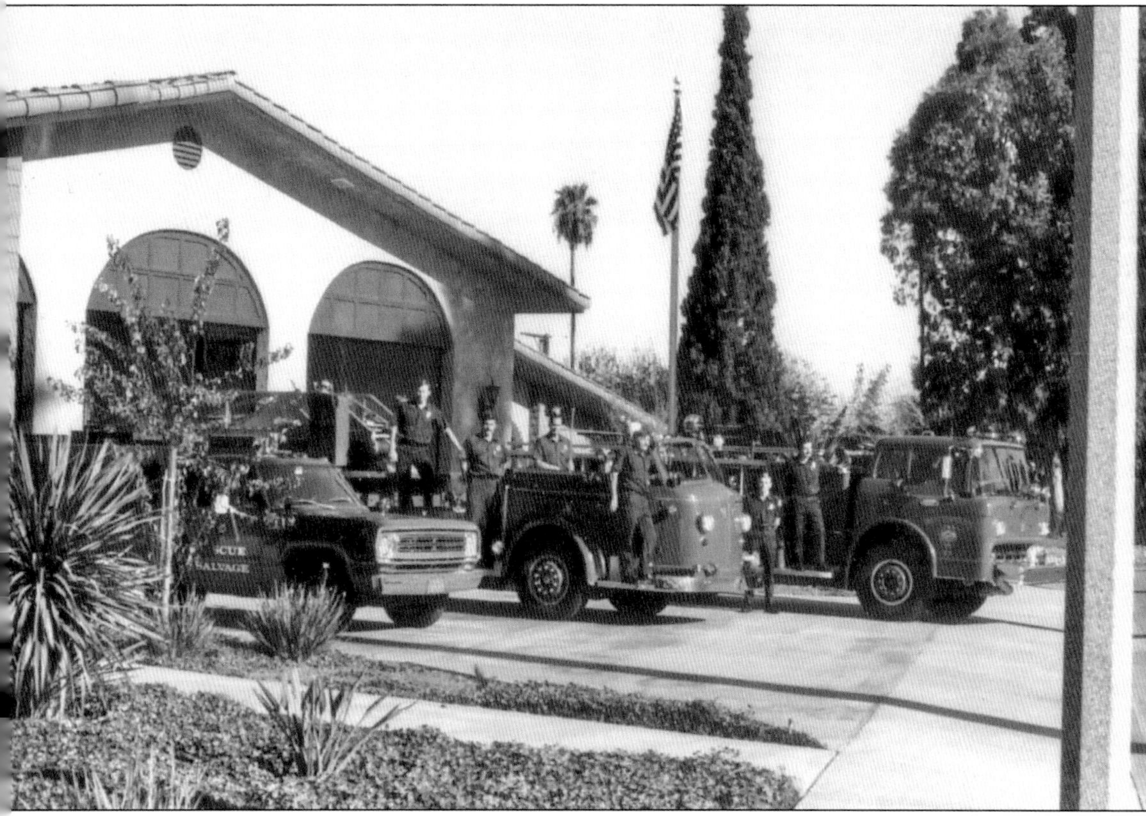

In the 1950s, the trucks from Arlington Fire Station No. 2 sit in front of the station, with six men looking as if they have just finished cleaning them. The rescue truck also appears ready for action. The flagpole is visible in the background. (Courtesy Daniel Balboa.)

Seven

Neighbors of Woodcraft

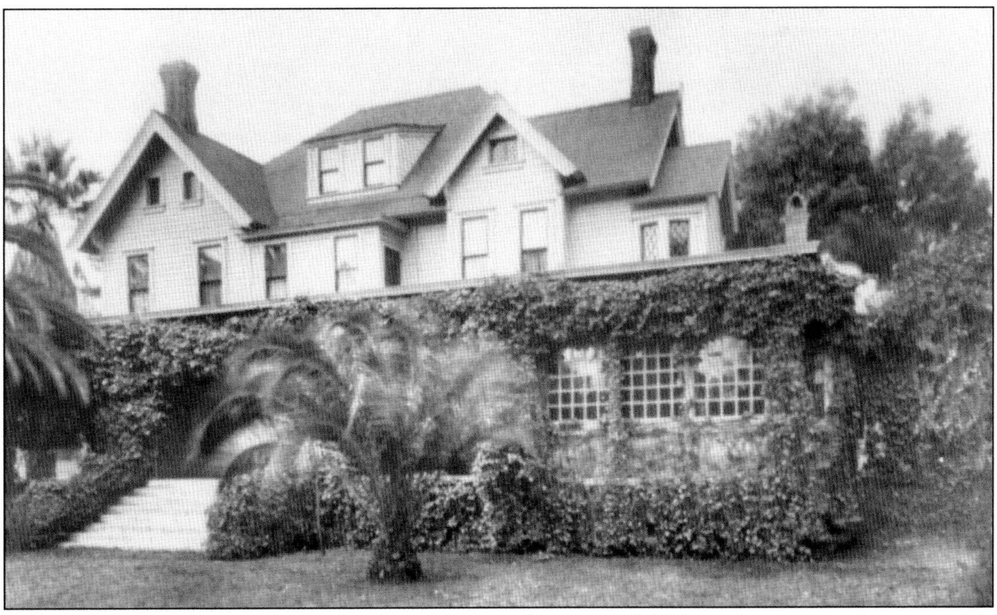

In 1920, the Neighbors of Woodcraft purchased this beautiful Magnolia Avenue home, which included large rooms, a high-ceiling sunroom, and wide verandas. The Neighbors used this original building for five years, as well as the 45 acres of land bought with the home. (Courtesy David Beaird.)

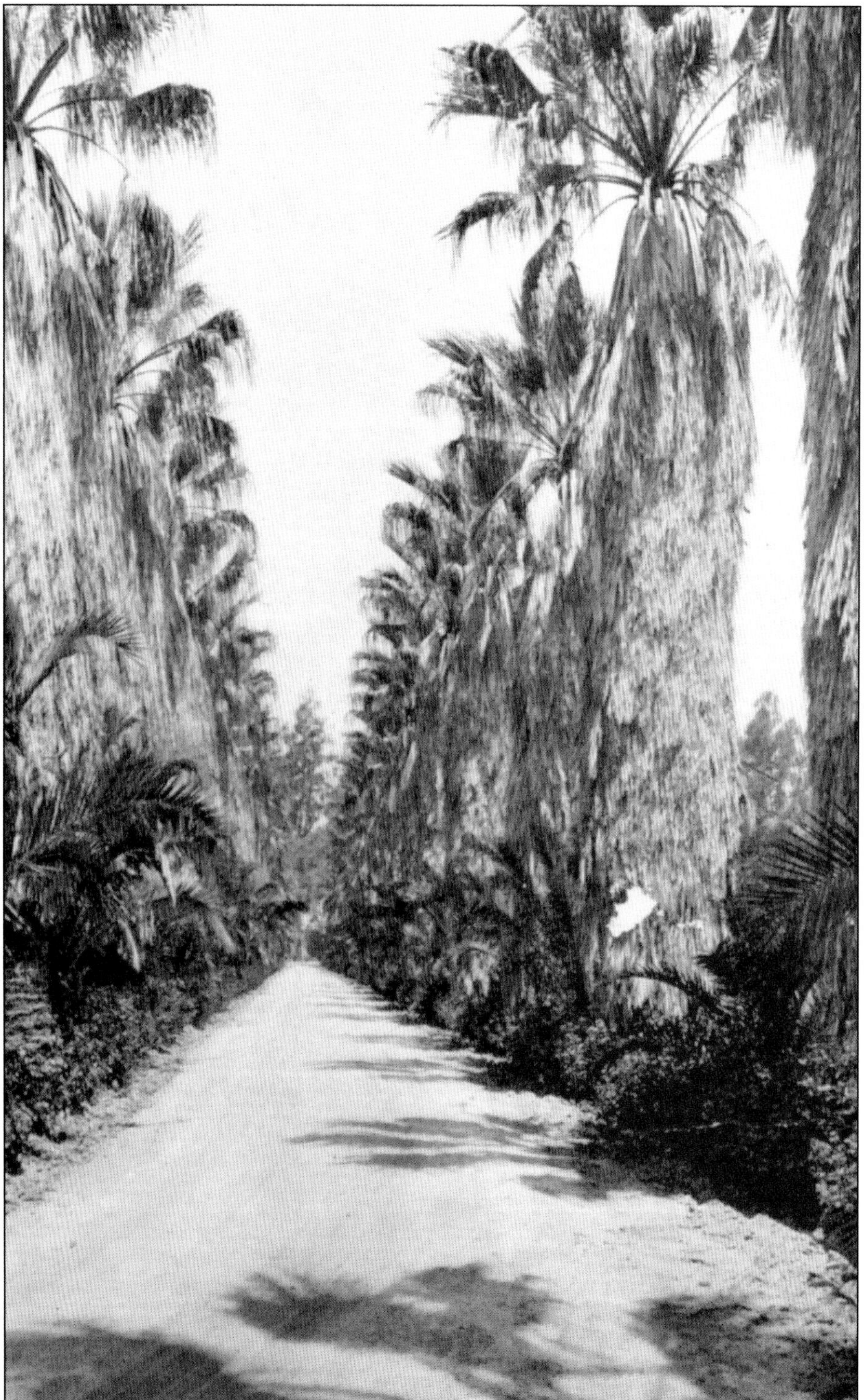

This very long driveway led to the Neighbors of Woodcraft Retirement Home. Sweeping, overgrown palms lined the drive to the front door. (Courtesy JoAnne Pease-Simpson.)

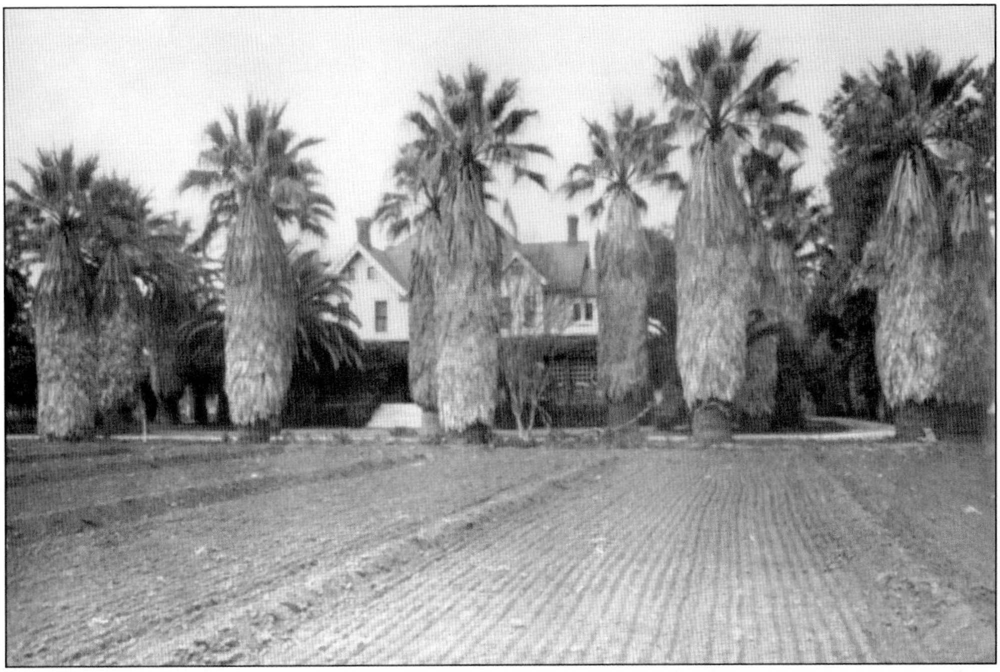

The Neighbors of Woodcraft Home was set far back from the road with a long driveway encircling it. A field of open land was planted with alfalfa, barley, wheat, orchards, and a garden. (Courtesy David Beaird.)

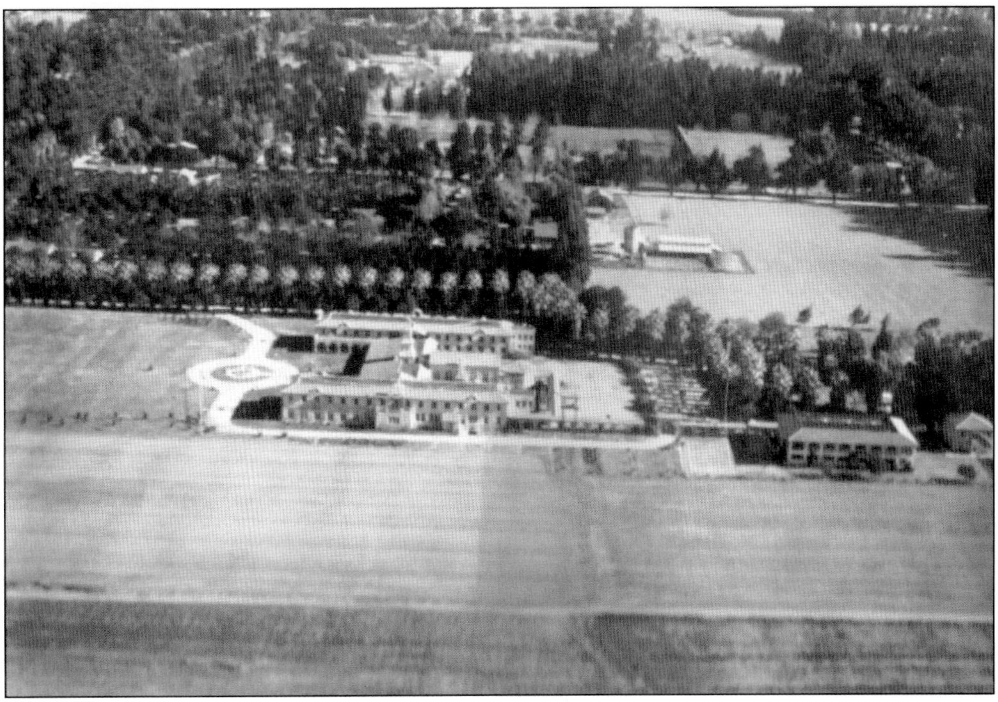

This *c.* 1934 aerial view shows the Neighbors of Woodcraft Home on Magnolia Avenue. The building standing alone to the right is the home's private hospital. To the left is north, facing Magnolia Avenue; to the right is south; and to the back is east, Adams Street. (Courtesy David Beaird.)

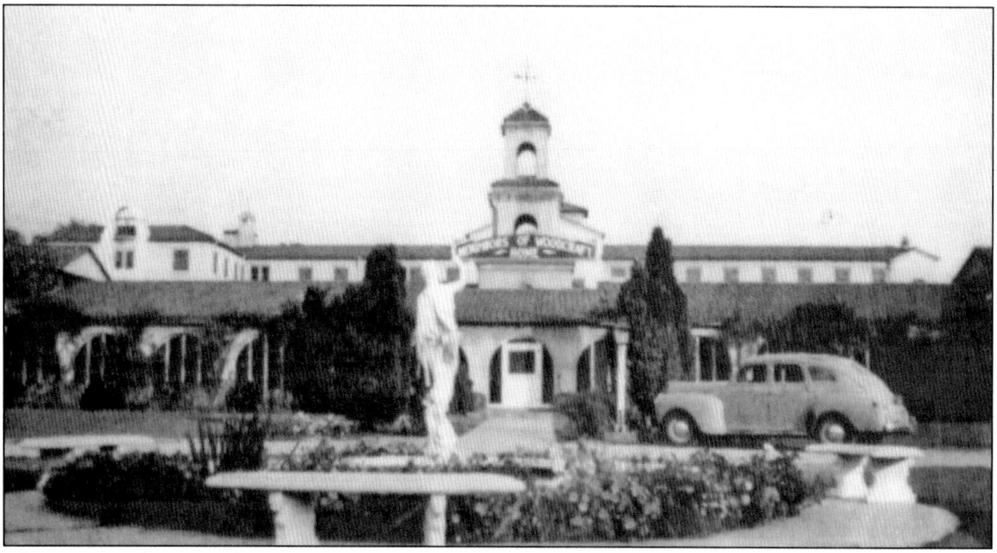

The Fortuna fountain, located in front of the Neighbors of Woodcraft Home, depicted the goddess of chance, who had the power to guide lives. This statue provided a popular resting place for guests of the home. (Courtesy David Beaird.)

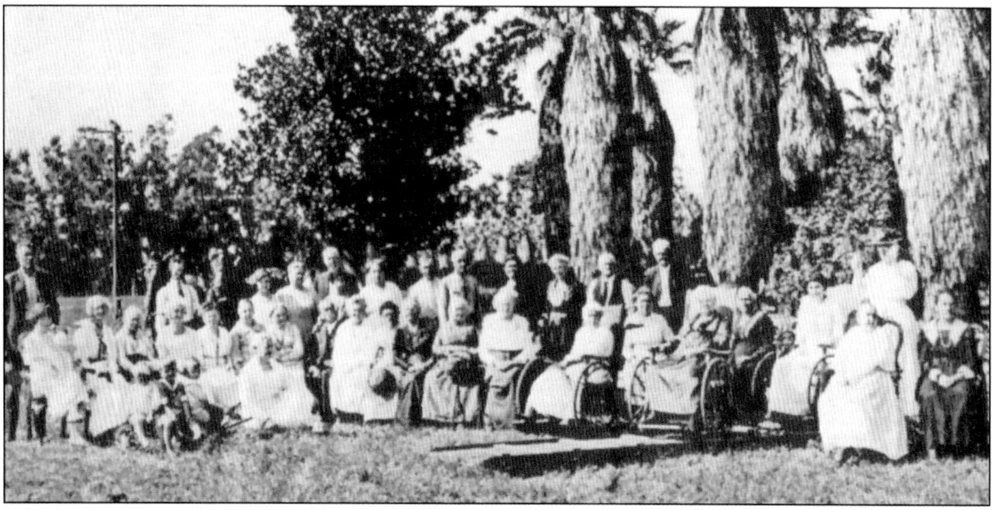

All the home residents, even some in wheelchairs, attend the groundbreaking for the hospital building on August 20, 1922. The hospital opened with a large reception in February 1923, and the cost of construction was $35,000. Still in need of more space, the Grand Circle session held in July 1925 advised the building of a new structure to replace the original three-story Woodcraft Home. (Courtesy David Beaird.)

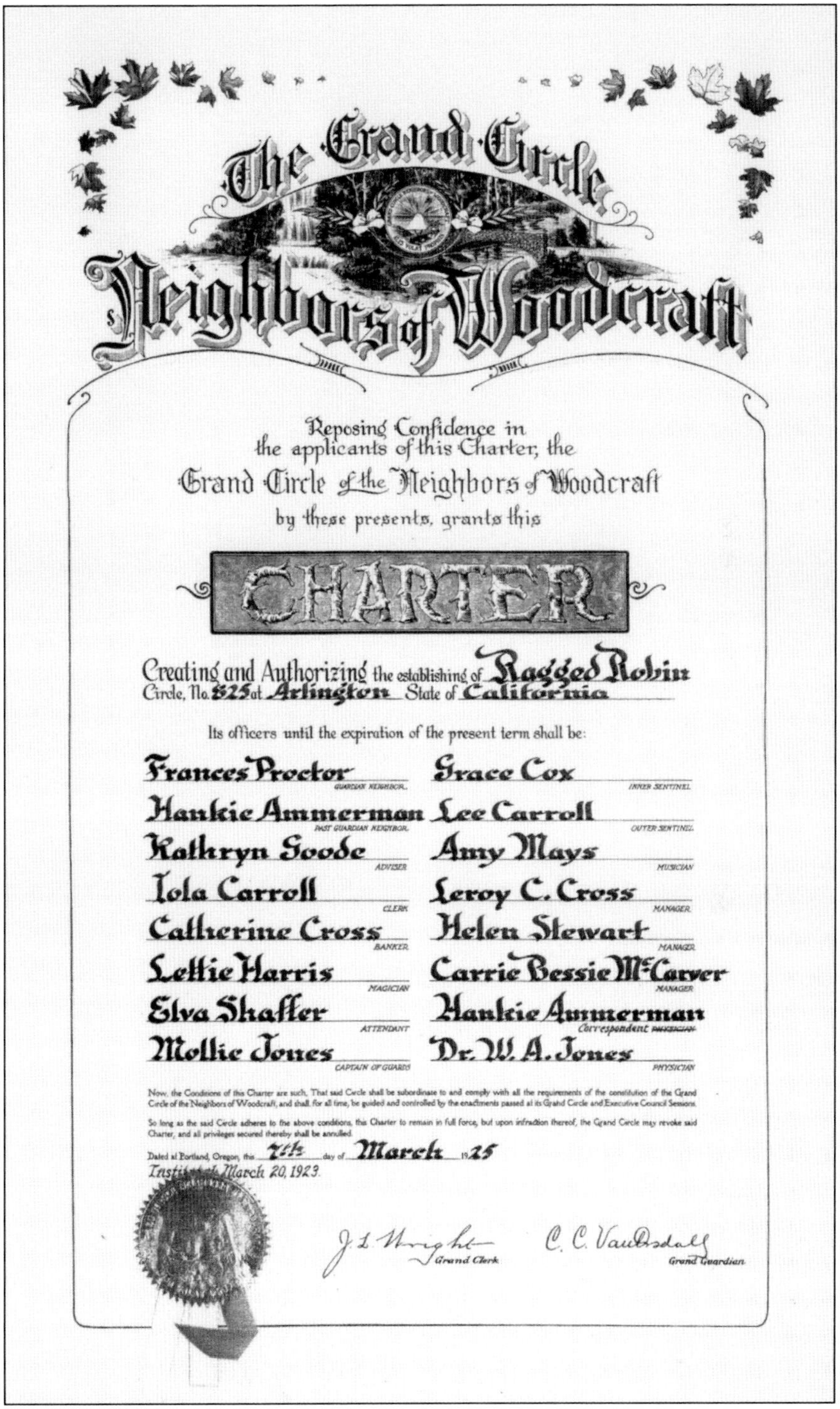

The Grand Circle
Neighbors of Woodcraft

Reposing Confidence in the applicants of this Charter, the Grand Circle of the Neighbors of Woodcraft by these presents, grants this

CHARTER

Creating and Authorizing the establishing of Ragged Robin Circle, No. 825 at Arlington State of California

Its officers until the expiration of the present term shall be:

Frances Proctor — Guardian Neighbor	Grace Cox — Inner Sentinel
Hankie Ammerman — Past Guardian Neighbor	Lee Carroll — Outer Sentinel
Kathryn Goode — Adviser	Amy Mays — Musician
Iola Carroll — Clerk	Leroy C. Cross — Manager
Catherine Cross — Banker	Helen Stewart — Manager
Lettie Harris — Magician	Carrie Bessie McCarver — Manager
Elva Shaffer — Attendant	Hankie Ammerman — Correspondent ~~Physician~~
Mollie Jones — Captain of Guards	Dr. W. A. Jones — Physician

Now, the Conditions of this Charter are such, That said Circle shall be subordinate to and comply with all the requirements of the constitution of the Grand Circle of the Neighbors of Woodcraft, and shall, for all time, be guided and controlled by the enactments passed at its Grand Circle and Executive Council Sessions.

So long as the said Circle adheres to the above conditions, this Charter to remain in full force, but upon infraction thereof, the Grand Circle may revoke said Charter, and all privileges secured thereby shall be annulled.

Dated at Portland, Oregon, this 7th day of March 1925

Instituted March 20, 1923.

Grand Clerk

Grand Guardian

The Grand Circle Neighbors of Woodcraft No. 825 at Arlington, California, consisted of officers Frances Proctor, Hankie Ammerman, Kathryn Goode, Lolo Carroll, Catherine Cross, Lettie Harris, Elva Shaffer, Mollie Jones, Grace Cox, Lee Carroll, Amy Mays, Leroy Cross, Helen Stewart, Carrie Bessie McCarver, and Dr. W. A. Jones on March 7, 1925. (Courtesy JoAnne Pease-Simpson.)

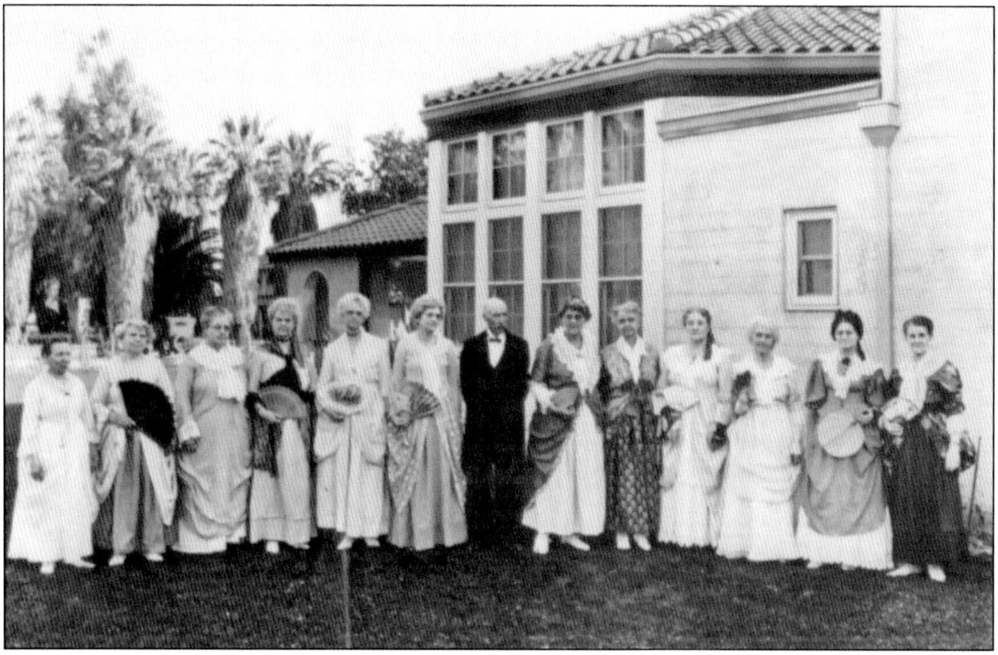

The Neighbors of Woodcraft often had what was called a dress-up day, when they dressed in their Sunday best. In this *c.* 1920s photograph, almost every woman holds a hand fan; they must have been very "hot" in all the clothing they were wearing, with dresses to the ground and long sleeves. (Courtesy David Beaird.)

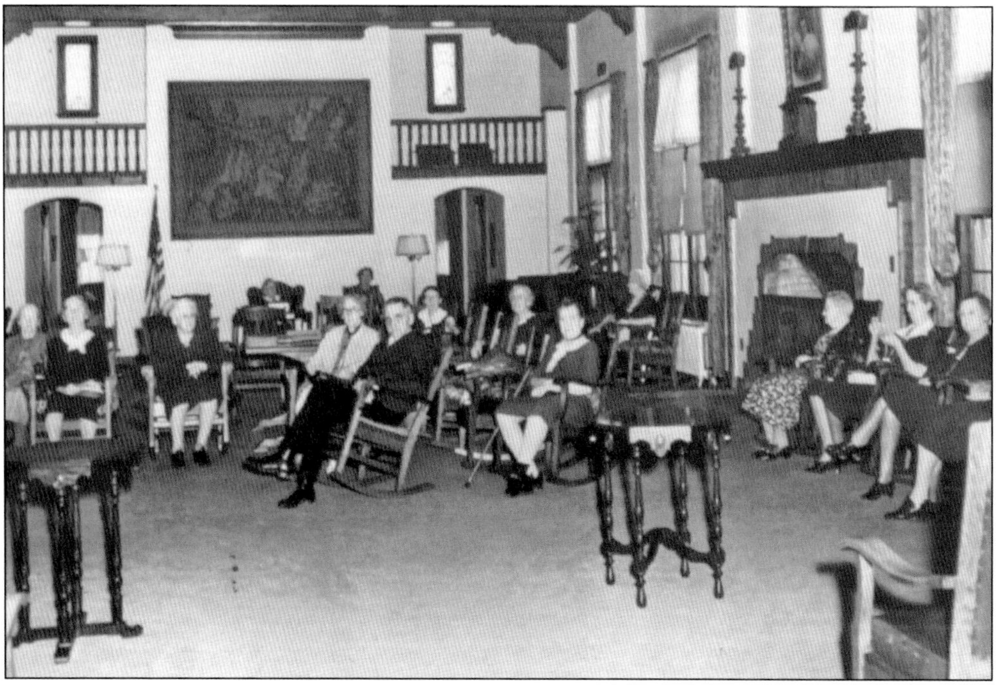

In the beginning, this room at Neighbors of Woodcraft was used for a chapel. Later it was used as a social area, to make the last days of the aged and infirm comfortable and happy. The furnishings were given by the Fraternal Insurance Society of Portland, Oregon. (Courtesy David Beaird.)

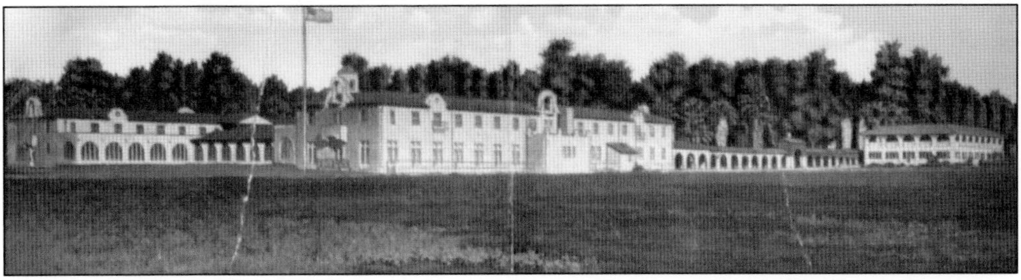

The beautiful Neighbors of Woodcraft Home was owned by the Fraternal Insurance Society of Portland, Oregon. There were 104 rooms, one for each elderly guest. A covered walkway from the main building led to the private hospital on the far right side. (Courtesy David Beaird.)

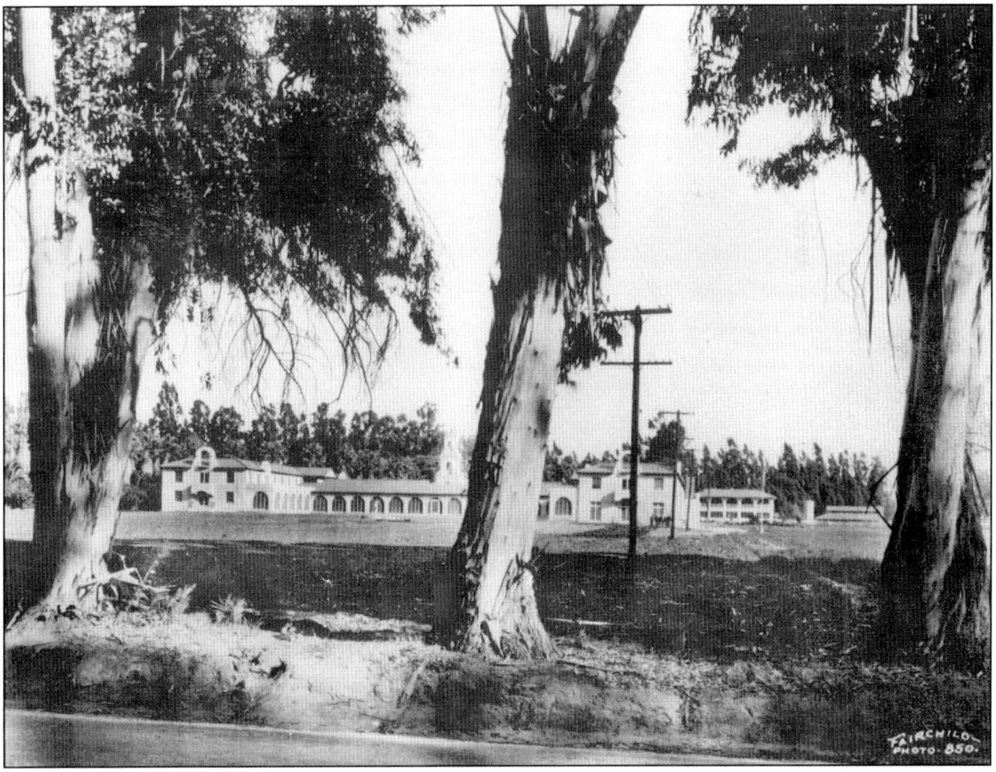

The Neighbors of Woodcraft Home was situated on the famous Magnolia Avenue in Arlington. In the administration building and living quarters (pictured here) were living rooms, parlors, sun parlors, a dining room, and a library—all the comforts one could want. The grounds had lots of wooded areas, and next to the avenue were large eucalyptus trees. (Courtesy David Beaird.)

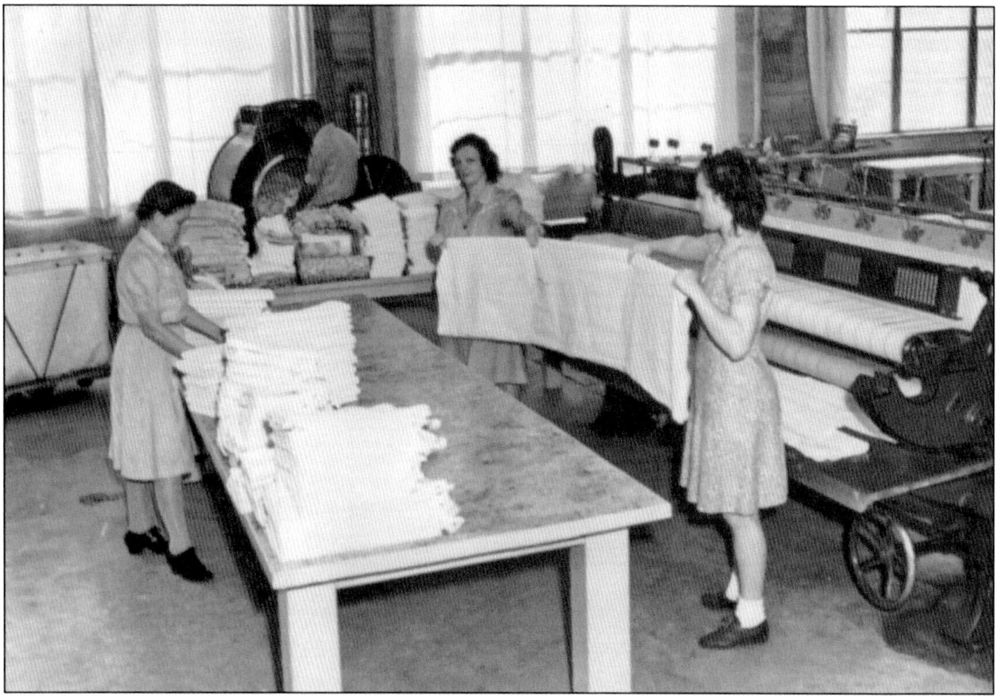

The laundry room at the Neighbors of Woodcraft Home worked round the clock, as there were between 114 and 137 guests at any given time. Ladies fold and stack bed sheets, blankets, and towels around 1929. (Courtesy David Beaird.)

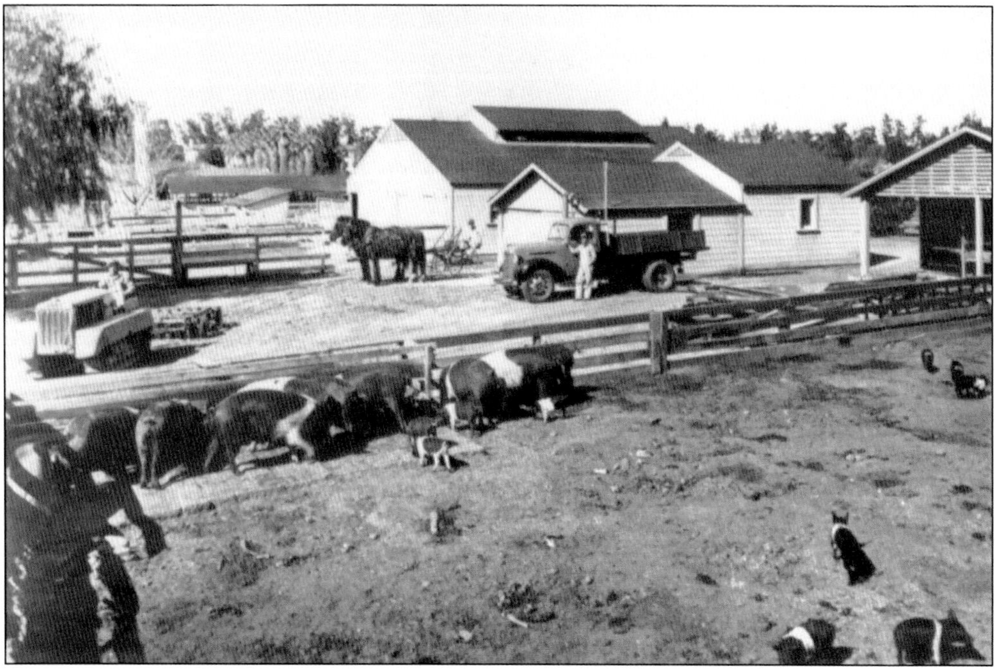

Home employees are going to work for the day: one on the tractor to rotate the land; one with a team of horses; and another standing by the old flatbed truck. The grounds consisted of many barns and sheds—and very large hogs with their many babies. (Courtesy David Beaird.)

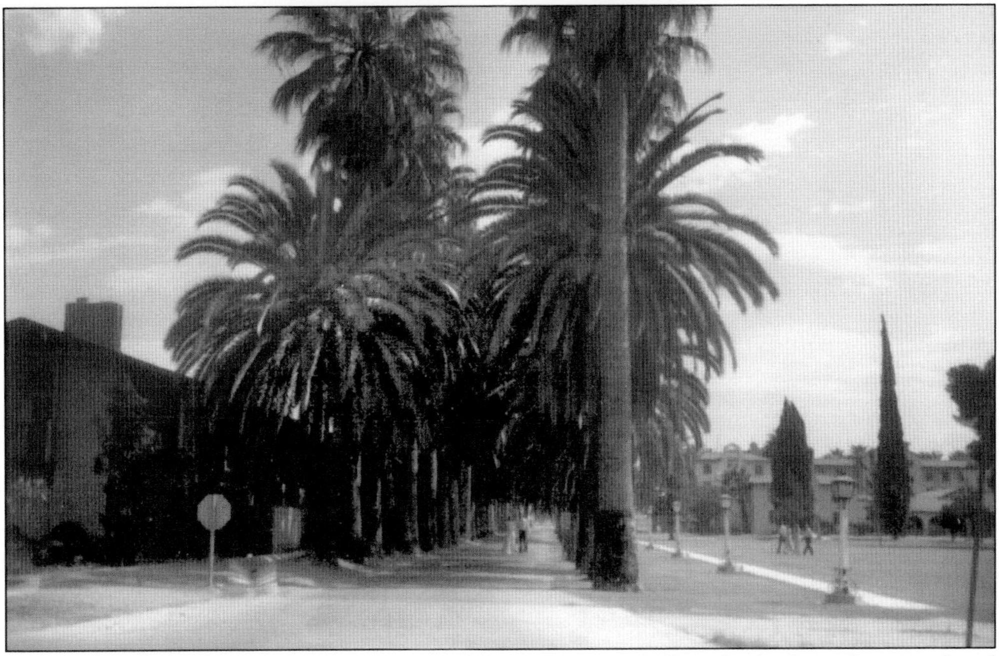

In the mid-1950s, the main entrance to California Baptist College had a long driveway lined with palm trees that were always kept nicely trimmed. Down the driveway and on the right side, students walk on the campus. To the left of the driveway are apartments. (Courtesy California Baptist University.)

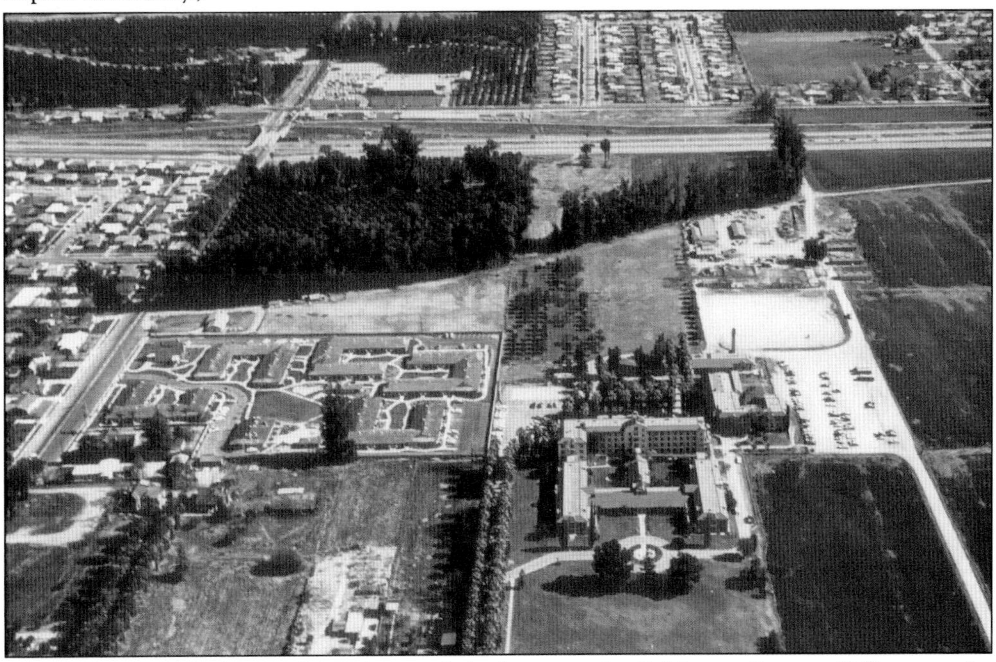

In this c. 1965 aerial view from the north looking south, California Baptist College can be seen to the right and the Royal Rose Retirement Home to the left at 3720 Adams Street. In the background is U.S. Highway 91. Today's familiar Adams Plaza and the Auto Center have not yet been built. (Courtesy California Baptist University.)

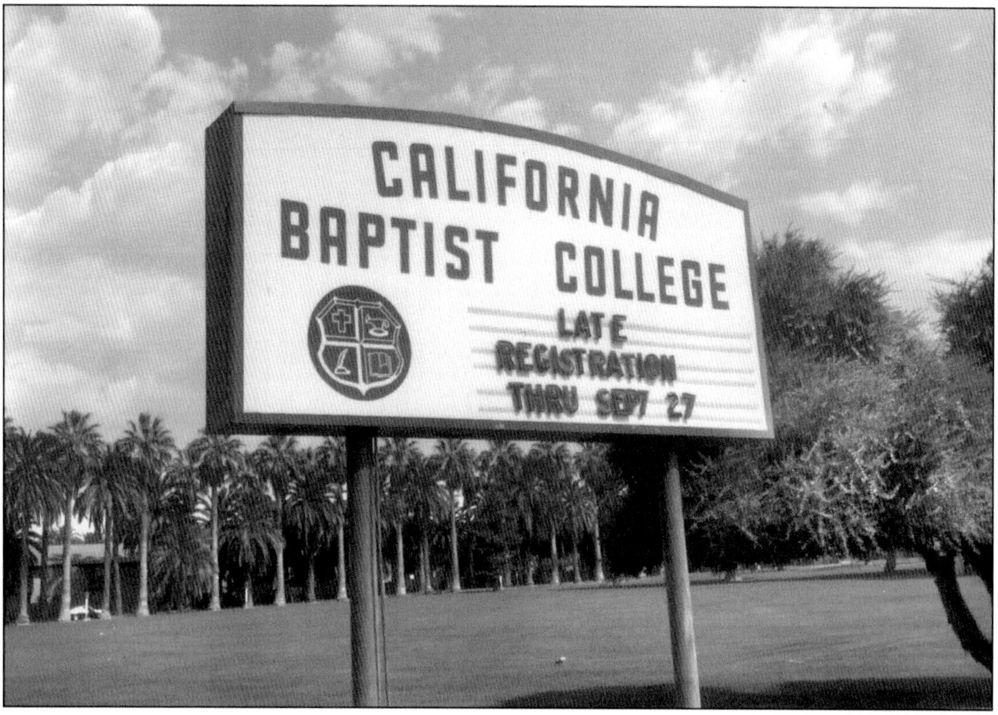

In 1955, the Southern Baptist Church acquired the property at 8432 Magnolia Avenue with the idea of opening a college. (Courtesy California Baptist University.)

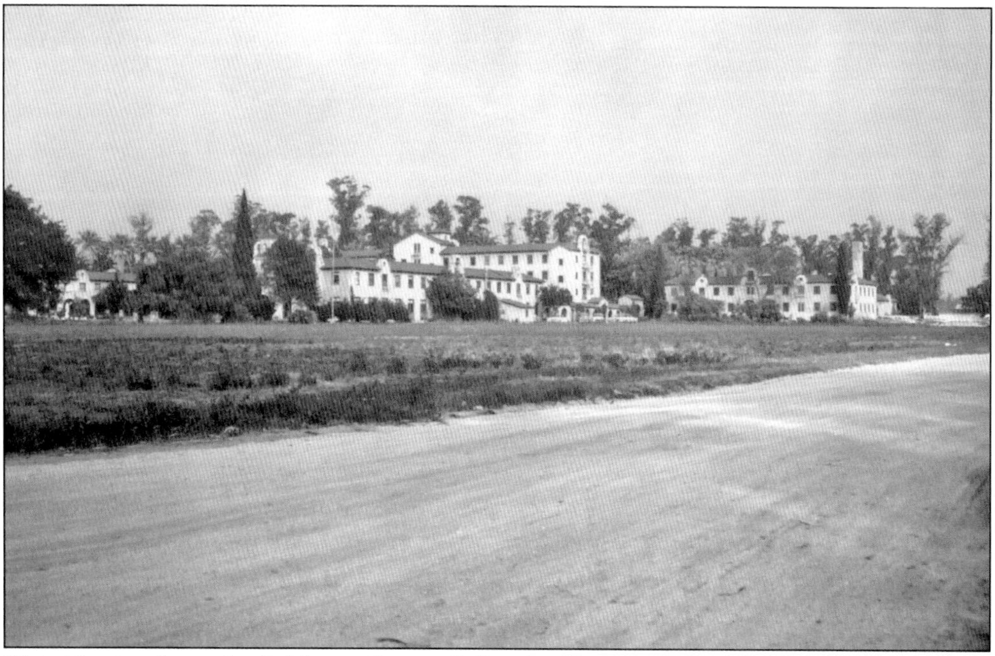

This side view shows the California Baptist College buildings around 1955. The church was lucky in its purchase because the land had created many interested parties. The local school board of education wanted the property for a future high school; the prison wanted it for a hospital for its elderly and infirm inmates. (Courtesy California Baptist University.)

Eight

ARLINGTON TODAY

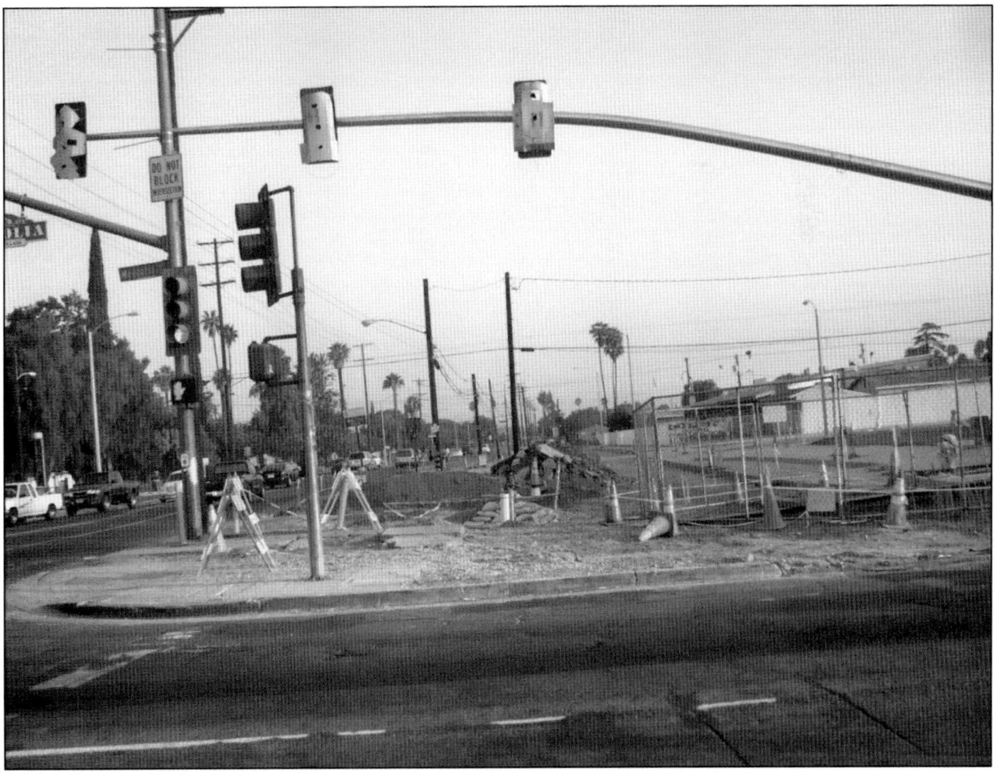

At the corner of Magnolia Avenue, looking south on Van Buren Boulevard, this 2007 view shows the street being widened to ease the flow of traffic. The road goes right up to the businesses, but there is still room for a sidewalk.

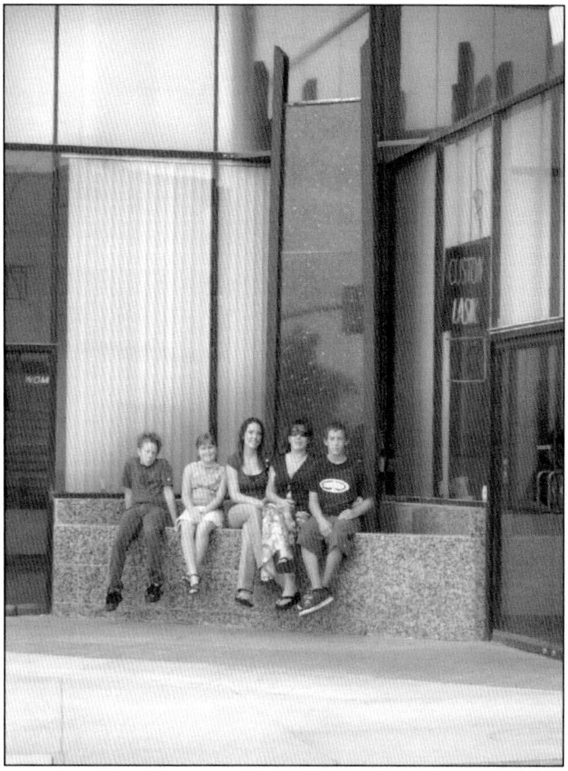

This building at the corner of Magnolia Avenue and Van Buren Boulevard is known as "the Jewel" because of all the glass and sparkle created by the sun. Sitting in front are, from left to right, Alex McDaniel, Jamie Sercl, Tori Williams, Tammy Williams, and Nick Williams in 2007.

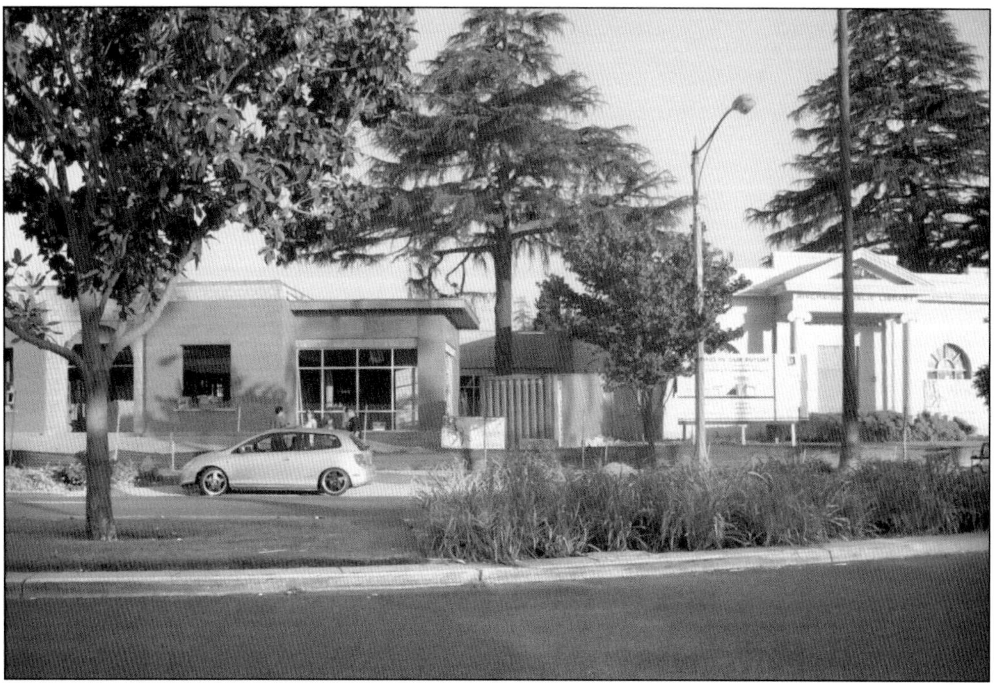

The Arlington Library is currently closed while construction is underway to double its size. The project should be completed near the end of 2007, and many local folk are anticipating the grand reopening. The library is located on Magnolia Avenue one block west of Van Buren Boulevard.

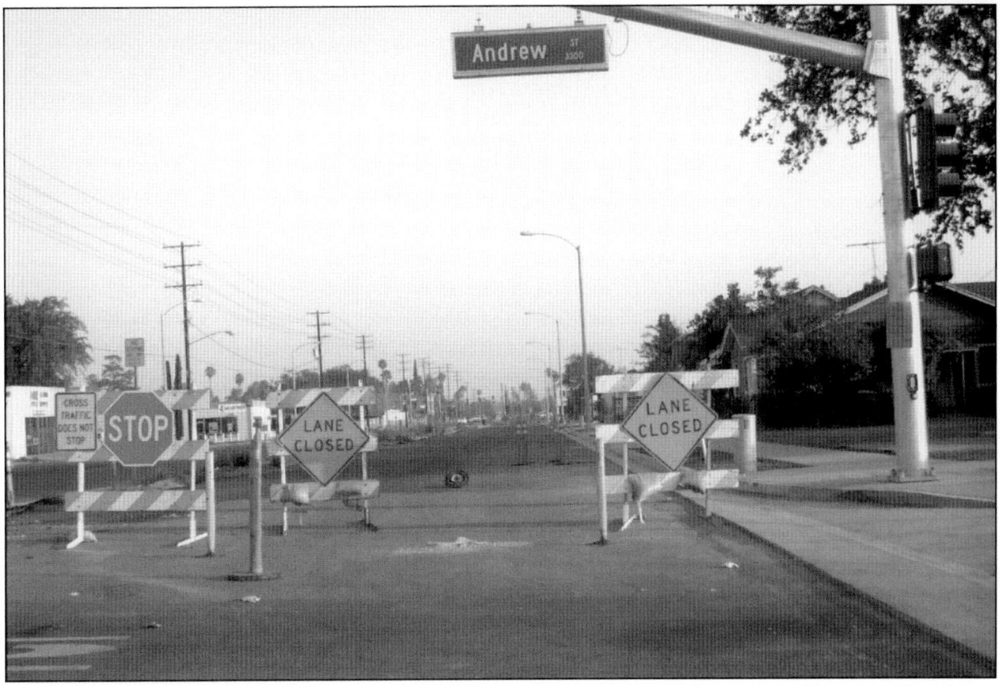

Van Buren Boulevard is now being widened at Primrose Drive, and a new traffic signal has been installed. Primrose has been lengthened to cross Van Buren to Franham Place and then go behind Fire Station No. 2.

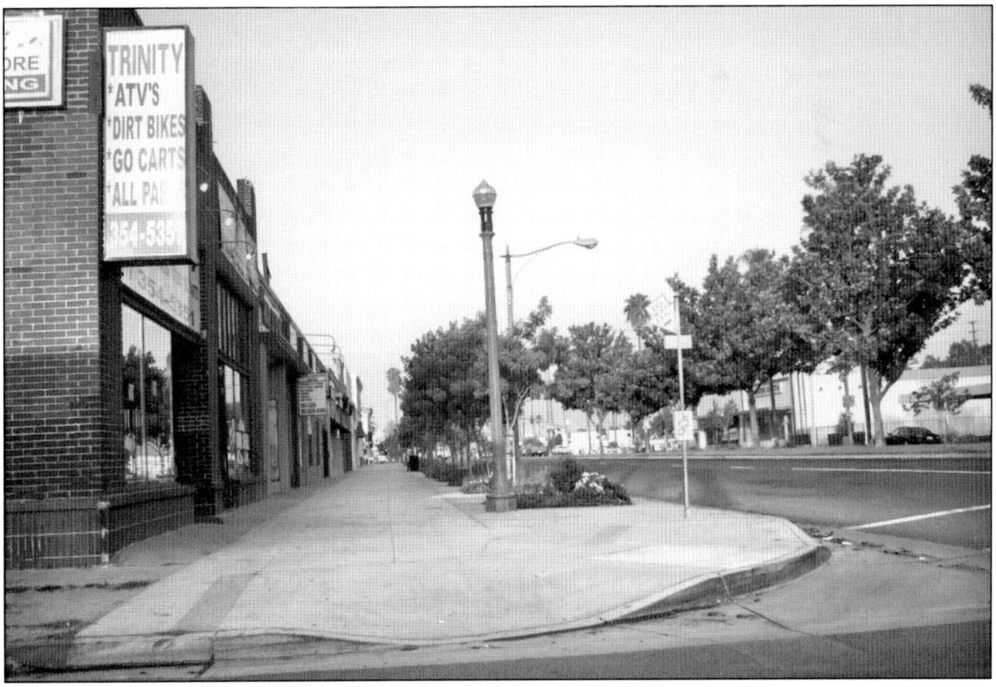

From this angle, looking west on Magnolia Avenue from the corner of Franham Place, the town of Arlington looks somewhat the same as it used to—with the old brick buildings and beautiful trees. Just a little bit more modern now, it is still a very nice town in which to live.